ISBN 978-3-409-12494-2   ISBN 978-3-322-90232-0 (eBook)
DOI 10.1007/978-3-322-90232-0

EDITORIAL BOARD

Professor Raj Aggarwal, Kent State University, Kent – U.S.A.
Professor Jeffrey S. Arpan, University of South Carolina, Columbia – U.S.A.
Professor Daniel van Den Bulcke, Universiteit Antwerpen – Belgium
Professor John A. Cantwell, University of Reading – United Kingdom
Professor S. Tamer Cavusgil, Michigan State University, East Lansing – U.S.A.
Professor Frederick D.S. Choi, New York University – U.S.A.
Professor Farok Contractor, Rutgers University, Newark – U.S.A.
Professor John D. Daniels, University of Miami, Coral Gables – U.S.A.
Professor Peter J. Dowling, University of Canberra – Australia
Professor Santiago García Echevarría, Universidad de Alcála de Henares, Madrid – Spain
Professor Lawrence A. Gordon, University of Maryland, College Park – U.S.A.
Professor Sidney J. Gray, University of Sydney – Australia
Professor Geir Gripsrud, Norwegian School of Management, Sandvika – Norway
Professor Jean-François Hennart, Tilburg University – The Netherlands
Professor Georges Hirsch, Centre Franco-Vietnamien de Formation à la gestion, Paris – France
Professor Neil Hood, University of Strathclyde, Glasgow – United Kingdom
Professor Andrew Inkpen, Thunderbird, The American Graduate School of International Management, Glendale – U.S.A.
Professor Eugene D. Jaffe, Bar-Ilan University, Ramat-Gan – Israel
Professor Erdener Kaynak, Pennsylvania State University, Middletown – U.S.A.
Professor Yui Kimura, University of Tsukuba, Tokyo – Japan
Professor Michael Kutschker, Katholische Universität Eichstätt, Ingolstadt – Germany
Professor Reijo Luostarinen, Helsinki School of Economics – Finland
Professor Klaus Macharzina, Universität Hohenheim, Stuttgart – Germany
Professor Roger Mansfield, Cardiff Business School – United Kingdom
Professor Mark Mendenhall, University of Tennessee, Chattanooga – U.S.A.
Professor Rolf Mirus, University of Alberta, Edmonton – Canada
Professor Michael H. Moffett, American Graduate School, Phoenix – U.S.A.
Professor Krzysztof Y. Obloj, University of Warsaw – Poland
Professor Lars Oxelheim, Lund University – Sweden
Professor Ki-An Park, Kyung Hee University, Seoul – Korea
Professor Robert D. Pearce, University of Reading – United Kingdom
Professor Lee Radebaugh, Brigham Young University, Provo – U.S.A.
Professor Wolf Reitsperger, Universität Hamburg – Germany
Professor Edwin Rühli, Universität Zürich – Switzerland
Professor Alan M. Rugman, Indiana University, Bloomington, U.S.A.
Professor Rakesh B. Sambharya, Rutgers University, Camden, U.S.A.
Professor Reinhart Schmidt, Universität Halle-Wittenberg – Germany
Professor Hans Schöllhammer, University of California, Los Angeles – U.S.A.
Professor Oded Shenkar, The Ohio State University, Columbus – U.S.A.
Professor Vitor Corado Simoes, Universidade Técnica de Lisboa – Portugal
Professor John Stopford, 6 Chalcot Square, London NW1 8YB – United Kingdom
Professor Daniel P. Sullivan, University of Delaware, Newark – U.S.A.
Professor Norihiko Suzuki, International Christian University, Tokyo – Japan
Professor Stephen Bruce Tallmann, University of Utah, Salt Lake City – U.S.A.
Professor George Tesar, Umeå University, Umeå – Sweden
Professor José de la Torre, Florida International University, Miami – U.S.A.
Professor Rosalie L. Tung, Simon Fraser University, Burnaby, BC – Canada
Professor Jean-Claude Usunier, University of Lousanne, Lousanne – Dorigny – Switzerland
Professor Alain Charles Verbeke, Vrije Universiteit Brussel – Belgium
Professor Lawrence S. Welch, Mt Eliza Business School, Melbourne, Australia
Professor Martin K. Welge, Universität Dortmund – Germany
Professor Bernard Yin Yeung, New York University – U.S.A.
Professor Masaru Yoshimori, Yokohama National University – Japan

BOOK REVIEW EDITOR

Professor Dr. Johann Engelhard, Universität Bamberg – Germany

EDITOR

MANAGEMENT INTERNATIONAL REVIEW, *Professor Dr. Profs. h.c. Dr. h.c. Klaus Macharzina, Universität Hohenheim (510 E), Schloss-Osthof-Ost, D-70599 Stuttgart, Germany, Tel. (0711) 4 59-29 08, Fax (0711) 459-3288, E-mail: klausmac@uni-hohenheim.de, Internet: http://www.uni-hohenheim.de/~mir Assistant Editors: Professor Dr. Michael-Jörg Oesterle, Universität Bremen, Germany, Professor Dr. Joachim Wolf, Universität Kiel, Germany, Editorial office: Mrs. Sylvia Ludwig*

© Gabler Verlag 2003

VOLUME 43 · SPECIAL ISSUE · 2003/3

CONTENTS

Guest Editors' Introduction	3
Peter J. Buckley/Martin J. Carter	
Governing Knowledge Sharing in Multinational Enterprises	7
Julian Birkinshaw/Carl F. Fey	
Organization of Research and Development in Large Multinational Firms	27
Volker Mahnke/Markus Venzin	
Governance of Knowledge-teams in the MNC: The Case of HeidelbergCement	47
Torben Pedersen/Bent Petersen/Deo Sharma	
Knowledge Transfer Performance of Multinational Companies	69
Jiatao Li/Oded Shenkar	
Knowledge Search and Governance Choice: International Joint Ventures in the People's Republic of China	91
Marjorie A. Lyles/Georg von Krogh/John Harald Aadne	
Knowledge Acquisition and Knowledge Enablers in International Joint Ventures and their Foreign Parents	111
Gabriel Szulanski/Robert J. Jensen/Tanya Lee	
Adaptation of Know-how for Cross-border Transfer	131
Alan M. Rugman/Alain Verbeke	
Multinational Enterprises and Clusters: An Organizing Framework	151

GUIDELINE FOR AUTHORS

mir welcomes articles on original theoretical contributions, empirical research, state-of-the-art surveys or reports on recent developments in the areas of

a) International Business b) Transnational Corporations c) Intercultural Management d) Strategic Management e) Business Policy.

Manuscripts are reviewed with the understanding that they are substantially new, have not been previously published in whole (including book chapters) or in part (including exhibits), have not been previously accepted for publication, are not under consideration by any other publisher, and will not be submitted elsewhere until a decision is reached regarding their publication in mir. The only exception is papers in conference proceedings, which we treat as work-in-progress.

Contributions should be submitted in English language in a Microsoft or compatible format by e-mail to the Editor at klausmac@uni-hohenheim.de. The complete text including the references, tables and figures should as a rule not exceed 25 pages in a usual setting (approximately *7000 words*). Reply papers should normally not exceed 1500 words. The title page should include the following elements: Author(s) name, Heading of the article, Abstract (two sections of about 30 words each), Key Results (20 words), Author's line (author's name, academic title, position and affiliation) and on the bottom a proposal for an abbreviated heading on the front cover of the journal.

Submitted papers must be written according to mir's formal guidelines. Only those manuscripts can enter the reviewing process which adhere to our guidelines. Authors are requested to

– use *endnotes* for clarification sparingly. References to the literature are indicated in the text by author's name and year of publication in parentheses, e.g. (Reitsperger/Daniel 1990, p. 210, Eiteman 1989). The references should be listed in alphabetical order at the end of the text. They should include full bibliographical details and be cited in the following manner: e.g.

    Reitsperger, W. D./Daniel, S. J., Dynamic Manufacturing: A Comparison of Attitudes in the U.S. and Japan, *Management International Review*, 30, 1990, pp. 203–216.

    Eiteman, D. K., Financial Sourcing, in Macharzina, K./Welge, M. K. (eds.), *Handwörterbuch Export und Internationale Unternehmung*, Stuttgart: Poeschel 1989, pp. 602–621.

    Stopford, J. M./Wells, L. T. Jr., *Managing the Multinational Enterprise*, New York: Basic Books 1972.

– avoid *terms* that may be interpreted denigrating to ethnic or other groups.
– be especially careful in dealing with gender. Traditional customs such as "... the manager wishes that **his** interest ..." can favor the acceptance of inequality were none exist. The use of plural pronouns is preferred. If this is impossible, the term "he or she" or "he/she" can be used.

In the case of publication authors are supplied one complimentary copy of the issue and 30 off-prints free of charge. Additional copies may be ordered *prior to printing*. Overseas shipment is by boat; air-delivery will be charged extra.

The author agrees, that his/her article is published not only in this journal but that it can also be reproduced by the publisher and his licensees through license agreement in other journals (also in translated versions), through reprint in omnibus volumes (i.e. for anniversary editions of the journal or the publisher or in subject volumes), through longer extracts in books of the publisher also for advertising purposes, through multiplication and distribution on CD ROM or other data media, through storage on data bases, their transmission and retrieval, during the time span of the copyright laws on the article at home and abroad.

© Gabler Verlag 2003

Guest Editors' Introduction

The objective of this special issue is to contribute to the understanding *of Knowledge Governance (KG) in the Multinational Corporation (MNC)*. Like the traditional literature on corporate governance we are concerned with the attraction of crucial capital, its efficient allocation, as well as the mechanisms used to achieve capital accumulation and optimal utilization. However, unlike the traditional literature we are concerned not with financial capital, but with knowledge as a particular sort of capital that is seen as increasingly crucial to the existence, boundaries, and economic organization of the modern MNC.

Intra-firm and inter-firm processes of knowledge-creation, sharing and exploitation have attracted increasingly managerial and international scholarly interest. However, the relation between particular knowledge processes, determinants of structural choices, governance mechanisms, their relevant costs and benefits, and associated strategic advantages remain less well understood. In part, this is due to complications in the conceptualization of process and outcome variable that effectively represent and measure impediments and enablers of such processes. There is also a lack of empirical understanding of governance modes (e.g. markets, hybrids, joint-ventures), including coordination mechanisms (e.g. incentive, trust) in the governance of knowledge in the MNC. To address these challenges, this special issue seeks to shed light on the following three questions:

- What are key challenges of governing knowledge in the MNC?
- How do contingencies influence relevant trade-offs?
- How do sets of governance mechanisms respond to problems of cognition and incentives?

The call for papers yielded a substantial number of submissions of which eight contributions were screened out through a double-blind review process for publication. Key criteria for inclusion included a sound combination of conceptualization and empirical grounding in response to the questions above.

Peter J. Buckley and Martin J. Carter in their paper *Governing Knowledge Sharing in Multinational Enterprises* examines knowledge-sharing processes in four UK MNCs. A key challenge is to design governance architectures so that application strategy (uses of a given portfolio of knowledge) and discovery strategy (new combinations of knowledge) can be supported through knowledge sharing. A key trade-off obtains here between integration and partitioning of knowledge assets, whereby increased partitioning facilitates local knowledge sharing but complicates global integration. In addition, coordination mechanisms employed in the governance of knowledge sharing may be organized centrally or decentrally, whereby central organization may lead to knowledge loss and managerial overload while decentral organization may lead to loss of control. An important contingency in resolving these governance problems is the extent to which firms follow application and discovery strategies. In addition, the authors recommend to closely integrate incentive systems with attempts for knowledge sharing including individual incentives and rewards.

Julian Birkinshaw and Carl F. Fey examine the *Organization of Research and Development in Large Multinational Firms* in a sample of 107 firms based in the UK and Sweden. The key challenge addressed in this paper is how knowledge creation is governed and how this impacts R&D performance. Several trade-offs obtain. First, headquarter centred vs. divisionalized R&D, whereby the former helps sponsoring strategic technologies that would not survive the short-term demands of the market but may also make technology development unresponsive to market needs. Second, while centralised R&D makes tacit knowledge sharing more likely and allows for cost economies, a MNC may also forgo learning benefits from locally dispersed R&D. Finally, freedom of choice among suppliers of R&D projects might allow for beneficial competition among R&D sites but on the other hand may also lead to duplication of research efforts and short-term orientation in the MNC. The authors suggest that the drawbacks of centralised R&D might be alleviated by developing strong vertical relationships between headquarter and business units. By implication, the way a particular knowledge governance structure is implemented may matter more than how the centralisation vs. decentralisation trade-off is resolved.

Volker Mahnke and Markus Venzin in their paper *Governance of Knowledge Teams in the MNC* use a grounded theory process in a large German MNC to investigate contingency factors for delegating alternative sets of decision rights to knowledge teams. A key trade-off obtains between granting autonomy to knowledge teams and compromising strategic alignment. Key contingencies in resolving this trade-off include the strategic impact of a knowledge team's activities as well as their relative focus on knowledge sharing or knowledge creation. In addition, the analysis reveals that institutionalising a knowledge management board prevents incentive conflicts and eases investments in monitoring knowledge.

Torben Pedersen, Bent Petersen, and Deo Sharma in their paper *Knowledge Transfer Performance of Multinational Corporations* examine whether and why the use of unsuitable knowledge transfer mechanisms impairs performance. When tacit knowledge transfer is supported by written media a knowledge loss obtains while explicit knowledge transfer supported by rich media drives up communication costs. Based on a large sample survey, they suggest that managerial discretion may be exercised to avoid impaired performance by addressing a trade-off between knowledge loss and communication costs in the governance of knowledge.

Jiatao Li and Oded Shenkar's paper on *Knowledge Search and Governance Choice* investigates learning strategies in international joint ventures in China from a local firm perspective. Interestingly both the local partner's intentions regarding governance forms and the actual formation of an international joint ventures is driven by knowledge types as well as overlap between knowledge bases. Results indicate that equity joint ventures are preferred if transferred knowledge is tacit and low knowledge overlaps exist between the local and foreign partner. A crucial trade-off in the governance of knowledge is thus indicated: the more knowledge is tacit and the greater learning possibilities between partners are, the more need is there for managers to deal with the alignment of incentives through equity arrangements up-front.

Marjorie A. Lyles, Georg von Krogh, and John Harald Aadne investigate *Knowledge Acquisition and Knowledge Enablers* in a study of 176 international joint ventures in Hungary. The focus is on knowledge acquisition by International Joint Ventures (IJVs) from foreign parents. The results indicate that foreign parents' knowledge sharing commitment, influence in decision-making, and ownership control predict high knowledge acquisition, whereas trust and business relatedness between the IJV and its foreign parent did not. In addition, they find that the IJV's interaction climate and performance predict high knowledge acquisition, whereas absorptive capacity did not. Again, careful management of interests and incentives facilitates learning.

Gabriel Szulanski, Robert J. Jensen, and Tanya Lee's paper deals with *Adaptation of Know-How for Cross-border Transfer* examining a case of franchising know-how transfer from the US to Israel. Ineffective knowledge transfer and poor local performance in receiver location may result if know-how transfer is managed wrongly. The authors recommend that not only environmental factors figure importantly when transferred knowledge is adapted to a local setting but also the characteristics of transferred knowledge itself. Furthermore, the authors draw attention to the trade-offs involved in applying standardised knowledge vs. adapting the knowledge to the local setting. Adapting knowledge incurs costs and if the receiver doesn't fully understand how to change the knowledge, the more

Guest Editors' Introduction

will a hasty and early adaptation of the practice on the receiver's site result in impaired transfer performance.

Alan M. Rugman and Alain Verbeke Verbeke in their paper the *Multinational Enterprises and Clusters: An Organizing Framework* investigate the interaction between MNCs including flagship firms. The MNE is now simultaneously a knowledge generator and a knowledge seeker, and it is necessary to carefully identify the organizational characteristics of its involvement in localized or trans-border clusters. To this end the authors offer insights into how MNE organization links with multiple local environments in its effort to govern knowledge.

Taken together the papers in this special issue show that advancing research on *knowledge governance* proceeds on several levels of analysis and through a variety of methods including grounded theory building, case studies, and large sample testing of theories. In response to the questions posed in this special issue the key challenges of knowledge governance concern trade-offs between alternative structural choices in a MNC's organizational design where coordination mechanisms employed deal with problems of cognition and conflicting interest that occur in processes of knowledge sharing and creation both within and across the boundaries of the MNC. Key contingencies influencing how these trade-offs are resolved include knowledge-types, knowledge-strategies pursued, and the costs of knowledge loss and communication. Importantly, however, there seems to be increasing empirical evidence on how the allocation of decision rights – be it in joint ventures or in the governance of teams – helps resolving conflict of interest to enable knowledge creation and transfer – an issue that much research on knowledge processes in the MNC has previously neglected.

We are very grateful to all colleagues who helped in the process of creating this special issue on knowledge governance – be it as reviewers, authors, or sponsors. We are also very grateful to Rudolf Hastenteufel and Joachim Wolf for supporting this special issue.

VOLKER MAHNKE
TORBEN PEDERSEN

Peter J. Buckley/Martin J. Carter

Governing Knowledge Sharing in Multinational Enterprises[1]

Abstract

- The paper examines knowledge sharing processes in four multinational firms. It derives five propositions from the literature on governing knowledge processes and utilises these propositions in an examination of the four firms.

- The propositions examine knowledge sharing, intra-organisational governance of knowledge, knowledge frontiers within and between firms and 'application' and 'discovery' strategies in governing knowledge.

Key Results

- A variety of knowledge governance problems are encountered in the four case studies and all involve resolving global /local issues. The coordination methods employed need to take account of this and other trade-offs (e.g. specialisation versus integration) and their resolution involves attention to the processes of knowledge sharing, the incentive structure within the firm and knowledge frontiers. These trade-offs are examined using the notions of partition and integration as architectural forms.

- Achievement of both application strategies (uses of a given portfolio of knowledge) and discovery strategies (new combinations of knowledge) are important goals of knowledge governance structures.

Authors

Peter J. Buckley, Professor of International Business and Director of the Centre for International Business, University of Leeds (CIBUL), Leeds University Business School, Leeds, UK.
Martin J. Carter, Lecturer in Economics, Leeds University Business School, Leeds, UK.

Peter J. Buckley/Martin J. Carter

Introduction

The paper examines knowledge sharing processes in four high technology multinational enterprises. It derives five propositions on governing knowledge processes and utilises these propositions in an examination of the four firms.

Knowledge and Knowledge Sharing in Multinational Enterprises

The starting-point of this paper is that knowledge is the converse of uncertainty. Shifts in demand and technology cause trade-inhibiting uncertainty in firms that lack relevant knowledge, but present opportunities for trade in firms who possess such knowledge (Buckley/Carter 1999). Just as uncertainty is a state of the human mind, so can effective knowledge only reside in the minds of people. Knowledge is a *quality* possessed by people, literally a *state of mind*.

The organisation's knowledge is an aggregation of the individual knowledge of its members (Grant 1996, pp. 112 et seq.). No individual possesses all the knowledge within a firm. Division of knowledge within the firm results in 'secondary' uncertainty, if individuals do not know what is in the mind of others. Koopmans claims that "[in] a rough and intuitive judgement the secondary uncertainty arising from a lack of communication, that is from one decision maker having no way of finding out the concurrent decisions and plans made by others . . . is quantitatively at least as important as the primary uncertainty arising from random acts of nature and unpredictable changes in consumers' preferences" (1957, pp. 162 et seq.). Secondary uncertainty can be reduced by sharing knowledge. The purpose of this paper is to examine the means which firms employ to achieve knowledge sharing amongst their members. Firms are communities of practice (Brown/Duguid 1991, 1998) which undertake "the integration of knowledge fragmented in various parts of the firm . . . confronting within the context of the firm Hayek's problem of utilizing knowledge not known to anyone in its entirety . . . "(Fransman 1998, p. 189). Our particular concern is with bringing together complementary knowledge. In multinational enterprises (MNEs) this includes, for example, knowledge of different national markets and knowledge of existing technologies within and outside the enterprise. The firm must understand how technology can be adapted or developed to meet the changing requirements of these markets. Such knowledge transfers are rarely one way flows and involve global/local interactions which have important implications for the governance of the firm (Buckley/Carter 2002).

The Governance of Knowledge

A fundamental tenet of received theory is that knowledge is shared more efficiently (at less cost) within the firm than between firms (Buckley/Casson 1976). Firms internalise the governance of knowledge by combining knowledge which is dispersed amongst individuals and applying it collectively towards a common purpose. The division of knowledge in a multi-person firm reflects the bounded rationality of individuals (Simon, 1945). Internal governance is motivated by several sources of gain in collective action. First are gains due to *complementarity* (*inseparability*), in which the value of the knowledge of in one part of the organisation is only realised when combined with knowledge held in another part of the firm (Buckley/Carter 1996, 2000). Second, there are gains from collective knowledge *processes*, particularly involving tacit knowledge, due to social characteristics of groups. These characteristics have been described as "higher order organising principles" and "tacit procedural knowledge" by Kogut and Zander (1992, 1996) and have also been discussed by Nonaka and Takeuchi (1995). Third are gains from internal *contracting* of which the classic example is the labour contract in Coase's (1937) rationale for the existence of the multi-person firm. These gains include monitoring and incentive allocation to overcome moral hazard (Alchian/Demsetz 1972), internalising the appropriation problem (Arrow 1962), avoiding complex price-setting problems (Rosen 1991) and providing better incentives than the market for individuals to develop co-specific human capital (Williamson/Wachter/Harris 1975, Williamson 1985, p. 249).

However, there are knowledge frontiers where an individual firm will find it more efficient to purchase inputs which embody the knowledge rather than internalise the knowledge transfer. Opportunities arise to economise on the transfer of knowledge when knowledge can be unambiguously codified or embodied in physical commodities. For example, a steel fabricator buys specified grades of metal rather than internalising the knowledge required for steel production (Demsetz 1991). Inseparability, processing, pricing and contracting problems diminish and market contracting is more attractive.

Proposition 1. Firms will recognise that some knowledge processes are better organised by another organisation and purchased through the market than by their organisation. Therefore, they will specialise in knowledge activities in a discrete but changing area. Specialised firms are separated from each other by the agency of the market.

Peter J. Buckley/Martin J. Carter

The Intra-firm Governance of Knowledge

The frontiers of knowledge specialisation *between* firms are drawn where uncertainty can be effectively borne by market contracting. Specialisation *within* firms produces internal knowledge frontiers between separate cognate areas, often corresponding to functional or divisional boundaries. Within each area, individuals specialise in knowledge of a broadly similar content, so that workers can interact and managers can monitor and guide their subordinates: integrated knowledge and 'organic' governance. Communication between specialised areas cannot depend on the full transfer of specialised knowledge, but requires the development of a sufficiently rich common code or language to allow each group to transmit and receive the messages which enable them to play their part in advancing the collective goals of the firm but which economises on knowledge transfer. This language, its knowledge content and the associated mechanics of communication, must allow senior managers to supervise and direct the firm's activities, even though no individual or small group holds, or could hold, all the firm's strategic knowledge.

Knowledge governance structures within firms must pay attention to

1. the boundaries between different knowledge holders (individuals, departments, functional areas)
2. the coordination and sharing of knowledge across frontiers
3. the incentives to individuals for sharing knowledge.

A potentially important boundary within MNEs is that between individuals from different countries. Our study focuses on two culturally close countries, the USA and the UK, and so reduces some of the factors that increase psychic distance (Hallen/Wiedersheim-Paul 1979). This enables us to isolate more distinctly the factors that arise from physical and time differences and from the need for adaptation to individual local markets. It is however possible that differences in managerial practice, style and linguistic nuances may exacerbate the separation of head office and affiliate.

Proposition 2. Governing knowledge within the firm requires attention to knowledge frontiers, to mechanisms of knowledge sharing and to the means of encouraging individuals to pool knowledge.

Knowledge Architectures in the Firm

Groups within the firm can coordinate their activities by sharing complementary knowledge. There is, however, a further problem concerning the coherence and reliability of knowledge exchanged in this way. An important dimension of knowledge intended for practical application is its degree of reliability or truth. A widely used shorthand in the business literature is that knowledge is "a justified true belief". Fransman (1998) points out that whenever there is uncertainty then firms do not act on "justified true beliefs" but simply on their *beliefs*, based on incomplete information, combined with insight, creativity and misconception. He suggests the term 'vision' for the *dominant* set of beliefs which guide its actions in the face of uncertainty. In an *organisation* different members of the firm can hold different beliefs. Furthermore, there may even be a lack of awareness that this is so as some individuals may keep their beliefs secret yet still base their actions upon them. This is potentially problematic, especially in the case of procedural norms and routines. A gap between the 'vision' adopted by top management and beliefs in other parts of the firm may result at the least in incoherence between parts of the organisation, and further in confusion, incomprehension, disaffection and even conflict. How routines and habits often embody hidden beliefs and assumptions is illustrated in Scott-Morgan (1994). This has radical implications for the governance of knowledge in firms. The firm might respond in two ways. One solution is *integration*, based on "heedful interrelating" (Weick/Roberts 1993) in which managers have an understanding of the knowledge possessed by those with whom they work. The alternative arrangement is *partition* in which the firm's structure is designed so that it is not necessary for managers to have a detailed understanding of the work of others or even the same beliefs. This has parallels with organic and mechanistic governance structures in managing the dynamics of knowledge development (Burns/Stalker 1961). The choice between integration and partition depends on a trade-off between breadth and depth in the domain of knowledge governance, so that some groupings are based on coherence of beliefs and widening the scope of collective action whereas other are based on specialisation and depth of knowledge. Partition and integration will coexist in the architecture of any firm insofar as some knowledge remains within knowledge frontiers and some is shared across frontiers.

One important aspect of hidden beliefs is Williamson's concept of opportunism as 'self-seeking with guile' (Williamson 1975, 1985). Incentives need to be created at the individual or group level to encourage actions to conform to the objectives of the firm. Such incentives can be individual rewards or benefits to the group. The culture of the firm can be engineered towards collective goals which over-ride opportunistic behaviour. The incentive structure must ensure that group goals are consistent with the firm's goals and that individual goals are consistent with group goals. Observation of an individual's behaviour may lead to the view that his action is inconsistent with the firm's objectives. However, this could only be verified by examining the intermediate level of the group. The hierarchy of incentives may provide a coordinating mechanism which brings individuals' 'deviant' behaviour into line with the collective purpose of the firm. We would expect to observe different incentive structures in the two architectural forms of integration and partition.

In multinationals based on high technology, professionalism and a common educational background may be factors around which groups cohere which can overcome cultural differences, nuances of language and other barriers to knowledge sharing. This shared background and language transcends local differences in the internal knowledge markets where employees are highly educated individuals sharing a common training based on the natural sciences. This may create internal knowledge frontiers and foster partition along the lines of particular scientific sub-disciplines.

The next proposition we derive is:

Proposition 3. Two ways to achieve coherence and coordination are architectural forms which we designate as *integration* and *partition*. Both may be present in a single firm as firms seek solutions to problems of uncertainty.

New Knowledge Configurations

Over-concentration on perceived current capabilities may well lead management astray (Bercovitz/de Figueiredo/Teece 1997). Over time, other producers can learn what the firm already knows, or learn other ways to achieve the same capabilities, or capabilities that will supercede them. Over time rents will dissipate. Firm specific advantages must be defined over a given time period (and possibly over a given cultural space) before they atrophy (Buckley 1983).

Protection of existing knowledge can include finding new capabilities based on *new combinations* of knowledge, redeploying and extending existing assets, including by the acquisition of or joint venture with the owners of other, complementary, assets. Existing knowledge assets with multiple applications are similar to the 'core competencies' discussed by Prahalad and Hamel (1990). Strategies concerned with applying and protecting rents from existing knowledge might be termed *application strategies*. When the firm has developed multiple applications, this an *application portfolio strategy*. The internal structures of firms reflect the need to facilitate the application of specialised knowledge and the collaboration between firm members with complementary knowledge. Von Hippel (1998) draws a strong relationship between 'sticky information' and the locus of problem solving. There are several strategies available to deal with stickiness. (1) Carry out the problem solving at the locus of the sticky information. (2) Iterate problem solving between sites (where there is more than one source of sticky information. (3) "Task partitioning" where the problem is split into sub-problems where each draws on one sticky source. (4) Invest in "unsticking" information. Examples of unsticking information include: training and the replication of existing knowledge, expert systems, easily transferable software, a centrally accessible database. This general issue, that needed information and problem solving capacity have to be brought together physically or virtually at a given point to solve a problem is central to knowledge management and reflects the facts that information is costly to acquire, transfer and use – and that it is sticky. This helps to determine the information structure within the firm, in which knowledge is partitioned to meet the requirements of each distinct applications and communication channels designed for the supervision of and development of the applications portfolio. The divisional type of organisation has the advantage that knowledge that is specialised to divisions can stay within divisional boundaries, allowing each group of specialists to increase their division-specific knowledge and avoid the overload which would arise if all specialists were expected to be cognisant of all application areas. The divisionalised organisation is particularly well adapted for the delivery of a *portfolio of applications*.

As Langlois (1991) has pointed out, whether a firm is avoid the complete diffusion of capabilities into the market place depends on the relative learning abilities of the market and of the firm. The search for new applications of existing knowledge can only take the firm so far, and sooner or later it must engage in the development of new capabilities based on new knowledge. Failure to engage in the 'creative destruction' of existing competencies can result in the choice of an incorrect growth path for the firm. Decision-making biases may come from bounded rationality in which managers preserve erroneous beliefs or theories of the world. According to North (1990), erroneous beliefs are a failure of "instrumental rationality", representing the impact of information costs on individual or group decision making. When information feedback is inadequate to convey to the participants in a process the correct theory of how their world operates, this will impact upon the individual's decision and in turn the outcome of the process and the further information which it generates (Dixit 1996, p. 45). This can take place even in the face of information which would suggest revision if it were not for the common practice of de-selecting information which does not support our established beliefs (Fransman 1998). There is a connection here with the notion of scientific paradigms and research programmes, which may only be revised some time after the evidence which first challenges them (Kuhn 1962, Lakatos 1970). Core capabilities become *core rigidities* (Leonard-Barton 1992). Furthermore there is path dependency of knowledge creation, so that experience gained in the past may reduce the cost of developing knowledge in areas with similarities or with complementarities (Dierickx/Cool 1989). The resulting increasing returns to knowledge creation can provide significant first mover advantages for knowledge-intensive firms although simultaneously they carry the risk for firms to be 'locked-in' to technologies which may be superseded (Arthur 1989).

A possible term to use for strategies which seek new capabilities based on new knowledge is *discovery strategies*. The forms of organisation adopted for application strategies may present some constraints to the pursuit of *discovery* strategies. Of course, there is no obstacle to the development of new capabilities using the expertise within a particular division, and many diversified companies have long experience of research and development. But an implication of divisionalisation is that discovery activities are either centralised, or are conducted independently in separate divisions. In either case, discovery capabilities of the firm are constrained in particular locations within the firm. This does not prevent innovation, but it places some limits on the scope of the innovation that is likely to take place. It is likely to be restricted to particular areas of application drawing on a sub-set of the expertise within the firm. Furthermore, it may be hard to disseminate any discoveries which have potential applications in other divisions of the firm. Therefore, a divisionalised firm may engage in a *portfolio of applications* and some individual discovery, but will have difficulties if it wishes to develop a strategy comprising a portfolio of discoveries.

The recent developments in global knowledge sharing provide responses to these limitations. MNEs thus provide channels of communication and planning and policy formation between functional specialists in different application areas. As a result, new specialist knowledge is disseminated across application boundaries, so that new capabilities can be integrated across the portfolio of the firm's activities. Furthermore, if ideas for innovation arise in one part of the organisation, perhaps derived from contact with a particular customer, this offers better access to the full range of knowledge and expertise in other parts of the corporation which may be able to contribute to the innovative development. Thus these forms of organisation offer the potential for a firm to move from a strategy based around an *application portfolio* to one based around a *discovery portfolio*.

Proposition 4. Long run success depends on processes of knowledge sharing that encompass both *application* and *discovery* strategies. The implementation of the latter will be crucial to sustained success.

Furthermore, the architectures (combination of partition and integration) which are adapted for application strategies may not be well suited for discovery strategies.

Proposition 5. Governance structures for application strategies may obstruct discovery strategies.

Applying the Propositions to Four Multinational Enterprises

The following section confronts these *propositions* with material drawn from repeated interviews with a number of executives in each of four multinational companies. These longitudinal studies covered not less than a year in each case. This research uses multiple case design, the results of which can be extended to a wider context based on "analytical generalisation" (Yin 1994, p. 10). This is an appropriate method for our purposes because we are engaged in an exploratory theory building exercise rather than theory testing. The choice of cases was determined by the wish to reduces influences of extreme cultural and language difference and therefore the four companies are all US or UK owned. Company names are disguised.

Braxia PLC: Buying Technology in a Global Market

The Braxia case is an example of the development of a new capability to buy technology by embodying valuable organisational knowledge in a new process architecture. This not only facilitated the company-wide dissemination of a nascent organisational capability, but incorporated a degree of continual learning.

Braxia is a UK owned firm with a long history of developing ethical pharmaceuticals in the traditional whole-cycle method from basic research and development through trials, registration, production and marketing. Scientific knowledge deepens continuously, and there is an increase both in the number of technologies that can be applied in a particular therapeutic area and a widening of potential therapeutic applications of particular technologies. A single firm can no longer internalise all the knowledge relevant to even a selected group of strategically chosen therapeutic areas. One result is that the basic research for novel therapies is increasingly carried out by independent biotechnology firms who then offer their discoveries to be licensed and marketed by the large pharmaceutical companies. Independent firms provide a greater variety of approaches by each specialising in their particular technology, and can rely on the large pharmaceuticals to provide production, marketing and distribution capabilities. Furthermore, these technology suppliers are spatially dispersed in various locations around the world. Similarly, final markets are globally distributed. Braxia and other MNEs provide the means of linking disparate consolidating technologies and adapting them to the particular needs of individual markets. Thus, there is a need for access to information on both internal and external technological developments and on market needs in a managed fashion. The domain of internalised knowledge needs to be integrated with the external across the interface with other firms.

This trend creates a requirement for a new organisational capability for buying technology in large pharmaceutical firms. Such a capability needs to combine alertness to potential developments with technological and commercial assessments of prospective 'purchases' and with legal and commercial expertise in drawing up agreements. Its application must be integrated with the strategic goals of the firm as a whole, with its continuing research plans and its market strategy. Expertise in buying (licensing) is complementary to detailed technological knowledge and marketing knowledge of relevant therapeutic areas. The firm must somehow strike a balance between benefits of increased specialisation, through a division of expertise between specialists, and the difficulties that such division of expertise creates in then combining one area of expertise with other complementary expertise.

A mechanism for knowledge sharing is therefore essential. One form of the 'partition' solution to achieving coherence (*Proposition 3*) is to locate all the firm's licensing expertise together in a separate specialist group which would provide a service for the corporation. This arrangement would facilitate the development of expertise and the deepening of knowledge in this area. This would have the advantages which functional groups provide: advantages of managing and monitoring performance, as managers have expertise in common with their team; mutual support through flexibility of individuals amongst tasks; exchange of ideas and experience; consistency of practice and coordination of activities. Appropriate communication channels would be needed between the licensing group and the therapeutic groups in order to combine licensing expertise with specialist technical and marketing knowledge. Such communications take time and often use summarised information, which can result in delays and misunderstandings. It may be difficult for members of the licensing group to internalise all the knowledge that would be desirable of the different therapeutic areas and the different national markets in which products would be sold. Furthermore, even though this group is formally providing a service to the other groups, there is a risk of competing strategic goals between therapeutic area groups and the group with licensing responsibility.

An alternative 'partition' is for responsibility for licensing to be allocated to specialists within each therapeutic or marketing unit. That is, for expertise to be combined within each therapeutic area. This would help to overcome difficulties of combining knowledge of licensing with that of therapeutic strategy and marketing, because licensing experts in each group concentrate on the needs of the group. But different experience in different groups may lead to different practices and different capabilities dispersed through the organisation. Furthermore, there is now a problem of coordination. Both Braxia and the independent suppliers of new technologies are geographically dispersed as well as representing a wide range of scientific and therapeutic applications. One part of the organisation may be unaware of actions taken by another operating unit. For example, a biotechnology company may approach more than one group and be rejected by one part of the organisation and yet be accepted by another.

Braxia's chosen solution resulted in the establishment of a 'virtual department', which provides benefits of both specialisation of expertise and of combination of expertise. This solution also creates a clear division of knowledge between Braxia and outside organisations as in *Proposition 1*. Expertise in buying is developed collectively by individuals who are located in each therapeutic area but who are also able to share their knowledge as though they were in a distinct unit specialised in licensing. This is made possible by adopting a common process of knowledge sharing for evaluating prospective offers and a management and information system which is embodied in customised computer software. This is accessible to all firm members who have responsibilities for licensing. The 'virtual department' is made up of a group of specialists, who support and manage the system, together with members of operating groups who have responsibility for licensing. The expertise of licensing specialists is available to all operating groups as needed while the decision-makers in each client group to comprise a 'virtual' licensing group while continuing to be fully integrated members of their own operating unit. The arrangement provides benefits of both forms of knowledge partition.

This form of organisation successfully overcomes trade-offs in knowledge specialisation paying attention to perceived knowledge frontiers as suggested by *Proposition 2*. The incentives to knowledge sharing are not individual monetary rewards but collective returns from "making the job easier and more rewarding" (Braxia senior manager). Managers in Braxia were dismissive of using monetary incentives to individuals because is deemed to devalue the process and the team ethic. This might otherwise require a greater division of labour amongst more specialised individuals, but is overcome through the application of a piece of organisational knowledge. This knowledge is the recognition that all acquisitions of products and technologies (including companies) could be achieved through the same process in all therapeutic areas and all countries. Furthermore, this process could be embodied in computer software which would automate many of the administrative requirements, and facilitate the required information flows, record keeping and documentation.

The embodiment of organisational knowledge, together with some licensing knowledge, in an information technology system provides an alternative to the internalisation of such knowledge in the minds of separate specialists. This improves the firm's ability to exploit the complementarities between its therapeutic-marketing knowledge and developing licensing expertise and to move on to integrating separate knowledge flows in a discovery process (*Proposition 4*). The Braxia case provides a good example of a governance structure for knowledge management which facilitates discovery strategies (*Proposition 5*).

Peter J. Buckley/Martin J. Carter

Devonian PLC: The Sale of Technology in a Global Market

Devonian is a UK owned global telecommunications company which owns and operates cable systems, fibre-optic networks and satellite earth stations. It is a leading supplier of global communications services to international firms such as banks, information technology companies, oil and gas companies and shipping companies. Two aspects of this business which strongly affect the nature of the knowledge creation requirements are firstly the rapid rate of innovation in telecommunications technology and secondly the wide local variations in the needs of individual customers. Designs must be tailored to customer requirements and bidding is intensely competitive. Integration of Devonian's internalised knowledge governance processes with its clients' needs are key elements in a successful strategy (*Proposition 1*). Bids often comprise several rounds. The client may use the first round to select two or three competitors who submit more detailed bids. Bidders can be asked to carry out partial or pilot projects in competition with one another.

The preparation of bids is a complex process drawing on many specialisations within Devonian including: general and specialised network design work, costing and pricing, commercial and financial appraisal, legal services, sales and service contacts with client, liaison with third party suppliers, project management for implementation of successful bids. Due to economies of specialisation, these skills are located in different groups. Furthermore, Devonian is a global corporation, serving international customers with headquarters in many different parts of the world and with international service requirements. Therefore customer contacts and Devonian's own sales and customer service personnel may be widely dispersed geographically as well as being members of different regional business units. Like Braxia, Devonian must find the balance between the architectural forms of partition and integration for coherence and coordination (*Proposition 3*).

Devonian needs to direct many diverse knowledge resources towards each potential client, when the needs vary between clients. Different clients have different technical problems and different geographical distributions of their head offices and operating divisions. Devonian has to call on whatever specialised resources are required, and also to align the sales and service communication channels with those of the client. The number of possible governance structures is very large, with some areas of expertise separately specialised and others combined. The ideal structure is likely to be different for different clients, particularly for high value projects for large international clients. Thus there is a variable domain of internalised knowledge with heavy reliance on information in the (potential) client base.

Devonian's solution to the problem of governance of knowledge is a flexible form of organisation which matches the organisation to the requirements of individual bids. This knowledge sharing is achieved by assembling 'bid teams' under the control of a specialist section called 'Major Bids'. Rewards are psychic returns from successful team working and a higher number of bids won, which feeds directly into the firm's pay structure via individual bonuses (*Proposition 2*). A 'virtual team' (the bid team) is appointed with membership from each of the key areas of expertise required for the bid. The Major Bids section supplies the lead design engineer, called the 'bid consultant' and the most appropriate regional business unit provides the sales account manager, who forms the primary channel of communication with the client. Knowledge sharing is thus within the team across functional areas and across teams by retaining key personnel in sequential bids (*Proposition 4*). However, this potential for discovery is sometimes negated by the phenomenon which the company describes as 'executive burn-out'. The pressure on individual managers of the bid process can be so great that over a period of two to three years the managers have to be replaced because they simply cannot function effectively in subsequent teams. Discovery strategies over time are inhibited by this excessive pressure. This represents a confirmation of *Proposition 5*.

Verona Inc.: Global Supply

The global supply arrangements of Verona (a US owned MNE) are similar to those of most large pharmaceutical manufacturers. The corporation has a network of approximately thirty manufacturing facilities which are distributed throughout the world. Supply management in Verona is concerned with both the short-term, tactical realisation of the current operating plan and the long-term, strategic planning and construction of production capacity for future market expectations. On both time-scales supply adopts a following rather than a leading role. Its senior managers perceive that its function is to make happen what has been determined elsewhere. In our terms, the supply function is separately partitioned and works to given objectives (*Proposition 3*). Nevertheless, both strategic planning and operational planning must allow for supply constraints. Therefore, in practice there are flows of knowledge both into the supply function as an output of the planning processes and from the supply function as one of the inputs into planning.

In common with many corporations, Verona has deployed enterprise resource planning (ERP) software at the heart of its global supply management in order to achieve coordination between its spatially distributed supply network in meeting the global market plan. Consequently, a large part of the information which must be captured and transferred is collected and disseminated through its ERP system. The system provides ready-defined relations between marketing, manufacturing and distribution and captures knowledge supplied by the supply system as parameters for the capacities and capabilities of the global supply network. This is both internalised and external knowledge from outside suppliers covering the interface with the market (*Proposition 1*). When the forecast is generated from marketing, the responses of purchasing, manufacturing, sales and distribution are therefore determined by processes which have been rationalised and are effectively standardised. The value-creating knowledge relating to supply is thus embodied in its planning software. Knowledge is codified in a form which turns its use into a set of *routines*. Data processing and data transfer is automated wherever possible.

This codification of operating knowledge enables the corporation to maximise the value achieved on the tactical, operational time-scale. It provides real-time monitoring and control of inventories, production schedules and distribution. Changes can be made with minimal response times if there are changes in the market environment in order to capture advantages, or minimise disadvantages. Standardisation eliminates many costs and time delays of knowledge transfer which would result from differences in understanding, selective capture of data, different mental models of business processes by the individuals concerned, differences in priorities and so on. Operational effectiveness requires many complementary activities to be co-ordinated in concert, with separate but related activities often taking place simultaneously, providing a challenge to the firm to go further to identify knowledge frontiers across which knowledge sharing is to take place. These activities must be based on mutually consistent understandings of the immediate goals and of the prevailing circumstances. The ERP system is central to achieving this common operational world-view within the business for controlling concurrent operations. However, this process of knowledge sharing is imperfect, because some kinds of knowledge are less susceptible to codification and quantification, and may depend wholly on judgement and on trust of the judgement of others.

Frecknall Inc.: Pharmaceutical Product Development

Frecknall Inc. is a US owned global research-based pharmaceutical company. In the last two years it deployed a set of related computer-network based tools in its efforts to increase the success rate of its product development activities and reduce the product development cycle time. Several factors prompted the development of these tools, including cost and competitive pressures in the industry and the complexity of global product development. The aim of the network systems it developed is to facilitate communication amongst all those engaged in product development. There are four systems, which are intended to achieve knowledge sharing. These are: portfolio information for senior management, project management system for project managers and participants, team communication system and an expertise support tool for members of individual functions.

Compared with the previous cases, the correspondence between the structure of these systems and the product development process itself is less transparent. This is partly because of the relative complexity of product development in a globally dispersed pharmaceutical company. At least twenty one distinct functional specialisations can contribute to any given project, and many of these have further geographical sub-specialisation.

The absence of a clear identification between process and structure is reflected in an internal evaluation conducted by Frecknall itself. In an appraisal of the system, there is a significant variation between systems in the perceptions of their users. The Expertise Support system (which is *not* cross-functional) is assessed the most positively across all dimensions and the Portfolio Information system the least positively. Most notably, the contribution to an identifiable business process is the lowest or equal lowest rated characteristic in all cases, and the technology is the highest rated characteristic. The significance of this result for the discussion here is that technology appears to have been the leading influence in designing all these systems, and the contribution to business processes has played a smaller part.

Frecknall's system has the objective of creating a coordinated product development process, but it has paid little attention to knowledge frontiers within and across the boundaries of the corporation and its methods of knowledge sharing are unsystematic and patchy (*Proposition 2*). Although designed to achieve new combinations of knowledge (discovery strategies as in *Proposition 4*), there is little evidence that this top-down approach has yet achieved consistency in governing knowledge across the firm. There is as yet little evidence of discovery strategies as outcomes of the knowledge governance process (*Proposition 5*).

Conclusion

A variety of knowledge governance problems are encountered in the four case studies and all involve resolving global /local issues. The coordination methods employed need to take account of this and other trade-offs (e.g. specialisation versus integration) and their resolution involves attention to the processes of knowledge sharing, the incentive structure within the firm and knowledge frontiers. These trade-offs are examined using the notions of partition and integration as architectural forms. Achievement of both application strategies (uses of a given portfolio of knowledge) and discovery strategies (new combinations of knowledge) are important goals of knowledge governance structures.

Table 1. The Propositions in Practice

	Propositions	Braxia	Devonian	Verona	Frecknall
Proposition 1	Internalised knowledge versus the market	Licensing in specialised knowledge and combining with internal skills	Integration of internalised knowledge with clients' needs.	Combining internal knowledge with external market/supply information	Little attention to boundaries.
Proposition 2	Knowledge frontiers, knowledge sharing. Global/local issues	World-wide sources of technology combined and disseminated to global markets	1. Bid specialisation and experience versus local and technical expertise. 2. Loss of information from each separate bid team versus executive 'burn-out' Local bids/clients. Globally distributed expertise.	Global primacy over local conditions. Hierarchical decision-making.	Unsystematic approach. E.g. status of local knowledge inputs is unclear.
Proposition 3	Knowledge architectures. Integration-partition. Trade-offs Resolution. Implications for Incentives.	Integrating through a company-wide licensing system which coordinates the partitioned therapeutic areas. Specialised licensing department versus therapeutic expertise Virtual department liases with individual therapeutic areas. Psychic rewards across organisation	Integration across functional areas by means of flexible teams, partitioned for each client. Major Bid Team acts as a repository of information and same people on repeat teams Both individual incentives and psychic rewards for members of successful teams.	Enterprise Resource Planning system. Codified knowledge in short term leading to operational efficiency versus inflexibility in planning system. Loss of autonomy, local control and flexibility Partial feedback of knowledge from supply function into plan. No obvious integration of knowledge sharing with incentive structure.	Portfolio information system. Global information system loses (local) detail. Insufficiently developed and unclear to participants.
Proposition 4	Need for application and discovery	Exploiting complementarities between therapeutic marketing knowledge and inward licensing expertise.	Knowledge sharing within team across functional areas.		Top-down software development process
Proposition 5	Application/discovery conflicts	Governance structure for knowledge management facilitates discovery.	Successive creation of appropriate teams. Knowledge maintained across teams by retaining key personnel in sequential bids.		Little evidence of discovery strategies as outcomes of the knowledge governance process.

Examination of the cases suggests optimism in the applicability of our five propositions to the governance of knowledge sharing in multinational firms (see Table 1). Our suggestion that 'integration' and 'partition' are separate and identifiable architectural forms of achieving this requires more research. The specialisation of firms around particular knowledge domains is a product of past research to which our cases contribute additional support. Mechanisms of knowledge sharing are found to be diverse, even within such a small sample of firms. The achievement of both application strategies (uses of a given portfolio of knowledge) and discovery strategies (new combinations of knowledge) are found to be important goals of knowledge governance structures, and our findings provide preliminary evidence that controlling information may, in certain circumstances, conflict with discovery strategies. Top-down approaches to governing knowledge sharing seem to be inappropriate and the phenomenon of executive burn-out are examples of unsuccessful attempts to control information. The introduction of sophisticated IT systems for storing and sharing information are not necessarily successful in rectifying problems of the knowledge architecture of the firm unless they are introduced with great care, consultation and in accord with appropriate incentives.

Possible extensions of this research include extending the case study method to include cases with wider cultural and psychic distance between units of the firm in order to refine the propositions and derive hypotheses which will then be testable by the use of survey methodology. The results can also be refined by further longitudinal studies at the level of the individual managers and groups within firms. The incentive structures implied by our findings need further investigation together with their implications for the methods of knowledge sharing.

Acknowledgements

1 This research was conducted with financial support from the Carnegie Bosch Institute for Applied Studies in International Management, Carnegie Mellon University, Pittsburgh, PA, USA.
The authors would like to thank the editors of this special issue and three anonymous referees for their insightful and helpful comments on earlier drafts.

References

Alchian, A./Demsetz, H., Production, Information Costs and Economic Organisation, *American Economic Review*, 62, 5, 1972, pp. 777–795.

Arrow, K. J., Economic Welfare and the Allocation of Resources for Invention, in *The Rate and Direction of Inventive Activity*, National Bureau of Economic Research, Princeton University Press 1962, pp. 609–626.

Arthur, B., Competing Technologies, Increasing Returns and Lock-in by Historically Small Events, *Economic Journal*, 99, 1989, pp. 106–113.

Bercovitz, J. E. L./de Figueiredo, J. M./Teece, D. J., Firm Capabilities and Managerial Decision Making: A Theory of Innovation Biases, in Garad R./Naygar, P. R./Shapira Z. B. (eds.), *Technological Innovation: Oversights and Foresights*, Cambridge, UK: Cambridge University Press 1987.

Brown, J. S./Duguid, P., Organizational Learning and Communities of Practice: Towards a Unified View of Working, Learning and Innovation, *Organization Science*, 2, 1991, pp. 40–57.

Brown, J. S./Duguid, P., Organizing Knowledge, *California Management Review*, 40, 3, 1998, pp. 90–111.

Buckley, P. J., New Theories of International Business: Some Unresolved Issues, in Casson, M. (ed.), *The Growth of International Business*, London: George Allen and Unwin 1983.

Buckley, P. J./Carter, M. J., The Economics of Business Process Design: Motivation, Information and Coordination within the Firm, *International Journal of the Economics of Business*, 3, 1996, pp. 5–25.

Buckley, P. J./Carter, M. J., Managing Cross-Border Complementary Knowledge: Conceptual Developments in the Business Process Approach to Knowledge Management in Multinational Firms, *International Studies of Management and Organisation*, 29, 1, 1999, pp. 80–104.

Buckley, P. J./Carter, M. J., Knowledge Management in Global Technology Markets: Applying Theory to Practice, *Long Range Planning*, 33, 2000, pp. 55–71.

Buckley, P. J./Carter, M. J., Process and Structure in Knowledge Management Practices of British and US Multinational Enterprises, *Journal of International Management*, 8, 2002, pp. 29–48.

Buckley, P. J./Casson, M. C., *The Future of the Multinational Enterprise*, London: Macmillan 1976.

Burns, T./Stalker, G. M., *The Management of Innovation*, London: Tavistock 1966.

Coase, R. H., The Nature of the Firm, *Economica*, New Series, 4, November 1937, pp. 386–405.

Demsetz, H., The Theory of the Firm Revisited, in Williamson, O. E./Winter, S. G. (eds.), *The Nature of the Firm: Origins, Evolution and Development*, Oxford: Oxford University Press 1991.

Dierickx, I./Cool, K., Asset Stock Accumulation and the Sustainability of Competitive Advantage, *Management Science*, 35, 12, 1989, pp. 1504–1511.

Dixit, A. K., *The Making of Economic Policy*, Cambridge, MA: MIT Press 1996.

Fransman, M., Information, Knowledge, Vision and Theories of the Firm, in Dosi, G./Teece, D. J./Chytry, J. (eds.), *Technology, Organization and Competitiveness: Perspectives on Industrial and Corporate Change*, Oxford: Oxford University Press 1998.

Grant, R. M., Toward a Knowledge-based Theory of the Firm, *Strategic Management Journal*, 17, Winter Special Edition 1996, pp. 109–122.

Hallen, L./Wiedersheim-Paul, F., Psychic Distance and Buyer-seller Interaction, *Organisasjon, Marked og Samfund*, 16, 5, 1979, pp. 308–324.

Kogut, B./Zander, U., Knowledge of the Firm, Combinative Capabilities and the Replication of Technology, *Organization Science*, 3, 1992, pp. 383–397.

Kogut, B/Zander, U., What Do Firms Do? Coordination, Identity and Learning, *Organization Science*, 7, 5, 1996, pp. 502–518.

Koopmans, T. C. *Three Essays on the State of Economic Science*, New York: McGraw-Hill 1957.

Kuhn, T. S., *The Structure of Scientific Revolutions*, Chicago: University of Chicago Press 1962.

Lakatos, I., Falsification and the Methodology of Scientific Research Programmes, in Lakatos, I./Musgrave, A. (eds.), *Criticism and the Growth of Knowledge*, vol. 4 of Proceedings of the International Colloquium in the Philosophy of Science, Cambridge: Cambridge University Press 1970.

Langlois, R. N., Transaction Costs in Real Time, *Industrial and Corporate Change*, 1, 1, 1991, pp. 99–127.
Leonard-Barton, D., Core Capabilities and Core Rigidities: A Paradox of Managing New Product Development, *Strategic Management Journal*, 13, 1992, pp. 111–125.
Nonaka, I./Takeuchi, H., *The Knowledge-creating Company*, Oxford: Oxford University Press 1995.
North, D., *Institutions, Institutional Change and Economic Performance*, Cambridge: Cambridge University Press 1990.
Prahalad, C.K/Hamel, G., The Core Competence of the Corporation, *Harvard Business Review*, 66, 1990.
Rosen, S., Transaction Costs and the Internal Labor Market in Williamson, O. E./ Winter, S. G. (eds.), *The Nature of the Firm: Origins, Evolution and Development*, Oxford: Oxford University Press 1991.
Scott-Morgan, P., *The Unwritten Rules of the Game*, New York: McGraw-Hill 1994.
Simon, H. A., *Administrative Behaviour*, New York: Free Press 1945.
von Hippel, E., "'Sticky Information' and the Locus of Problem Solving: Implications for Innovation", in Chandler A. D./Hagström, P. Sölvell, Ö., (eds.), *The Dynamic Firm: The Role of Technology, Strategy, Organisation and Regions*, Oxford: Oxford University Press 1998.
Weick, K. E./Roberts, K. H., Collective Mind in Organisations: Heedful Interrelating on the Flight Deck, *Administrative Science Quarterly*, 38, 3, 1993, pp. 357–381.
Williamson, O. E., *Markets and Hierarchies*, New York: Free Press 1975.
Williamson, O. E., *The Economic Institutions of Capitalism*, New York: Free Press 1985.
Williamson, O. E./Wachter, M. L./Harris, J. E., Understanding the Employment Relation: the Analysis of Idiosyncratic Exchange, *Bell Journal of Economics*, 6, 1975, pp. 350–80.
Yin, R. K., *Case Study Research: Design and Methods* (2nd edition), London: Sage 1994.

mir *Edition*

Andreas Wald

Network Structures and Network Effects in Organizations

A Network Analysis in Multinational Corporations

2003, XVIII, 238 pages, pb., € 49,90 (approx. US $ 49,90)
ISBN 3-409-12395-4

Network structures have been praised as the organizational form of today's multinational corporation. Building on conceptual work on network organizations, a quantitative network analysis of formal and informal organizational structures is performed in this study. It is tested whether network structures can be identified empirically. Moreover, the effects of organizational structures on strategic decision making in two multinational corporations are analyzed. A theoretical framework is provided by an exchange model and by social capital theory.

The book is addressed to scholars of international management and organizational studies.

Betriebswirtschaftlicher Verlag Dr. Th. Gabler GmbH, Abraham-Lincoln-Str. 46, 65189 Wiesbaden

mir Special Issue 2003/3, pp. 27–46

Management
International Review
© Gabler Verlag 2003

Julian Birkinshaw/Carl F. Fey

Organization of Research and Development in Large Multinational Firms[1]

Abstract

- This paper examines how research and development is organized in large multinational firms. The paper identifies three key criteria which differentiate the different organizational systems firms use: doing R&D at the corporate level vs. divisions, the degree of geographic dispersion of R&D activities, and the degree of choice in where to conduct R&D. Results are tested on a sample of 107 firms based in the UK and Sweden.

Key Results

- Results indicate that choice is the most important organizational dimension to facilitate superior firm performance. In-depth case studies of ABB, HP, Ericsson, and Electra (disguised name) are then used to put the large sample results into context.

- Case study analysis reveals a high level of variation in systems of R&D organization and reveals that regardless of the organization system used, it is possible to create checks and balances to guard against the worst drawbacks of the chosen system.

Authors

Julian Birkinshaw, Associate Professor of Strategic and International Management, London Business School, London, England, UK.
Carl F. Fey, Assistant Professor of International Business, Institute of International Business, Stockholm School of Economics, Stockholm, Sweden.

Julian Birkinshaw/Carl F. Fey

Introduction

Most large firms recognise the importance of their R&D activities – as the primary source of new products and technologies – to their sustained competitiveness. However, the issue of how to organize R&D effectively is a matter of considerable debate. One model that has been used widely (e.g. AT&T, IBM, Philips) was based around a central R&D laboratory that undertook everything from basic research through to new product development. However, more recently large firms have increasingly realised that the speed and scope of technological development makes it impossible for them to do everything in-house at headquarters. As a result, many firms now spread their R&D activities more around the world. Many firms have also developed partnerships and alliances as a means of tapping into external sources of technology. And, many firms have sought to make their R&D activities more cost-effective – by focusing on the more applied end of the R&D spectrum, or by creating a higher level of accountability around their R&D investments. However, the performance implications of different organizational designs for a firms' R&D activities remain unclear.

These changes in the organization of R&D have been underway for many years, but while the literature on external sources of technology has become quite extensive (e.g. Coombs/Richards 1993, Croisier 1998, Narula/Hagedoor 1999) and an abundant amount is written on R&D strategy (e.g., Pavitt 1990, Tidd/Bessant/Pavit 2001, Tidd/Trewhella 1997), the literature on internal R&D organization is much thinner (e.g., Gassmann/Zedtwitz 1999, Coombs/Richards 1993), and mostly written from a rather applied perspective (e.g. Peters 1994, Reger 1999, Roussel et al. 1991). The purpose of this paper, then, is to report on a detailed theoretical and empirical analysis of internal structures and systems used in R&D organizations. Using case-study data collected in four companies as well as questionnaire responses from 107 companies, the paper addresses two broad questions. First, what structures and systems are used in the R&D organizations of large firms to allocate resources to market and technological opportunities? Second, what, if any, is the impact of the chosen structures and systems on R&D performance?

Research and Development Organization

The management literature has long underplayed the design of international R&D activities of firms (Cheng/Bolon 1993, Granstrand et al. 1993). While, substantial economic analysis has been done to explain why firms locate in different countries, little research has focused on how they are actually designed (DeMeyer 1993). Several researchers have developed taxonomies of R&D subsidiaries' organizational activities (e.g., Chiesa 1996, Kummerle 1997, Pearce 1989, Ronstadt 1997), but a comprehensive model for organization of international R&D is still lacking (Gassmann/Von Zedwitz 1999). Further, more work has gone into classifying the roles of subsidiaries rather than the overall design of a firm's R&D activities. For example, among more recent contributions, Kuemmerle (1997) discusses how new R&D laboratories were formed and how the main objective of most laboratories can be defined as either home-base augmenting or home-based exploiting. Chiesa (1996) has also developed a taxonomy of R&D which differentiates between R&D site role being experimentation and exploration. Medcof (1997) presents a useful review of other R&D unit taxonomies and also develops an extensive eight category taxonomy. Gassmann and Zedwitz (1999) develop a useful categorization of overall R&D organizational systems of a firm including ethnocentric cenralized R&D (all R&D is cenralized), geocentric R&D (R&D is centralized, but R&D employees are sent abroad to collaborate with local local suppliers, manufacturing, and customers or just to sense what is going on in the environment), polycentric R&D (local R&D sites are established), and the R&D hub model (Most R&D is centralized, but there are smaller R&D centers focusing on special areas and acting as listening posts which are geographically dispersed), and the integrated R&D network (a true network of R&D sites around the world with no clear center). While Gassmann and Zedwitz do a good job of presenting different possible ways of organizing a firm's R&D activities, they leave investigating the performance implications of different systems for future researchers.

There are several dimensions that are of particular importance when considering design of international R&D activities of a firm. One issue which R&D managers wrestle with is what role corporate R&D should play compared to the divisions (Coombs/Richards 1993, Reger 1999, Roussel/ Saad/Ericksson 1991). Based on a sample of 25 UK companies Coombs and Richards (1993) analyze the balance of responsibility between the corporate level and the business unit level and suggest that this is an important dimension to consider when evaluating organizational design of R&D systems. To simplify our discussion somewhat, it is possible to make out two polar approaches to R&D organization. At one extreme research is the responsibility of the corporate level. This can be seen as the traditional model that firms like AT&T, IBM and Philips used successfully for many decades (Leonard-Barton 1995). The chief benefit of this design is essentially that it provides protection for technological innovations that would otherwise be killed off by the short-term demands of the market (Schumpeter 1934). However this can also be seen as a weakness, because its focus on technology-driven innovations makes it unresponsive to market demands, historically slow, reluctant to switch away from technologies which have been years developing in the pipeline, and expensive to maintain. Having R&D be the responsibility of the divisions is the other extreme and has the exact opposite strengths and weaknesses as those mentioned above for the corporate model.

A second important question is how geographically dispersed R&D facilities of an MNC should be (Terpstra 1977, Zander 1999)? Much work has been done to describe how globally-distributed a firm's R&D activities are (e.g. Pearce 1989, Zander 1999), however, the performance implications of geographic dispersion of R&D remains murky. It is argued that R&D requires much sharing of tacit knowledge which is best done in person and thus it is best for researchers to be co-located. Having a central R&D facility also decreases costs since less equipment is needed (much equipment is only needed occasionally and can be shared). Further, co-location saves costs in terms of travel costs and time. However, different parts of the world are good at doing different things and thus there is a benefit for an MNC's R&D being present to learn from different local environments. There are clearly costs *and* benefits to decentralisation of R&D.

A third important issue to consider in design of R&D is how much choice exists about where a given R&D project will be conducted, both internally and externally. The issue of choice relates to the concept of internal markets. The internal capital market is a well recognized concept (Williamson 1975). There is also a line of thinking around the use of transfer-pricing within the firm (Cook 1955, Eccles 1982, Hirschleifer 1956). Further, some recent work in economics (e.g., Baker et al. 2001) also addresses internal markets. And there is a more practically-oriented body of literature that applies market-like thinking inside large firms (Birkinshaw 1999, Halal 1994, Hamel 2000, Peters 1994). These authors suggest that internal choice inside of a firm is helpful. Increased choice will increase efficiency as R&D groups understand they will not get business if they do not deliver value. However, some argue that such pressure is counter-productive for R&D and will create a situation where nobody is willing to do the risky projects that may pay big dividends if they succeed. Further, for a system of internal choice to work, some degree of duplication is necessary – if there are no duplicated facilities and competencies then there can not be any decision about where to do a given project. These duplicated facilities may be pursuing competing technologies which can be beneficial when it is unclear which technology is superior. However, on the downside, duplication costs money. Further, if the decision is made to go with a superior external lab instead of awarding the project in-house, the company may end up with a better project short-term, but by not developing in-house competence the company may be less competitive in the future. Clearly, there are pros and cons to having an R&D system which allows either internal or external choice.

Our research seeks to understand the current approaches to R&D resource-allocation used in large firms. And in keeping with the above discussion, we are primarily concerned about three dimensions of R&D organization – the extent that R&D is conducted at corporate R&D labs or in divisions, how geographically dispersed R&D activities are, and the extent that customers have a free choice in their source of R&D. Thus, we arrive at our first research questions:

Research Question 1. What structures and systems are used in large R&D organizations, in terms particularly of: (a) the extent to which R&D is conducted at corporate rather than division level, (b) geographical dispersion of R&D activities, and (c) the extent to which customers have a free choice in their source of R&D.

Our second research question is concerned with the impact of the various designs of a firms' R&D activities on R&D performance. Given the lack of strong *a priori* expectations, then, our preference is to work with a research question, as follows:

Research Question 2. What impact, if any, do different forms of R&D organization (as identified above) have on the performance of the R&D organization and thus the firm's performance?

Research Methodology

Research Design

This research was conducted in two phases. Phase one involved in-depth case studies of four firms based on interviews with 55 executives. Phase two was a mail questionnaire that yielded 107 responses from R&D – intensive firms in Sweden and Great Britain. The clinical phase of research provided the insights into the resource allocation processes in R&D that allowed us to operationalize the constructs and put together the questionnaire.

In phase one of the research we undertook comparative case studies of four firms operating in the electronic-electrical engineering sector – ABB, Ericsson, HP and Electra[2]. These firms were chosen to represent a variety of different organizational approaches to R&D, as will become clear. However, in order to facilitate comparison we focused our research in ABB on the automation and control side (where R&D is focused on electronics and software), and in Ericsson we restricted ourselves to a study of the mobile systems division (which is one of three divisions at Ericsson and also predominantly is a software and systems business, rather than consumer electronics). Table 1 provides an overview of the four firms' R&D organizations, in terms of where their R&D activities are located and their size.

Table 1. Characteristics of Sample Firms and Data Collected

Dimension	ABB Automation and Control	Ericsson Radio Systems	HP	Electra
Total sales revenues 1997	$31.3 billion	$24.1 billion	$43.2 billion	$19.0 billion
R&D headquarters	Zurich	Stockholm	Palo Alto, CA	East Coast, USA
R&D expenditure 1997	$2.6 billion	21b SEK	$3.1 billion	$1.1 billion
Amount of total R&D done at Corporate level	$300m	0**	$250m	$350m
Major R&D locations	Switzerland, Sweden, US, Germany, Finland, Italy, Norway	Stockholm, US, Germany, UK, Canada, smaller sites in another 40 countries	US, Japan, UK, France	US, Japan, UK, France
Interviews				
Senior managers in R&D organization	5	7	3	7
Technical people & lab managers	3	11	3	6
Managers in business units	3	4	6	4
Locations for interviews	Sweden, Germany, Finland, US	Sweden, US, Japan, Canada, UK	US, UK, Canada	US, Japan, Canada
Questionnaires returned	10	12	11	10

** R&D in Ericsson is all conducted either at the business area or business unit level, rather than through corporate research labs.

Data in these four companies were collected between December 1997 and April 1999. We conducted a total of 55 interviews (each one to two hours in length) with R&D vice presidents, lab managers, and business unit managers (see Table 1). These interviews were semi-structured around issues of resource allocation. Questions were gradually refined as the research progressed and we began to get a more detailed understanding of each firm. We also conducted a questionnaire survey in the companies. It was put together as the interview stage neared completion, and it was then mailed to all the interview subjects. 43 of the 55 questionnaires were returned. The questionnaire aimed to provide quantitative verification for our qualitative findings. We developed multi-item scales for what appeared to be the main constructs emerging from the interviews. These scales were examined for reliability using the 43 responses and refined accordingly. The analysis then consisted of a series of Kruskal Wallis ANOVA models to identify differences in mean levels between the four firms.

The second phase of data collection was a large sample survey using the questionnaire that was developed in the four-company study. For practical reasons this survey was undertaken in Sweden and Great Britain. In Sweden, we assembled a database of R&D-intensive firms using the sources *Hugin* (owned by magazine Veckans Affärer) and by using the Swedish Institute of Statistical Information's (SCB) database. Foreign-owned firms were excluded from this database, as were holding companies. The questionnaire was sent to 160 companies. In Great Britain we used the Financial Times list of the largest 500 R&D intensive firms in the country, which after removing foreign-owned companies resulted in a database of 220 firms. In both countries, we phoned each of these firms to get the name of the R&D director. The questionnaire was then mailed to that individual, and after a follow-up mailing we ended up with 52 responding firms in Sweden (31%) and 55 responding firms in Great Britain (24% response rate). This response rate is within the norms for questionnaire research, and higher than many international surveys (Harzing 2000).

Construct Operationalization

The constructs were operationalized in the course of the case-study and pilot-testing phases of research. This section describes how they were measured on the questionnaire.

Dimensions of R&D Organization

Doing R&D at the corporate level vs. divisions, the degree of geographic dispersion of R&D activities, and the degree of choice in where to conduct R&D have been identified above as three key dimensions of R&D organization which managers and academics alike need to consider. These three dimensions are operationalised below.

Doing R&D at the Corporate Level vs. Divisions

1. Divisionalisation of Research. How is (a) pure research, (b) applied research split in your firm? 1 = done at a corporate level, 2 = split between corporate and divisions, and 3 = done by the divisions. Inter-item correlation = 0.79.
2. Commercial input into R&D decisions. Assess the relative input of commercial and technical managers into the following decisions: (a) overall funding levels, (b) definition of specific projects, (c) definition of long-term research trajectories, (d) identification of new research opportunities, (e) "killing" a project that is delayed or in difficulties, (f) paying additional costs when projects are delayed. 1 = decided by technical managers, 5 = decided by commercial managers. Cronbach's Alpha = 0.76.
3. Contract research funding. Which of the following systems are used for funding research? (a) Projects are contracted by divisions; (b) a fixed tax paid by divisions (reverse coded). 1 = not used at all to 7 = used to a great extent. Cronbach's Alpha = 0.80.

The Degree of Geographic Dispersion of R&D Activities

Number of R&D locations. Please indicate the number of locations around the world where your company performs R&D work.

The Degree of Choice in Where to Conduct R&D

1. Internal choice. Assess the extent to which you agree with the following statements where 1 = disagree completely and 8 = agree completely: (a) Managers of different sites can influence the decisions about where specific projects are located; (b) There is an active "bottom-up" process whereby managers of different sites bid for or request specific projects; (c) For any given R&D project there are several sites that could potentially undertake the work; (d) There is a "market-like" system for allocating projects between different sites; (e) R&D work is sometimes moved between sites as a result of performance differences between sites; (f) Sites often undertake R&D projects on the basis of ideas picked up in the local marketplace. Cronbach's Alpha = 0.70.
2. External choice. Indicate the extent to which the following approaches are used in your firm where 1 = not used at all, 7 = used to a great extent: (a) Business managers contract with external R&D sources if they do not believe the necessary capability exists in-house; (b) Business managers use both in-house R&D and external sources *at the same time* for their development work; (c) Technology is bought or licensed from other firms; (d) R&D managers sell their services or technology to *other firms*. Cronbach's Alpha = 0.71.

Measures of Performance

For the large sample study we collected secondary performance information on firm performance including return on equity for 1997 and average sales growth from 1994–1997. For the four case studies we collected data on operating margins for three years and asked respondents to self-rate several aspects of R&D performance including: (1) getting new products to market quickly, (2) coming up with radical/breakthrough technologies, (3) bringing breakthrough technologies to market, (4) making good use of outside sources of technology, (5) making efficient use of R&D expenditure, (6) technological leadership in your chosen industry.

Findings

The findings from the research are multi-faceted, with qualitative findings from the case studies and quantitative findings from both the case studies and the large-sample survey. Our approach is as follows. First, we describe how the four case-study firms organized their R&D. Second, we describe the quantitative findings, which provide support for the use of organizing R&D such that both internal and external choice exists to increase performance, but which does not provide support for geographic dispersion or divisionalization of R&D. Third, there is a discussion as to the reasons why the performance link is not stronger, which leads to the final part of the findings section in which we revisit the case-study data and show that equifinality between systems of R&D organization and performance can be observed.

Case Study Findings: Types of Organization of R&D Activities

The case study analysis indicates very large differences between the firms in the way that R&D activities were organized. ABB used a market-like system in which almost all R&D resources were tied to specific contracts and the business units had considerable choice as to where they sourced technology. HP used a more traditional hierarchical system, in which corporate research funding was obtained almost exclusively through a tax on business units, and there was relatively little choice for the business units as to where they sourced their technology. Ericsson

Table 2. Mean Responses From Four Companies to Resource Allocation Questions

	ABB Automation and Control	Ericsson Radio Systems	HP	Electra	Kruskal-Wallis Chi Square (sig.)
Divisionalisation of research	1.58	1.75	1.36	1.20	7.86**
Contract research funding	5.37	3.53	1.42	3.56	13.76***
Commercial input into R&D decisions	2.64	2.50	1.73	2.17	3.91*
Internal choice	29.35	20.08	10.94	15.80	11.83**
External choice	4.10	3.68	3.87	4.22	1.12
Number of R&D locations*	10 corporate + divisions	50	4	6	NA
Getting new products to market rapidly	4.6	4.75	4.18	3.50	1.98
Coming up with radical/breakthrough technologies	5.1	5.33	5.09	4.80	0.28
Bringing breakthrough technologies to market	4.7	4.75	3.91	3.90	1.43
Making good use of outside sources of technology	4.1	4.00	3.20	3.20	1.71
Making efficient use of R&D expenditure	4.40	4.75	4.73	3.90	0.95
Technological leadership in your industry	5.60	5.58	5.09	4.90	1.04
Average operating margins 1993–1997**	11.0	12.2	13.9	18.4	N/A

* This measure is based on estimates by highest ranking R&D manager we talked to in each firm
** Taken from Value Line financial reporting service

and Electra both used hybrid systems that lay in-between ABB and HP, though each also had some important distinctive features. Table 2 provides data to support this point. Below we describe the R&D organizations in greater detail.

ABB has approximately ten corporate research and development centers in different locations in Europe and North America. Most of their work is labeled "technical support" which is contract-based work undertaken for business units. The second category of work is "strategic development" in the form of projects that are co-funded by corporate and business units. The third category, which is only 2–3% of the total, is pure innovation research that is funded solely through corporate resources. Corporate research and development centers together account for around 10% of the total R&D budget of ABB, with the rest being done in business units. So taken as a whole, the model is highly market-driven, with almost all R&D activities focused around specific commercial propositions. One respondent commented that the "focus has been on market oriented research since

Percy Barnevik became CEO"; another said that "There is money for research (as opposed to development) within ABB but you have to fight for it".

In terms of creating choice, ABB allows business units high degrees of freedom in their decision of where to source R&D. Corporate research and development centers are set up as legal entities and while they are not seeking to make a profit *per se*, they are held accountable for their revenues and costs. One respondent observed that they "Compete with external firms for the right to do research for business units", so there is clearly a sense of customer responsiveness built into the corporate research and development centers. There is also some duplication between the capabilities of the corporate research and development centers, so to a limited degree they are also competing with each other. Finally, in terms of selling their services to external entities, one person observed that this is "not encouraged, and to some degree prohibited, but it happens anyway". A couple of instances were mentioned where corporate research and development centers had sold their services to non-competing firms.

Ericsson (the radio systems group) bears some similarity to ABB in the extent to which R&D is market-driven. Back in 1991 when the radio systems group was created, it was decided that the business units would control all R&D. Each business unit now has its own R&D responsibility, and partly as a result of this structure, the work they do is focused on development rather than research. However, it was recognized that this structure had the potential to be too short-term focused, so an additional unit was established to do applied research that was of interest to all three major business unit. This unit receives a small amount of its resources through a corporate fund that is agreed by the heads of the three business units; the rest of its funding is obtained on a contract basis with the business units.

The actual R&D work is carried out for the most part in semi-independent "design centers" of which there are more than 50 around the world. They work for business units on a contract basis, and as a result there is a form of market system at work, in that for a given piece of work there are potentially several internal design centers, and other external entities, who could all "bid" for the work. As one corporate respondent commented, "we have never forced a business unit to use a specific design center". In practice, while it is not realistic that there would be a choice between all 50 design centers, it is common that 2 to 4 design centers would be considered for a project. However, once a project has begun and a business unit has started to develop the competencies of a given design center for that project, it would be very costly in terms of time and money (and thus uncommon) to switch to another design center. In a few cases there are design centers that also sell their products on the external market.

Hewlett Packard operates with a very different model that is to a large degree technology-driven. There is a distinct group call HP Labs, which is funded exclusively through a corporate "tax" on the business units. HP Labs budget is 8% of the total R&D budget for HP, and its mandate is to work on technologies that the business units could do but are not prioritizing at the current time, and on new technological areas that lie beyond the business units' existing areas of interest. And unlike ABB or Ericsson, they are not interested in enhancing their funding through contract-based relationships with business units. As one lab manager explained, "we do not want business units to contribute to our funding – that would compromise our independence". The work done by HP Labs is defined through inputs from business units and from its own people, based on their areas of expertise and on the insights they gain from their scientific communities. The model gives them considerable independence from a funding perspective, but of course they still have to demonstrate that they are providing value to the business units who are ultimately paying for them.

In terms of choice, there is very little internal duplication within HP Labs, and while business units are free in principle to work with outside entities, their preference is typically to work with groups in HP Labs. There were no cases mentioned of HP Labs selling its services on the external market.

Electra operates a model that until ten years ago looked a lot like HP's. But in 1992 it became much more contract-driven so that now it is a hybrid between HP and ABB. Simply stated, the "Corporate Research and Technology" group (CR&T) is funded in three ways – a pure "tax" component that is based on the relative R&D expenditures of the business units, a "negotiated tax" component that the business units have some say over how it is spent, and a contract-research component. However, a key point to make is that the total CR&T budget is stable at 1.4% of Electra revenues, so that if the business units elect not to use CR&T for contract-based work, they end up paying more through the other components. The result is that CR&T is being held more accountable for what it does, but the customer (i.e. the business unit) does not have the option of withdrawing its resources. As one respondent observed, "if there are any delays or problems in a project, it is always the business unit who ends up paying". Business units have the option, in principle, of working with outside parties or even doing the relevant R&D work themselves, but they still end up paying CR&T anyway. The result is that the model ends up being close to that used by HP.

Summary: In terms of research question 1, we see that the four companies each has its own model for design of R&D. ABB is evidently closest to an internal market model, both in terms of being customer driven and allowing the customer a free choice in their source for R&D. Ericsson has a model that is internal market-like in principle but slightly less so in practice (see the numbers in Table 2). HP and Electra both have models in which R&D funding is allocated in a more hierarchical manner.

Design of R&D Activities and Performance

Moving on to research question 2, what is the impact of these differences on R&D performance? The large-sample questionnaire survey findings are indicated in Tables 3 and 4. Table 3 shows the means and standard deviations for all constructs and the correlation matrix. One can note that high correlations/multicolinearity is not a problem. Table 4 reports the OLS regressions on performance measures ROE and sales growth. The results indicate that there is there is good evidence to support that performance is positively affected when R&D is organized in such a way that choice exists as to which internal unit, or even an external unit compared to an internal unit, could conduct various R&D projects. Support was also provided suggesting that it was beneficial for performance if the divisions had a role in R&D (as opposed to only corporate). However, no performance effect for how

Table 3. Pearson Correlation Coefficients for Large Sample (n = 107)

Variable	Mean	SD	2	3	4	5	6	7	8	9	10	11
1. Divisionalisation of research	2.04	0.83	–0.097	0.152	0.230*	0.039	0.117	0.063	0.082	–0.074	0.153	0.224
2. Contract research funding	3.77	1.58		0.136	–0.151	0.161	–0.094	0.076	–0.005	–0.035	–281	–0.031
3. External choice	3.30	1.51			0.019	0.254*	–118	–0.058	–0.108	0.035	0.289**	0.079
4. Commercial input into R&D decisions	2.80	0.60				–0.003	0.112	–0.001	–0.119	–0.156	0.184	–0.060
5. Internal choice	3.13	1.11					0.223*	–0.058	–0.202	–0.184	0.285	0.178
6. Number of R&D locations	6.80	10.95						–0.173	–0.235	–0.251	0.164	0.171
7. Getting new products to market	4.42	1.25							0.323**	0.699***	0.189	0.358*
8. Coming up with radical/ breakthrough technologies	4.47	1.38								0.699***	0.141	0.142
9. Overall R&D performance	4.54	0.89									0.177	0.200
10. Growth in ROS 1994–1997	2.06	2.33										0.073
11. Return on equity 1997	28.59	90.64										

* $p < 0.05$; ** $p < 0.01$

Table 4. Regression on Performance Measures for Large Sample (n = 107)

	ROE 1997	Sales Growth 1994–1997
HQ Country (UK/Sweden)	−0.389*	0.181*
Commercial input	0.168	0.124
Contracting	0.128	−0.114
Split of R&D	0.354*	0.056
Number of R&D locations	0.232	0.025
External choice	1.00	0.193*
Internal choice	0.352*	0.140*
N	107	107
R^2	0.311	0.193
Adjusted R^2	0.138	0.136

geographically dispersed R&D was observed (regression coefficients did have the correct sign despite being non-significant). Admittedly, our measure of geographic dispersion of R&D activities could be better and this may be the reason for non-significant results.

However, the case studies indicate that the story is more complicated than the relatively simple picture portrayed by the regression results present above. Put simply, the case studies show that *how* R&D systems are implemented is very important. Different checks and balances can be used to mitigate (or increase if done incorrectly) the drawbacks of a particular design of R&D organization. As Table 2 and other information about the four case studies indicate, case study firms have significant differences in all but one of the dimensions characterizing the type of R&D organization, but no significant differences at all on the subjective measures of performance. There is also one objective measure of overall performance – average yearly operating margins for 1993–1997. This measure varied from 11.0% in ABB to 18.4% in Electra. These differences are relatively small, so there does not appear to be evidence of a material difference in performance between these companies either.

Case-Study Findings: Configurations of Structures and Systems

Our case studies highlight two basic approaches to R&D design – a hierarchical or technology-driven model exemplified by HP and to a lesser degree Electra; and an internal-market model exemplified by ABB and to a lesser degree Ericsson. These are treated as "ideal types" in the subsequent analysis. Table 5 provides a summary of the elements in the two configurations.

Table 5. Two Configurations of Structure and Systems in R&D

	Hierarchy-based Model	**Internal Market Model**
Dominant system for R&D resource allocation	1. Corporate R&D funded primarily through "tax" on business units 2. Limited commercial input into R&D funding decisions; 3. Limited internal and external choice in sourcing technology	1. Corporate R&D funded primarily through contracts with business units 2. High level of commercial input into R&D funding decisions 3. Considerable internal and external choice in sourcing technology
Primary weaknesses of system	1. R&D can become isolated from business units 2. R&D can be seen as expensive and irrelevant to the needs of business units	1. The company can become very short-term focused in its R&D activities 2. Business-unit goals can end up being prioritized ahead of corporate goals 3. There can be a lack of coordination between business units
Approaches used by sample firms to alleviate primary weaknesses	1. Development of vertical relationships between central R&D activities and business units 2. A strong entrepreneurial mindset in the central R&D activities 3. Brokering activities in the business units	1. Alternative funding vehicles for risky or long-term projects 2. Strong horizontal relationships across R&D units 3. Corporate veto rights over resource allocation decisions made by business units

The Hierarchy-based Model

Because of the emphasis in this model on making decisions centrally and focusing on technology-led decision making, its primary drawback is that the central R&D activities may become isolated from the business units, and as a result their efforts may end up being perceived as expensive and irrelevant. In HP and Electra this drawback was countered in three ways:

(a) Development of vertical relationships between central R&D activities and business units. HP had developed a very impressive set of vertical linkages between HP Labs and the business units. These include formal two-day reviews between Labs and their associated business units every year; exchanges of personnel from business units to Labs and vice versa; technology fairs at which the Labs presented their current projects to the business units; a proven methodology for "technology transfer" from Lab to business unit; and a number of computer-based systems for knowledge sharing. Respondents felt that these relationships worked very well. One business unit manager said that "Unless I take the time to talk to them, there will be little expectation that they come with anything we need." A Lab manager commented that "The divisions who are most successful at getting our time are the ones who work hard at getting me excited. The divisions that wait for great ideas to arrive will always be disappointed." In other words, there was a clear recognition on both sides that these relationships were the key to R&D success.

Electra also recognized the need to create these sorts of vertical relationships, but their systems were less well-developed. Electra did, however, have some co-production arrangements between CR&T and the BUs. Further, the Electra funding processes required significant discussions between the BUs and CR&T. Finally, Electra had monthly meetings between Chief Technology Officers (of the business units) and CR&T portfolio leaders. It is, however, worth noting that while HP had significant informal contact between the BUs and corporate research at all levels, Electra mostly had contact between top management.

(b) A strong entrepreneurial mindset in the central R&D activities. A consistent message emerging from HP Labs was the importance attached to "finding a customer". In other words, HP Labs managers were expected to act as entrepreneurs – taking their technology or idea and selling it to one or more business units. And this philosophy pervaded the organization – it cropped up in the appraisal and reward system, and it was frequently mentioned by senior Lab managers.

(c) Brokering activities in the business units. Finally, another useful system in HP was a brokering activity, by which we mean a relatively small number of senior managers who were on the lookout for synergies between business units, and ways to match up technological developments in the Labs with opportunities in the business units. For example, in one part of HP they had developed a "group champions program" to act as the interface between labs and business units.

Taken together, these systems allowed HP to avoid the potential problem of R&D activities becoming isolated, expensive and irrelevant. Interestingly, the story at Electra was less clear-cut. Certainly, they had developed some of the same systems to keep R&D and business units working together, but in addition a great deal of energy had gone into changing the funding mechanism to ensure that each business unit was getting value-for-money for its R&D expenditure. Our interpretation is that this change was actually detrimental, because it led to effort being devoted to contractual negotiations rather than relationship-building between the central labs and business units.

The Internal-market Model

Because the emphasis in this model is on market-driven contract funding with business units, the potential drawbacks it faces are a short-term focus, a lack of coordination among the business units, and a risk that corporate goals will be subordinated to business-unit goals. In ABB and Ericsson, these drawbacks were countered in three ways.

(a) Alternative funding vehicles for risky or long-term projects. ABB had developed a number of special funding vehicles for projects that were either too risky or too long-term oriented to be funded through the normal contract system. "High Impact Projects" were put forward by business units and if accepted were funded up to 50% by the corporate research group. In addition there was a small amount of money for corporate "programs" that were put forward by program managers in the corporate research and development centers. And some countries had their own arrangements as well, such as ABB Finland whose "step-up" fund was available to business units to underwrite high-risk projects. This money had to be refunded to ABB Finland if the project ended up being a success.

Ericsson had a similar arrangement in the form of an applied-research group who received a small amount of funding direct from the business units. This group had become very effective at leveraging its small amount of money by persuading the business units to invest additional amounts of money in projects they felt were important. In the words of one research manager, "they (the business units) think they control product development and we let them believe it". The implication being that she played a large part in setting the agenda, but she preferred to let them take the credit for it because they were ultimately paying for it. A second, and completely separate source of funding was the Ericsson Business Innovation group, a "corporate venturing" group who invested in new and risky projects that failed to get funded through traditional means.

(b) Strong horizontal relationships across R&D units. To avoid the problem of a lack of coordination among business units in their sourcing of R&D, both firms had put in place research advisory boards. These boards included senior corporate R&D managers who were in a position to judge whether there was unnecessary duplication across R&D sites, and where opportunities for coordination existed. As one of them observed, "our job is to review what we are doing, and whether we are missing big opportunities. But at the same time we have to avoid too much top down control".

(c) Corporate veto rights over resource allocation decisions made by business units. The final system, which we only saw limited evidence for, was the existence of a corporate right of "veto" over the resource allocation decisions of business units. The best example of this was in Ericsson, where one business unit had decided to award a development contract to a European design center purely because of its proven ability to do the work. However, in reviewing this decision at a corporate level, they ended up awarding the contract to an Asian design center on the basis that it would enhance their chances of selling equipment to a local Asian telecoms operator. This brief example illustrates an important point, namely that an internal market system runs the risk of prioritizing the narrow goals of the business unit (in this case, what was the most efficient way of getting a piece of development work done) rather than thinking in terms of the broader agenda of the corporation (in this case, selling equipment in the

Asian marketplace). Unless corporate management ultimately has the right to veto, or at least demand a reconsideration of, the resource allocation decisions of the business units, then they are essentially letting the market system take over. Taken together, these three systems allow ABB and Ericsson to counter the biggest potential drawbacks of operating with an internal-market system for resource allocation.

Conclusions

This paper makes several important points. First, the paper identifies three key criteria which differentiate the different organizational systems firms use: doing R&D at the corporate level vs divisions, the degree of geographic dispersion of R&D activities, and the degree of choice in where to conduct R&D. Empirical results form our large sample study suggest that designing a firm's R&D such that parties needing R&D can choose internally between different units which could carry out the project increases firm performance. Further, results indicate that allowing internal R&D customers to choose to source R&D either inside or outside the firm (what we call external choice) also increases firm performance. No result was observed for geographic dispersion being positively associated with firm performance (although the coefficients did have the correct sign).

However, the story is more complicated than the large sample results make out as the case studies show. The case studies show that how systems are implemented is very important. The case studies demonstrate that it is possible to implement various checks and balances such that a given R&D organizational design has either better or worse performance than would be expected by the basic characteristics of the system.

This paper represented a first attempt to get to grips with organizational design of a firms R&D. As with all inductive research it opened up as many new questions as it provided answers, but considerable progress was made on defining important dimensions for describing R&D organization and on providing some initial results to how type of R&D organization is related to performance. Future research should attempt to test the ideas developed here in a more rigorous manner and usefully extend this research into other industry and country settings.

Endnotes

1 Research assistance from Emma Lansing, Anna Norin, Henrik Kemkes and Andreas Svensson is gratefully acknowledged. The helpful comments of seminar participants at the University of Uppsala and Stockholm School of Economics are acknowledged.
2 Electra is a disguised company name.

References

Baker, G., R./Gibbons, K./Murphy J., Bringing the Market Inside the Firm, *American Economic Review*, 91, 2, 2001, pp. 212–218.
Baker, G., R./Gibbons, K./Murphy, J., Informal Authority in Organizations, *Journal of Law Economics and Organization*, 15, 1, 1999, pp. 56–73.
Birkinshaw, J. M., Multinational Strategy and Organization: An Internal Market Perspective, in Hood, N./Young, S. (eds), *The Globalization of Multinational Enterprise Activity and Economic Development*, Oxford: MacMillan 1999, pp. 230–248.
Cheng, J. L. C./Bolon, D. S., The Management of Multinational R&D: a Neglected Topic in International Buisness Research, *Journal of International Buisnes Studies*, 1, 1993, pp. 1–18.
Chiesa, V., Managing the Internationalization of R&D Activities, *IEEE Transactions on Engineering Management*, 43, 1, 1996, pp. 7–23.
Coase, R. A. The nature of the Firm, *Economica*, 4, 1937, pp. 386–405.
Cook, P. W. Jr., Decentralization and the Transfer-price Problem, *The Journal of Business*, 18, 2, 1955, pp. 87–94.
Coombs, R./Richards, A., Strategic Control of Technology in Diversified Companies with Decentralized R&D, *Technology Analysis & Strategic Management*, 5, 4, 1993, pp. 385–396.
Croisier, B., The governance of External Research: Empirical Test of Some Transaction-cost Related Factors, *R&D Management*, 28, 4, 1998, pp. 289–298.
De Meyer, A Management of an International Network of Industrial R&D Laboratories, *R&D Management*, 23, 2, 1993, pp. 109–120.
Eccles, R. G., *Transfer Pricing: A Theory for Practice*. Lexington, MA: Lexington Books 1982.
Gassmann, O./von Zedtwitz, M., New Concepts and Trends in International R&D Organization, *Research Policy*, 28, 2, 1999, pp. 231–250.
Granstrand, O./Håkanson, L./Sjölander, S., Internationalization of R&D – a Survey of Some Recent Research, *Research* Policy, 22, 1993, pp. 413–430.
Hamel, G., *Leading the Revolution*, Boston: Harvard Business School Press 2000.
Halal, W., From Hierarchy to Enterprise, Internal Markets are the New Foundation of Management, *Academy of Management Executive*, 8, 4, 1994, pp. 69–83.
Harzing, A. W., Cross-national Industrial Mail Surveys, Why do Response Rates Different Between Countries?, *Industrial Marketing Management*, 29, 3, 2000, pp. 243–254.
Hirschleifer, J., On the Economics of Transfer pricing, *The Journal of Business*, 29, 1956, pp. 72–84.
Kummerle, W. Builiding Effective R&D Capabilities Abroad, *Harvard Business Review*, March–April, 1997, pp. 61–70.
Leonard-Barton, D., Wellsprings of Knowledge, *Building and Sustaining the Sources of Innovation*, Boston, MA: Harvard Business Review Press. 1995.
Medcof, J. W., A Taxonomy of Internationally Dispersed Technology Units and its Application to Management Issues, *R&D Management*, 27, 4, 1997, pp. 301–318.
Moran, P./Ghoshal, S., Markets, Firms and the Process of Economic Development, *Academy of Management Review*, 24, 3, 1999, pp. 390–412.
Narula, R./Hagedoorn, J., Innovating through Strategic Alliances, Moving Towards International Partnerships and Contractual Agreements, *Technovation*, 19, 1999, pp. 283–294.

Pavitt, K., What we know about Strategic Management of Technology, *California Management Review*, 32, 3, 1990, pp. 17–26.

Pearce, Robert D., *The internationalization of Research and Development by Multinational Enterprises* New York, NY: St Martin's Press 1989.

Peters, T., Liberation Management, Necessary Disorganization for the Nanosecond Nineties, New York: Fawcett Columbine 1994.

Reger, G., How R&D is Coordinated in Japanese and European Multinationals, *R&D Management*, 29, 1999, pp. 171–188.

Ronstadt, R. C., *Research and Development Abroad by U.S. Multinationals*, New York, NY: Praeger Publishers 1977.

Roussel, P. A./Saad, K. N./Erickson, T. J. *Third Generation R&D*, Boston, MA: Harvard Business School Press 1991.

Schumpeter, J. A., The Theory of Economic Development, Cambridge, MA: Harvard University Press 1934.

Terpstra, V., International Product Policy: The Role of Foreign R&D, *Columbia Journal of World Business*, 12, Winter 1977, pp. 24–32.

Tidd, J./Bessant, J./Pavitt, K., *Managing Innovation, Integrating Technological, Market, and Organizational Change*, New York: Wiley 2001, Chapter 6.

Tidd, J./Trewhella, M. J., Organizational and Technological Antecedents for Knowledge Acquisition and Learning, *R&D Management*, 27, 4, 1997, pp. 359–374.

Williamson, O. E., *Markets and Hierarchies: Analysis and Antitrust Implications*, New York: The Free Press 1975.

Zander, I., How do you mean Global? An Empirical Investigation of Innovation Networks in the Multinational Corporation, *Research Policy*, 28, 2, 1999, pp. 195–213.

Management International Review
© Gabler Verlag 2003

Volker Mahnke/Markus Venzin

Governance of Knowledge-teams in the MNC: The Case of HeidelbergCement[1]

Abstract

- This study examines the governance of knowledge-teams as one particularly important mechanism to integrate and combine knowledge in the MNC.

- Specifically, the research assesses contingency factors for delegating alternative sets of decision rights to teams based on a grounded theory process in a large MNC.

Key Results

- The results indicate that team differences (strategic importance, knowledge sharing vs. knowledge creation focus) influence the initial delegation of alternative degrees of autonomy to knowledge teams. Team members also trade decision rights for group status and career prospects.

- The analysis also highlights that a knowledge-management board is instrumental in institutionalising knowledge management and serves as an efficient vehicle for developing monitoring knowledge.

Authors

Volker Mahnke, Associate Professor, Department of Informatics, Copenhagen Business School, Copenhagen – FDB, Denmark.
Markus Venzin, Assistant Professor, Department of Strategy & Entrepreneurship, Università Luigi Bocconi, Milano, Italy.

Volker Mahnke/Markus Venzin

Introduction

Recent research in international management views the MNC not as a hierarchy but as a network of diverse linkages and relationships (Bartlett/Ghoshal 1989, 1999, Kogut/Zander 1992, 1993, Gupta/Govindarajan 1991, 2000, Szulanski 1996, Argote 1999).[2] Particular emphasize has been put on the impact of lateral knowledge flows in a MNC to enable knowledge sharing and combination in knowledge teams of various types (e.g. Subramaniam/Venkatraman 2001, von Krogh et al. 2000, Snyder/Wenger/McDermott 2002). These, in turn, may contribute to better exploitation of dispersed knowledge and exploration of new knowledge (March, 1991). While it is well understood *why* knowledge teams are used to enable lateral knowledge sharing and combination in MNCs, little is known about how knowledge-teams should be governed?

Several authors suggest that knowledge teams should be self-governed rather than hierarchically controlled (Wenger/Snyder 2000, von Krogh et al. 2000). It has been argued that knowledge-based competition requires employee autonomy to unlock high involvement in work processes (Lawler 1996), empowerment (Spreitzer 1995), delegation (Leana 1986), and self-managed teams (Cohen/Ledford/Spreitzer 1996). Thus, contrary to bureaucratic methods of organizational control, new organizational forms may be signified by increasing self-governance of knowledge teams (Child/McGrath 2001). As Wenger/Snyder (2000, p. 140) note, 'the organic, spontaneous and informal nature of [...knowledge teams...] makes them resistant to supervision and interference.'

However, as Foss/Mahnke (2002) warn, delegating decision rights to autonomous knowledge teams has also its dangers. For example, teams use resources, but concrete strategic benefits are at times hard to identify. Moreover, self-governance of knowledge teams comes often at the cost of lost oversight and lacking control (Jensen/Wruck 1994). This is a particularly salient problem when knowledge-transfer and combination requires the alignment of team efforts with the strategic aspiration of the MNC. Hence, management may seek to actively monitor, provide team incentives, and strategically define tasks (Holmström/Milgrom 1994) to align a knowledge team's work with shareholder interests. The greater the knowledge gaps between managers and knowledge teams, however, the more difficult such managerial efforts become (e.g. Fama/Jensen 1983, Tosi/Gomez-Meija 1989, Gupta/Govindarajan 1986, Jensen/Meckling 1992). The current research adds to the understanding of governing knowledge teams in the MNC.

While delegation of decision rights to knowledge-teams may exhibit well-known advantages and dis-advantages of granting decision rights in agency relation in general (see for a summary Foss/Foss 2002), the answer to the question whether knowledge-teams should be self-governed rather than strategically managed may benefit from acknowledging empirical differences between knowledge teams in question. In addition, particular types of decision rights that may be delegated to knowledge teams can be distinguished (Zahra/Pearce 1989). The literature to date does not suggest empirically derived contingency factors that influence the delegation of particular decision rights to alternative knowledge-teams. Thus, this paper seeks to advance research through grounded theory building. The remainder of this paper proceeds as follows. First, we set the background and discuss the importance of knowledge teams as one type of lateral linkages in the MNC. Second, we discuss possibilities and limits of allocating decision rights to knowledge teams. Next we enrich our theoretical arguments through an in depth analysis of team practices in a large MNC that allows for pattern recognition through a grounded theory building process. Based on the findings we outline contingency factors that influence the allocation of sets of decision rights to such teams. Finally, we discuss emergent patterns and the implication of our finding for new organizational forms. Conclusions follow.

Background: The Importance of Lateral Knowledge Flows and Teams in the MNC

International competition has not only intensified, it has also become more knowledge based (Prahalad/Hamel 1990, Quinn 1992, Stewart 1997, Child/McGrath 2001). Where the sources of competitive advantage have shifted from physical assets to intellectual resources (Rajan/Zingales 2000), knowledge-based competition raises some particularly significant organizational challenges for firms competing internationally. For example, integrating knowledge development efforts across countries may become more important as this eliminates duplication of efforts and saves costs (Porter 1986, Kogut/Zander 1992, 1993). This may yield advantages over competitors who rely on knowledge development either as a purely domestic process or as a portfolio of independent activities in different countries (Ghoshal 1987, Porter 1986).

When firms leverage ideas generated in one geographic market into other geographic markets it may be too costly to communicate knowledge first from a subsidiary to the head quarters and then back to another subsidiary (Bartlett/Ghoshal 1989). Instead, local subsidiaries may benefit from engaging through lateral linkages with another. Bartlett/Ghoshal (1989, p. 89) argue, therefore, that an integrated network of lateral linkages is instrumental to achieve "... the multidimensional strategic objectives of efficiency, responsiveness and learning" However, because the MNC needs to combine the advantages of de-central learning with knowledge-sharing and the efficiency of central decision making

(Prahalad/Doz 1986), managing the 'transnational organization' poses sever challenges in practice as recent empirical studies show (e.g. Leong/Tan 1993, Turner/Henry 1994). Nonetheless, changes in power from owners of physical assets to owners of intellectual assets (Child/McGrawth 2001) do make the propositions of the 'transnational organization' as a 'new organizational form' in general, and the arguments on the lateral linkages in particular all the more relevant. A key element in the 'multinational organization' is the management of lateral linkages and knowledge teams, but little empirically corroborated advice is given on how to govern them.

More recent literature is concerned with why and when knowledge teams are used. General determinants of knowledge transfer and combination include knowledge types (Kogut/Zander 1992, 1993), media richness (Daft/Lengel 1986), motivation of participants (Gupta/Govindarajan 2000), and relative absorptive capacity (Lane/Lubatkin 1998). For example, it has been argued that 'combinative capabilities' and 'relative absorptive capacity' ease knowledge-sharing and combination across countries (Kogut/Zander 1993, Lane/Lubatkin 1998). In addition, alternative governance mechanisms such as job rotation, intranets, or teams might be chosen because alternative knowledge types (e.g. tacit vs. explicit) require alternative communication channels (e.g. Szulanski 1996, Hansen 1999, Gupta/Govindarajan 2000). In particular, research suggests that cross-national and cross-functional teams are a particularly important lateral mechanism where tacit knowledge is involved because such teams facilitate rich communication.

Teamwork may bring knowledge together that hitherto existed separately, resulting in "new combinations" (Schumpeter 1950), it may facilitate cross-functional communication, cross-fertilization of ideas and enhance worker involvement (Snyder et al. 2002). Through the integration of knowledge of individual members, teams may not only blend knowledge and insights beyond what individual members may achieve; the development of new knowledge may also be stimulated by conversations and language-based learning in teams (Brown/Duguid 1991, Nonaka/Takeuchi 1995). Because of these benefits, contributions to the knowledge management and MNC literature recommend the use of teams in the form of work groups, inter-disciplinary and cross-functional teams to foster knowledge sharing and combination in lateral linkages between functional and geographic boundaries (e.g. Bartlett/Goshal 1989, von Krogh et al. 2000). Thus research on lateral knowledge flows in the MNC literature suggests when and why teams are used to share and combine knowledge. Next we turn to the question how knowledge teams may be governed.

The Governance of Knowledge Teams

The answer to the question how knowledge-teams should be governed may depend on where one thinks decision-making power on knowledge-issues should be concentrated. In the hands of the knowledge team itself or in the hands of a principal, for example, a manager in a line function, a steering committee, or a knowledge management board, which acts on behalf of shareholders in the MNC. For what regards the governance of knowledge teams, 'normative integration' may be achieved through attempts of managers to provide vision and common cognitive grounds (von Krogh et al. 2000) that enable organizational socialization (Nonaka/Takeuchi 1995, Bartlett/Goshal 1989), for example, when employees from different regions engage in joint work-teams, task forces and committees. Because knowledge-based competition may require employee autonomy to unlock high involvement in self-managed teams (Cohen/Ledford/Spreitzer 1996) governing possibilities in the MNC may be exhausted in what one might call 'normative leadership' that relies on providing 'common grounds' and 'cultivating sozialization' processes rather than managerial control and intervention.

For example, communities of practice "... are groups of people internally bound together by shared expertise and passion for a joint enterprise ... its primary output is knowledge" (Wenger/Snyder 2000, pp. 139–140). For communities of practice to function, managers "... must legitimize and support the myriad enacting activities perpetrated by its different members." This support cannot be intrusive, however, because such knowledge teams "...must be allowed some latitude to shake themselves free of received wisdom". (Brown/Duguid 1991, p. 53). While the authors remain unclear regarding what they mean with 'some latitude', others suggest knowledge-teams organize themselves, they set their own learning agendas, establish their own leadership, and membership should be self-selected (Wenger/Snyder 2000, p. 142). Nonetheless, for knowledge teams to function, managers may need to legitimise and support the myriad of activities, but this support should be merely concerned with cultivation (von Krogh et al. 2000). In sum, the authors suggest that knowledge teams need to work autonomous. By implication decision rights may need to be delegated to teams so that knowledge creation and sharing can thrive – largely without managerial inference.

Other authors suggest that knowledge teams may not be of one kind. Thus, at times, the corporate headquarter of an MNC can also deliberately establish knowledge teams by pointing out strategically relevant areas of knowledge development while leaving the activities of knowledge-sharing and learning to the team. For example, expert groups are usually initiated by top management to investigate certain areas of strategic concern including industry trends, competitor moves etc. In sum, we expect that alternative sets of decision rights might be delegated contingent on the type of knowledge team in question. By implication, an empirical investigation benefits from acknowledging empirical differences between knowledge teams.

While there are different opinions on whether and to which degree knowledge teams should be self-managed, the recent literature suggests general determinants of delegating decision rights in agency relations (e.g. Foss/Foss 2002). These may shed light on the question whether knowledge teams should be self-governed rather than actively managed. Granting autonomy by delegating decision rights to knowledge teams economizes on vertical knowledge transfer cost (Jensen/Meckling 1992), frees overburdened manager's cognitive constraints (Aghion/Tirole 1995, 1997), avoids costly delays in decision-making (Marchak/Radner 1972), and may intrinsically motivate skilled employees (Osterloh/Frey 2000). On the other hand, when knowledge teams are entirely self-governed, lack of control may result in moral hazard (Jensen/Meckling,1992), coordination of knowledge development and sharing efforts might be compromised, resources might be wasted and the alignment of knowledge management initiatives with the strategic aspirations might be impeded (Bartlett/Goshal 1999).

While delegation of decision rights to knowledge-teams exhibits well-known advantages and dis-advantages of granting decision rights in agency relation in general empirical research may benefit in addition from considering alternative types of decision right. To do so, we draw on one application of agency theory to board roles (for a review see Zahra/Pearce 1989) to distinguish the following set of decision rights for our empirical investigation: (1) Initiation rights: The right to initiates knowledge groups; (2) Member selection rights: The right to determine who should be member of the knowledge groups, (3) Task definition rights: The right to limit the scope of the knowledge sharing and knowledge development activities, (4) Resource allocation right: The right to allocate and withdraw resources from the team, (5) Monitoring and reward rights: The right to control and reward performance. Finally, because the literature to date does not suggest particular contingency factors that influence the delegation of alternative decision rights to knowledge-teams we seek through a grounded theory process to identify contingency factors related to team differences.

Research Setting and Methodology

The current study is part of a larger project mapping the determinants of performance implication of knowledge management in large MNCs. The research design is based on multiple cases of alternative types of lateral knowledge teams, their tasks environment as well as their governance practice, allowing a replication logic whereby we used each case to test emerging theoretical insights (Yin 1989). This method allows for a close correspondence between theory and data, a process whereby the emergent theory is grounded in the data (Eisenhardt 1989, Glaser/Strauss 1967). The setting for our study is the cement industry in the period of 1998 to late 2001. The focal organization – HeidelbergCement – is one of the key players in the cement industry and one of the leading firms in the industry. We choose HeidelbergCement based on a theoretical sampling logic. The organization has a very rich past of experimenting with teamwork and knowledge management. It is also one of the industry innovators, being frequently copied by other firms. The richness of the case made the process of delegating authority regarding particular decision rights to knowledge teams more transparent and visible to the researchers (Eisenhardt 1989). In addition, since we were able to participate in company processes, we could analyze how the decisions on delegating decision rights to teams were shaped over time. In addition, we adopted an embedded design in which each delegation decision to or from knowledge teams is treated as a different case embedded in a higher-level analysis of the knowledge governance at HeidelbergCement (Yin 1989).

This article is the result of an 18-month field study of knowledge team practices involving the headquarter-level, 6 geographical divisions, 3 suppliers and one industry association of this large MNC located in Germany. HeidelbergCement has more than 36,000 employees in about 1,500 locations in over 50 countries and more than 60 cement plants. HeidelbergCement grew mainly by acquisitions and a major challenge was therefore to integrate the new companies into their global network. The objective was to create new knowledge involving the global network of companies and to make sure that everyone has access to the global knowledge base. This knowledge exists in many different places such as databases, reports, and books but also in peoples' heads, skills and experiences are or should be distributed right across the whole company. A problem for intensively geographically diverted companies like HeidelbergCement is that one part of the company repeats work of another part simply because it is difficult to keep track of and make use of knowledge developed in other parts or plants.

In the first phase of the project, 15 unstructured interviews have been carried out that allowed the research team to get a general understanding of the industry and the functioning of the company itself. Based on these, 51 semi-structured interviews of 60 to 120 minutes have been conducted in different geographical regions (Germany, Czech Republic, Sweden, Africa, Asia, Turkey, Belgium and the US). Informants (around 100 in total) included the corporate vice president responsible for each group, general managers (one per division), functional managers (multiple managers for each division), and project managers. Informants were briefed beforehand regarding the scope of the research. Notes regarding each interview were written within 24 hours of the interview. Interviews typically lasted 90 minutes, although some went on for several hours. The interview data was supplemented with data relating to the company, its strategy and its business environment drawn from participant observation, published articles, and internal company documents. Based on workshop results and on these interviews, we were able to identify, describe and categorize several distinct international k-Teams: Communities of Practice, Expert Groups, Regional Coordinators, and the Information and Documentation Services. The unit of analysis was autonomy of knowledge teams defined as the ability to perform several pre-selected governance roles that were delegated from the knowledge governance board and left to the team itself. A delegation of decision rights occurred when a knowledge team obtained a particular decision right in a particular area of responsibility.

Data analysis used familiar approaches for inductive studies (Eisenhardt 1989, Yin 1989). Analysis began with detailed written accounts and schematic representations of each group formation process. After constructing the case histories, we conducted within-case analyses, which were the basis for developing early constructs surrounding the delegation of decision rights as experienced by knowledge-groups and leading managers. Cross-case analysis produced our working framework of the determinants for delegating decision rights to teams as indicated in Figure 1.

Based on our discussion with the knowledge teams at HeidelbergCement and those responsible for delegating decision rights to them two contingency factors

Figure 1. Governance of Knowledge-teams in the MNC

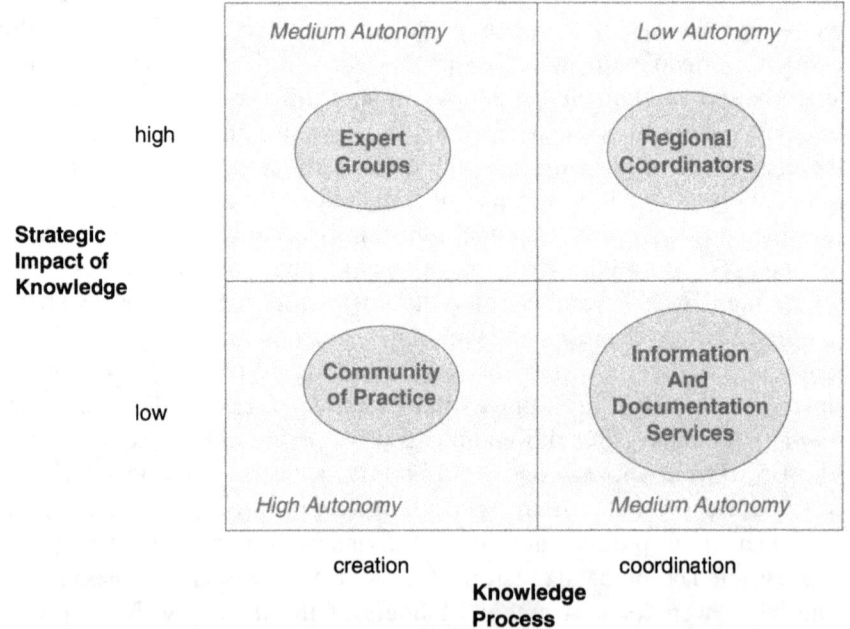

emerged in the process: (1) the main focus of the team on knowledge sharing or new knowledge creation; and (2) the strategic importance of the knowledge team. Both, in the opinions of the informants influence as independent variables the degree of autonomy of the knowledge management teams as well as the decision rights granted to it. Interestingly, strategic importance is perceived as potential impact of knowledge teams on cost and differentiation drivers related to particular industry trends and value chain activities. As one knowledge-board member put it: "We want to have control on attempts to knowledge sharing and creation whenever the team work has an immediate and/or important impact on our strategic orientation."

Findings: Delegating Decision Rights to Knowledge Teams

The integrated HC Knowledge Management Model has 3 main components: (a) The World of Cement (WOC) portal, (b) the four promoters team, and (c) the knowledge management board. The WOC portal is believed to build the foundations for effective knowledge exchange because it makes explicit knowledge easily accessible for everyone in the company worldwide. Experiences have however shown that a knowledge portal as an island-solution contributes little to facilitate knowledge transfer. In addition to data storage and retrieval systems, the human side of knowledge sharing requires support. The so-called 'promoters' that drive this aspect of knowledge management are the communities of practice, the expert groups, the regional coordinators and the information and documentation service. The knowledge management board as a third building bloc attempts to measure the effect of knowledge and knowledge management on the company performance and to influence the knowledge promoters accordingly.

Knowledge Management Board

The knowledge management board (KMB) is composed of 8 members. All of them directly report to the board of directors and mainly have a technical background. Five of them have a regional responsibility and the remaining three are directing the Heidelberg Technology Center – the engineering think tank and corporate center of excellence. Two committees in the field of technical marketing and environmental issues support the KM Board. The KMB is responsible for the implementation and closure of Expert Groups as well as the nomination of their members. In addition, it monitors their activities underway. This includes the authority to make sure that experts are available for cross unit projects. Furthermore, the KMB initiates and monitors specific studies or projects that aim at

Figure 2. The Integrated KM Business Model of HeidelbergCement

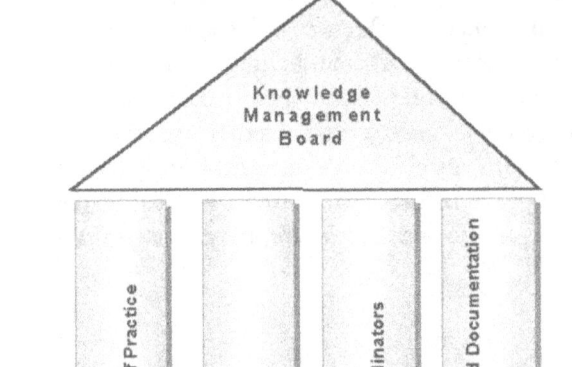

enlarging the knowledge base of the company in a specific field of expertise. The Knowledge Management Board has been initiated to ensure continuity and institutional framing of knowledge management at HeidelbergCement after an initial pilot-project terminated. The steering committee of the KM project was by definition responsible for the use of the project results and the implementation of the recommendations made by the project team including external consultants. At the point where the project itself terminated, the steering committee was resolved. As a consequence, a new institutional entity was created to take up the task of the former steering committee. Since the line functions themselves throughout the world would not be able to take up those tasks, a "board" function was created: the knowledge management board directly reports to the board of directors and ensures that the knowledge management initiative was implemented and maintained as intended. As such, it is neither a line function with operational responsibilities nor a staff function with merely supportive tasks, but a unit with decision rights and responsibilities regarding the international production and dissemination of knowledge. In the following, we address the relation of each particular group with the knowledge management board in terms of delegating decision rights.

Communities of Practice

A Community of Practice is a group of experts who are informally bound to one another by exposure to and interest for a common class of tasks. An expert group (see next paragraphs) is at the core of each community of practice. They exist for an undefined period of time, and come together virtually (Intranet) or face-to-face to exchange knowledge. Members of a community of practice can come from different units, functions, and hierarchical positions within the organization. The participation in a community is not mandatory; hence employees are not assigned to a specific community of practice. The main goals are to generate new knowledge for personal use in operational activities and thereby to utilize knowledge generated by the expert groups as well as to support the expert groups by contributing with their own experiences. Therefore, it is the community itself – or more precisely the individual members – which defines the tasks of the community. The scope of the tasks and activities has to be however within the limits of the personal time and resources those individuals obtain from their operational units. If more resources are needed to further explore interesting topics, a community of practice has to propose to the Knowledge Management Board to be converted into an expert group, or they can indicate areas for further knowledge creation to expert groups, if the interest goes beyond a mostly individual one. The monitoring and rewards of the results is therefore not standardized and not intense. It is up to the line superiors of each participant to decide whether the time spent by an employee is beneficial for the personal development of the single member of the community.

Expert Groups

An expert group is composed of members nominated by the Knowledge Management Board. The expert groups develop project reports, collect existing best practices and carry out technical projects by order of the Knowledge Management Board in contact with the communities of practice. Furthermore, expert groups are responsible for group-internal knowledge transfer and dissemination of this knowledge to the rest of the company through seminars, conferences or the like. In addition, external literature is screened and disseminated. *The initiation rights are clearly allocated at the Knowledge Management Board.* Proposals to initiate can however come from a variety of areas within the organization. Furthermore, the members – and firstly the practice leader – are selected by the Knowledge Management Board. The reason for installing a "filter" function for membership of expert groups was mainly due to different self-perceptions of what it means to be an expert: in some cultures employees might expose themselves too early as experts and in other cultures the true experts are hiding themselves because they fear to be covered with additional work. The filter also ensures the strategy fit of the expert groups, i.e., they concentrate on strategically important knowledge areas.

Whereas internally in a community of practice no significant hierarchy can be identified, it is a major career step for an expert to be nominated leader of an expert group. The tasks of the practice leader are however more linked to coordination than to control. The Knowledge Management Board is also responsible for defining the general tasks of the expert groups. It is then up to the expert group to translate the task into a work program. Resources can be requested by the expert groups and are then assigned by the Knowledge Management Board, which has also the right to withdraw the resources and thereby close an expert group. It is sometimes a challenge for the Knowledge Management Board to negotiate time of experts with the line managers of those experts. Since the Knowledge Management Board is assigning tasks and resources, it is also monitoring the performance. Whereas the line management rewards the group members, the knowledge management board is responsible for feedback to the line managers regarding performance of individuals. The Knowledge Management Board supported by the marketing committee and group environmental committee is composed of experts that are able to assess the technical quality of the project work. In addition, the success (measured by downloads and hit-rates as well as an online survey) of the publications of the expert group on the internal web-site is an indicator for the performance of the expert group. The members of expert groups are highly self-motivated because they are given the possibility to follow their interests and work on the edge of the research front in their knowledge area. However, the Knowledge Management Board can influence career decisions of members of expert groups and thereby provide additional incentives.

Regional Coordinator Group

Regional coordinators (RCOs) are experienced engineers of the Heidelberg Technology Center. They dispose of an overview of existing knowledge within the company. The tasks of the RCOs is the development of a directory of expertise in key knowledge areas, connect people who are in search for solutions with experts or written expertise. In their operational activities, RCOs are regularly in contact with members of the board of directors, general managers, HTC management, cement plants (mainly plant managers), project engineers/managers, production and maintenance engineers, HTC employees, and regional competence centres. As knowledge brokers, RCOs make knowledge available every time, use feedback to make sure knowledge transfer was successful, arrange knowledge connections, have a knowledge map, and are able to appropriately assess existing knowledge.

The RCOs directly report to the Managing Directors of the Heidelberg Technology Center, the engineering unit of HeidelbergCement. It is therefore a line function not directly dependent from the Knowledge Management Board. Since the governing mechanisms of RCOs are even more intense than the ones of expert groups, it would be too difficult and complex to be done by the Knowledge Management Board, which personally meets only twice a year. Hence the tight monitoring and rewarding, the task definition, and the nomination of Regional Coordinators is executed by the line management of HTC. The Regional Coordinators do not have a direct connection with the Knowledge Management Board. Whereas expert groups take on the responsibility of mainly creating knowledge in a particular field of expertise, the RCOs focus on the coordination of knowledge sharing activities of plants in a specific geographical area as indicated by Figure 3.

Information and Documentation Services (IDS) – World of Cement Portal

Information and Documentation Services as administration function ensures in cooperation with RCOs and Expert Group Leaders the strategic and operational flow of technical information within HeidelbergCement. The "World of Cement" – portal builds the basis for the knowledge management model at Heidelberg

Figure 3. Task Definition of Expert Group vs. Regional Coordinators

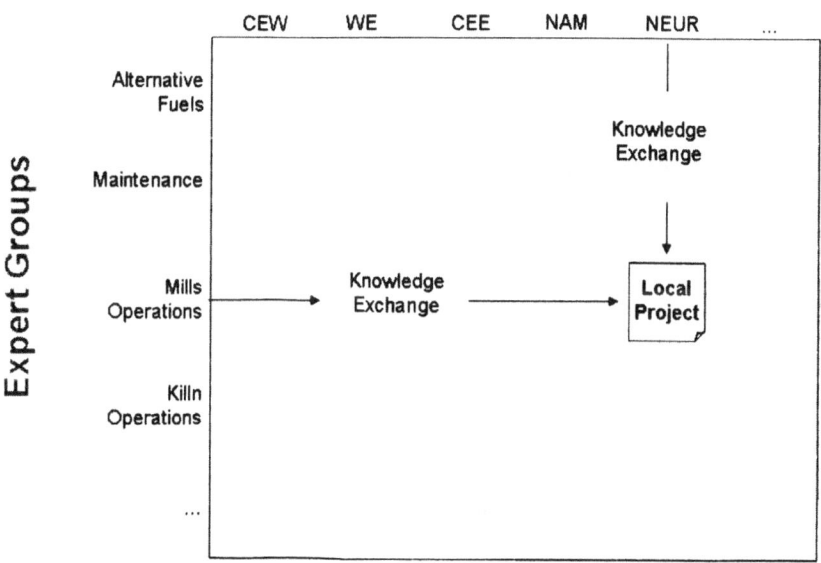

Cement. It is the medium where explicit knowledge is stored and made accessible. The portal has the following functions: Newsgroups – chat rooms, special sites for communities of practice and main functions, helpdesk, news-services, subscription services, general search engine, editorial feedback. The portal has the following content:

- Project portfolio: A brief description of the most significant realized and ongoing projects. At least meta-information about the projects is mentioned (project title, abstract of project objectives, status, location, project manager, available reports). A filter function for selection of projects has to be defined. The goal is not necessarily to save project data in the portal itself but to get clear indications on where to find further information.
- Guidelines and standard procedures: The collection of general guidelines allows a further harmonization of global procedures. The main issue is to store them centrally and thereby make them available for everyone in the company.
- Technology updates – results of basic research: Journals, conferences and other sources of technical knowledge generated both inside and outside the company are periodically screened and made available in a concise form.
- List of training programs: Internal (and eventually external) training offers are published as well as online-courses. Furthermore, a database should be prepared to allow course participants of mostly external courses to describe the course content and judge the quality of the course.
- Best practices of past projects

Information and Documentation Services as administration function ensure, in cooperation with RCOs and Expert Group Leaders, the strategic and operational flow of technical information within HeidelbergCement. Similar to the RCOs, the IDS group is directly reports to the HTC management team: Monitoring and rewarding, task definition is centrally taken care of by HTC senior staff, as is the nomination of IDS – members. The Knowledge Management Board, however, is supporting the IDS group with issues that go beyond the influence of the HTC mainly regarding investments in new information technology or the integration of different IT platforms across national boundaries.

Discussion

The analysis of delegating decision rights to knowledge teams in the MNC suggests three main themes: First, contrary to the recommendations in the knowledge management literature, communities of practice are actively governed rather than completely autonomous. Second, knowledge teams differ in their focus on knowledge sharing and creation and the strategic importance of their knowledge focus. These differences lead to the delegation of alternative sets of decision rights to knowledge teams. Finally, the institutionalisation of the HC knowledge management initiative illustrates a way to deal with knowledge asymmetry that complicates the management of knowledge teams in the MNCs. All three themes inform the possibilities of active management of knowledge teams in the MNC.

Active Management Intervention in Communities of Practice

Contrary to claims in the knowledge management literature our explorative study shows that communities of practice might be actively managed rather than self-governed. Although communities of practice at HeidelbergCement enjoy many decision rights such as initiation right and member selection, their freedom to decide on team work is restricted by (a) line managers who must agree on team members spending their working time in such communities, and (b) the relation to expert groups around which communities of practice evolve.

In other words, while communities of practice enjoy the right to initiates issues for knowledge creation and sharing and the right to determine who should be member of the knowledge groups, the right to define the scope of the knowledge sharing and knowledge development activities of the community is co-determined by line managers who provide resources to the community by granting or withholding managerial time. In addition, the right to allocate and withdraw financial resources from the knowledge team is maintained by the knowledge management board and restricted to the case where a community applies successfully for change of status to an expert group.

Interestingly, relatively self-governed knowledge-teams at times sought to constrain initial sets of delegated decision rights. By gaining the status of an expert group former communities of practice traded the right to appoint and attract members, to freely initiate knowledge creation as well the autonomy to select knowledge issues on the one hand against financial support and career prospects of its members. In sum then, the direct line managers of community participants retain monitoring and reward rights lest there is a change of team status whereupon the relevant principal changes from line management functions to the knowledge management board as a direct superior and principal. The management of communities of practice in our case substantially deviates from the perhaps romanticised ideal suggested in the knowledge management literature – the ideal of autonomous knowledge-work in teams. While members of the community can decide with whom and how they learn, rewards for participation that motivate individual members may lay more in their own wish for professional development in a strategically relevant area rather than explicit rewards given by the knowledge management board or other principals on which the knowledge team may depend.

Delegation of Alternative Decision Rights to Different Knowledge-teams

Knowledge-teams in the MNC are not of one kind. Far from restricting managerial intervention to providing 'normative control' (Bartlet/Gosha, 1989), and cultivating influence (Snyder et al. 2002) our exploratory study shows that knowledge teams may be actively managed through the selection of sets of delegated decision rights to alternative knowledge teams.

Key contingency factors that drive the delegation of decision rights to teams appear to include the team's strategic importance, the team's knowledge focus and the primary focus on knowledge generation or knowledge sharing. In general we find that the higher the strategic importance, the more control is exercised and less autonomy is granted by the principal of knowledge teams. Where strategic importance is low, knowledge teams whose focus is on knowledge creation are delegated more decision rights compared to teams whose focus is on knowledge sharing. Put differently: key contingency factors that drive the delegation of decision rights to teams are a team's strategic importance and respective focus on knowledge creation or sharing. The empirical analysis also adds to the MNC literature on lateral linkages and knowledge teams by illustrating how decision rights are delegated from the knowledge management board and other relevant principals to alternative teams as illustrated in the Table below.

The KMB as Knowledgeable Principal and Institutional Guarantee

One reason for the existence of agency relations is the principal's lack of know what, know how, and know why. At the same time, a key complication in controlling for opportunism in the form of adverse selection and free riding in agency relations are knowledge gaps between agents and principals. Where knowledge gaps exist between principal and agent, measurement of input, process, and output might be noisy (Ouchi 1980, Alchian/Demsetz 1972). By implication, metering and rewarding agent's performance is complicated. One way to deal with this control dilemma is to shift performance risk to agents in teams, but agents may be risk adverse or unable to carry the risk due to budget constraints. An alternative way for the principal is to invest in control knowledge so that a measurement base can be developed e.g. through monitoring. Seen this way, the knowledge management board may be interpreted as an investment in common knowledge that allows metering of performance of experts in teams by other

Table 1. Decision Rights and Contingency Factors Differ with Group Type

	Communities of Practice	Expert Groups	Regional Coordinators	Information and Documentation Services
Principal	(KMB – Line function)	(KMB – Line function)	(HTC)	(HTC)
Purpose	Individual knowledge development; stimulation of expert groups	Development of best practices; special projects; regional knowledge transfer; screening of external knowledge carriers; make knowledge available to CoP; feed portal with data	Transfer technical knowledge within specific region	Information and Documentation Services ensures in cooperation with RCOs and Expert Group Leaders the strategic and operational flow of technical information
Contingencies for delegating decision rights	Knowledge creation and low strategic importance	Knowledge creation and high strategic importance	Knowledge sharing and high strategic importance	Knowledge sharing and low strategic importance
Initiation	Initiated by members and evolution around expert groups	Expert Groups are initiated by KMB in collaboration with line managers from SBUs	RCOs are in a line-subordination to HTC and therefore recruited by HTC managing directors	Members are in a line-subordination to HTC and therefore recruited by HTC managing directors
Ratification	No influence	Project milestones have to be ratified	HTC board as well as (internal) clients	Performance ratified by HTC board
Nomination of group leaders & members	No influence	Practice leaders as well as group members are nominated by KMB	Nominated by HTC board	Nominated by HTC board
Task definition	No influence	Projects are assigned by KMB	Projects are assigned by HTC board	Projects and operational job description done by HTC board
Resource allocation	No influence – CoP that need substantial resources might apply for becoming an expert group	Resources are allocated by KMB	Resources are allocated by HTC board	Resources are allocated by HTC board
Monitoring of performance	No influence – possibility to restrict participant's time by line managers	Done through project review meetings and project reporting	HTC board monitors performance supplemented by an (internal) customer satisfaction report	HTC board monitors performance
Rewarding performance	Little influence – awards for best practices and innovative ideas are given; nonstandard through line manager's evaluation	Being part of an expert group means to make a functional career	"Deals with knowledge" as performance item in MbO system for RCOs	According to job description

experts that can judge what agents do when they develop knowledge on behalf of the MNC. Such investments in control knowledge by a principal may be only justified where expert groups perform tasks of high strategic relevance as defined from the principal's perspective. Where this is not the case, e.g. with communities of practice with low strategic relevance, control loss might be accepted.

Another solution to the control dilemma is made possible through the KMB. When agents in communities of practice are convinced that a certain knowledge area is strategically relevant for reasons that line managers may not understand or are willing to support, a knowledge team might signal strategic importance of their knowledge domain or issue. This is done, by changing from less informed line managers to more informed principals in the KMB through applying for a change in team status. While the KMB appears as a novel institutional solution to control problems in agency relations with large knowledge gaps, it is also an institution that guarantees continuity of the KM initiative in the face of knowledge team failure and lack of continuing fascination with knowledge management in the MNC. Not only does the knowledge management board maintain the right to withdraw resources from failing knowledge management teams or from teams that have reached their useful life span. Even if knowledge teams fail despite the support of knowledge management board (which may be the case as knowledge creation is risky), the knowledge management board ensures the continuity of knowledge management at HeidelbergCement through embedding the concept in a routine-based institutional form.

Conclusion

Using the context of a large MNC to analyse various types of knowledge-teams as a context for grounded theory development, the current paper identified contingency factors (strategic importance and focus on knowledge creation vs. knowledge sharing) that influence the governance of k-teams. These contingency factors appear to influence the selective allocation of decision rights to knowledge teams in the MNC.

Not much empirical research to date has focussed directly on the process contingencies for delegating decision rights and institutional framing of agency relation in context of knowledge teams in the MNC. In contrast to claims in the MNC and knowledge management literature on knowledge teams our empirical investigation finds that degrees of hierarchical governance may be beneficial for knowledge management performance. In particular, knowledge management teams are not of one kind. We find that selectively delegated decision rights according to team contingencies suggest much more managerial discretion and possibilities for intervention than usually assumed in the literature on knowledge teams and deemed possible in arguments on the limits of selective intervention (Williamson 1996). Thus, we support empirically recent arguments suggesting that knowledge work might benefit from hierarchical elements (e.g. Zenger 2002). On the other hand we also find that simple reward/risk trade offs suggested in conventional agency theory do contribute little to explaining how decision rights are allocated to teams.

Conceptually, this paper contributed to the understanding of knowledge governance in the MNC by describing the functioning of the knowledge management board as an explanatory element of a new organizational form. This board represents an institutional vehicle for investing in common shared knowledge that helps resolving agency conflicts. At the same time the design of the knowledge management board also serves as institutional framing and guaranteeing function through embedding knowledge management in the routines of an MNC. Finally, an emergent issue for future research in knowledge governance is how managerial authority is rented from key asset holders (which may be the employees) who cede autonomy in exchange for career prospects and financial resources.

Endnotes

1. The authors would like to thank Dr. Dienemann and his colleagues from HeidelbergCement for their support and comments on the article.
2. This shift in perspectives – from hierarchical views towards network view – is motivated by a need to explore and integrate knowledge from locally dispersed sources and, in part, by a belief that the MNC's ability to explore, share and integrate knowledge rests on the empowerment of capable and willing managers engaged in international operations (Goshal/Bartlett, 1989).

References

Aghion, P./Tirole, J., Formal and Real Authority in Organization, *Journal of Political Econom*, 105, 1997, pp. 1–29.
Aghion, P./Tirole J., Some Implications of Growth for Organizational Form and Ownership Structure, *European Economic Review*, 39, 1995, pp. 440–455.
Alchian, A./Demsetz, H., Production, Information costs, and economic Organisation, *American Economic Review*, 625, 1972, pp. 772–795.
Argote, L., *Organizational learning: Creating, Retaining and Transferring Knowledge*, Norwell, MA: Kluwer 1999.
Bartlett, C. A/Ghoshal, S., *Managing across Borders: The Transnational Solution*, Cambridge, MA: Harvard Business School Press 1989.
Bartlett, C. A./Ghoshal, S., *The Individualized Corporation*, Whiley 1999.

Bartlett, C. A./Ghoshal, S., Beyond the M form: Toward a Managerial Theory of the Firm, *Strategic Management Journal*, Winter Special Issue, 14, 1993, pp. 23–46.
Brown J. S./Duguid, P., Organizational Learning and Communities-of-practice: Toward a Unified View of working, Learning, and Innovation, *Organization Science*, 2, 1, 1991, pp. 40–47.
Child, J./McGrath, R., Organization Unfettered: Organizational Forms in an Information Intensive Economy, *Academy of Management Journal*, 44, 6, 2001, pp. 1135–1148.
Cohen, S. G./Ledford, G. E./Spreitzer, G. M., A Predictive Model of self-managing Work Team Effectiveness, *Human Relations*, 49, 1996, pp. 643–676.
Daft, R. L./Lengel, R. H., Organizational Information Requirements, Media Richness, and Structural Design, *Management Science*, 32, 1986, pp. 554–571.
Eisenhardt, K. M., Building Theories from Case Study Research, *Academy of Management Review*, 14, 1989, pp. 532–550.
Fama. E. F./Jensen, M. C., Agency Problems and Residual Claims, *Journal of Law and Economics*, 26, 1983, pp. 327–349.
Foss, K./Foss, N., Authority and Discretion: Tensions, Credible Delegation and Implications for New Organizational Forms, *LINK working paper* 2002.
Foss, N./Mahnke, V., Knowledge Management: What Organizational Economics can Contribute, in Easterby-Smith, M./Lyles, M. (eds.), *The Blackwell Companion to Organizational Learning and Knowledge Management*, Oxford: Basil Blackwell 2003 (forthcoming).
Ghoshal, S., Global strategy: An Organizing Framework, *Strategic Management Journal*, 8, 5, 1987, pp. 425–440.
Gupta, A. K./Govindarajan V., *Knowledge Flows within Multinational Corporations*, Strategic Management Journal 21, 4, 2000, pp. 473–496.
Gupta, A. K./Govindarajan, V., Resource Sharing among SBUs: Strategic Antecedents and Administrative Implications, *Academy of Management Journal*, 29, 1986, pp. 695–714.
Gupta, A. K./Govindarajan, V., Knowledge Flows and the Structure of Control within Multinational Corporations, *Academy of Management Review*, 16, 1991, pp. 768–792.
Hansen, M., The search-transfer problem: The Role of Weak Ties in Sharing Knowledge across Organization Subunits, *Administrative Science Quarterly*, 44, 1, 2000, pp. 82–111.
Holmström, B./Milgrom, P., The firm as an incentive system, *American Economic Review*, 84, 1994, pp. 972–991.
Jensen, M. C./Meckling, W. H., Specific and General Knowledge, and Organizational Structure, in Werin, L./Wijkander, H. (eds.), *Main Currents in Contract Economics*, Oxford: Basil Blackwell 1982, pp. 189–207.
Kogut, B./Zander, U., Knowledge of the Firm and the Evolutionary Theory of the Multinational Corporation, *Journal of International Business Studies*, 24, 1993, pp. 625–645.
Kogut, B./Zander, U., Knowledge of the Firm, Combinative Capabilities, and the Replication of Technology, *Organization Science*, 3, 3, 1992, pp. 383–397.
Lane, P. J./Lubatkin, M., Relative Absorptive Capacity and Inter-Organizational Learning, *Strategic Management Journal*, 19, 8, 1998, pp. 461–477.
Lawler, E. E., *From the Ground up: Six Principles for Building the New Logic Corporation*, San Francisco: Jossey-Bass 1996.
Leana, C. R., Predictors and Consequences of Delegation, *Academy of Management Journal*, 29, 1986, pp. 754–774.
Leong, S./Tan, C., Managing across Borders: An Empirical Test of the Bartlett and Ghoshal (1989), *Journal of International Business Studies*, 1993, pp. 449–464.
March, J. G., Exploration and Exploitation in Organizational Learning, *Organization Science*, 2, 1991, pp. 71–87.
Marschak, J./Radner, R., *The Theory of Teams*, New Haven: Yale University Press 1972.
Nonaka, I./Takeuchi, H., *The Knowledge Creating Company*, Oxford: Oxford University Press 1995.
Osterloh, M./Frey, B., Motivation, Knowledge Transfer and Organizational Form, *Organization Science*, 11, 2000, pp. 538–550.
Ouchi, W., Markets, Bureaucracies and Clans, *Administrative Science Quarterly*, 25, 1980, pp. 129–141.
Porter, M. E., *Competition in Global Industries*, Boston, MA: Harvard Business School Press 1986.

Prahalad, C. K./ Hamel, G., The Core Competence of the Corporation, *Harvard Business Review* 68, 3, 1990, pp. 79–91.
Prahalad, C. K./Doz, Y,. *The Multinational Mission: Balancing Local Demands and Global Vision*, New York: Free Press 1986.
Quinn, J. B., *Intelligent Enterprise: A Knowledge and Service Based Paradigm* for Industry, New York: Free Press 1992.
Rajan, R. G./Zingales, L., *The Governance of the New Enterprise*, NBER working pape 2000.
Schumpeter, J. A., *Essays on Entrepreneurs, Innovations, Business Cycles, and the Evolution of Capitalism*, New Brunswick: Transaction Publishers 1950.
Snyder, W./Mc Dermott/Wenger, E., *Cultivating Communities of Practice*, HBR Press 2002.
Spreitzer, G. M., Psychological Empowerment in the Workplace: Dimensions, Measurement, and Validation, *Academy of Management Journal*, 38, 1995, pp. 1442–1465.
Stewart, T. A., *Intellectual Capital: The New Wealth of Organizations*, New York: Currency Doubleday 1997.
Subranamian, M./Venkatraman, N., Determinants of Transnational New Product Development Capability. *Strategic Management Journal*, 22, 2001, pp. 359–378.
Szulanski, G., Exploring Internal Stickiness: Impediments to the Transfer of Best Practice within the Firm, *Strategic Management Journal*, 17, 1996, pp. 27–43.
Tosi, H. L./Gomez-Mejia, L. R., The Decoupling of CEO Pay and Performance: An Agency Theory Perspectiv, *Administrative Science Quarterly*, 34, 1989, pp. 169–189.
Turner, I./Henry, I., Managing International Organizations: Lessons from the Field, *European Management Journal*, 12, 4, 1994, pp. 417–431.
Von Krogh, G./Ochijo, K./Nonaka I., *Enabling Knowledge Creation*, Oxford University Press 2000.
Wenger E./Snyder, W., Communities of Practice: The Organizational Frontier, *Harvard Business Review*, 2000, pp. 139–145.
Williamson C., *The mechanisms of governance*, New York: Oxford University Press 1996.
Wruck, K./Jensen, Science, Specific Knowledge, and Total Quality Management, *Journal of Accounting and Economics*, 18, 1994, pp. 247–287.
Yin, R. K., *Case Study Research – Design and Methods*, Thousand Oaks, CA, Sage Publications, 1989.
Zahra, S. A./Pearce, J. A., Boards of Directors and Corporate Financial Performance, *Journal of Management*, 15, 1989, pp. 291–334.
Zenger, T., Crafting internal hybrids: Complementarities, Common Change Initiatives, and Team Based Organization, *LINK WP*, 2002.

Neuerscheinungen

Doris Lindner
Einflussfaktoren des erfolgreichen Auslandseinsatzes
Konzeptionelle Grundlagen – Bestimmungsgrößen – Ansatzpunkte zur Verbesserung
2002
XX, 341 S. mit 38 Abb., 21 Tab.,
(mir-Edition),
Br. € 59,–
ISBN 3-409-11952-3

Tobias Specker
Postmerger-Management in den ost- und mitteleuropäischen Transformationsstaaten
2002
XX, 431 S. mit 60 Abb., 28 Tab.,
(mir-Edition),
Br. € 64,–
ISBN 3-409-12010-6

Jörg Frehse
Internationale Dienstleistungskompetenzen
Erfolgsstrategien für die europäische Hotellerie
2002
XXVI, 353 S. mit 48 Abb.,
(mir-Edition),
Br. € 59,–
ISBN 3-409-12349-0

Anja Schulte
Das Phänomen der Rückverlagerung
Internationale Standortentscheidungen kleiner und mittlerer Unternehmen
2002
XXII, 315 S. mit 17 Abb., 2 Tab.,
(mir-Edition),
Br. € 59,–
ISBN 3-409-12375-X

Andreas Wald
Netzwerkstrukturen und -effekte in Organisationen
Eine Netzwerkanalyse in internationalen Unternehmen
2003
XVIII, 238 S. mit 19 Abb., 61 Tab.,
(mir-Edition),
Br. € 49,90
ISBN 3-409-12395-4

Nicola Berg
Public Affairs Management
Ergebnisse einer empirischen Untersuchung in Multinationalen Unternehmungen
2003
XXXIV, 471 S. mit 20 Abb., 67 Tab.
(mir-Edition),
Br. € 64,–
ISBN 3-409-12387-3

Betriebswirtschaftlicher Verlag Dr. Th. Gabler GmbH, Abraham-Lincoln-Str. 46, 65189 Wiesbaden

Torben Pedersen/Bent Petersen/Deo Sharma

Knowledge Transfer Performance of Multinational Companies

Abstract

- The effective dissemination throughout the MNC organization of valuable knowledge acquired by its local affiliates is seen as an important source of competitive advantage.

- Knowledge differs in characteristics and so do the available transfer mechanism. As such, it is essential that the MNC employ the mechanism of transfer that suits the specific knowledge characteristics. The use of unsuitable transfer mechanisms may cause loss of knowledge in the process of transmission or may involve unnecessarily high communication costs – both with potentially negative effects on the performance of the MNC.

Key Results

- Focusing on internationalization knowledge this large-scale empirical study explores the performance implications of fit between knowledge characteristics and transfer mechanism as used by Danish MNCs. It is found that a substantial proportion of the observed MNC knowledge transfer transactions may be classified as 'misfits' and to some extent do these 'misfits' result in impaired performance of the MNCs.

Authors

Torben Pedersen, Professor of International Business, Department of International Economics and Management, Copenhagen Business School, Copenhagen, Denmark.
Bent Petersen, Associate Professor of International Business, Department of International Economics and Management, Copenhagen Business School, Copenhagen, Denmark.
Deo Sharma, Professor of Marketing, Department of Marketing, Copenhagen Business School, Copenhagen, Denmark.

Torben Pedersen/Bent Petersen/Deo Sharma

Introduction

To an increasing extent is the success of multinational companies (MNCs) considered to be contingent upon the ease and speed by which valuable knowledge is disseminated throughout the organization (Hedlund 1986, Bartlett/Ghoshal 1989, Gupta/Govindarajan 1991). Thus, creation of knowledge in the spatially dispersed multinational organization is a necessary, but not sufficient condition for success in the global marketplace. If valuable knowledge remains in, or only diffuses slowly from, the individual MNC affiliates, opportunities for worldwide leverage are lost. Therefore, appropriate incentive structures and proper knowledge transfer mechanisms should be in place ensuring swift dissemination to other units of the multinational organization. It is essential that the MNC employs a medium suiting the specific characteristics of the knowledge subject to transfer. The use of unsuitable transfer mechanisms may cause loss of knowledge in the transmission process or may involve unnecessarily high communication costs – both with potentially negative effects on the overall performance of the organization.

It is an open question to what extent MNCs managers are capable of realizing the right 'fit' between, on the one side, the *characteristics* of the knowledge, and – on the other side – the *medium*, or *mechanism*, by which the knowledge is transferred. The combination of knowledge characteristics and transfer mechanism represents an important choice that is expected to have severe implications for performance. This study explores the knowledge transfer processes as they take place in Danish MNCs. Our focus will be on transfer of one specific type of knowledge, namely internationalization knowledge, i.e. knowledge that enables the organization to expand its activities across national borders. Internationalization knowledge includes a broad range of knowledge of conducting international operations, such as knowledge of customer preferences, supply structure, business culture, and industry standards in foreign markets.

As far as we know, our study is the first one to explore empirically the performance consequences of different combinations of knowledge characteristics and transfer mechanisms – including both appropriate and inappropriate combinations – as made by MNCs. In a research field where empirical studies are in short supply, as ascertained by Simonin (1999), the study may contribute to the advancement of the field of knowledge transfer of MNCs in a more normative and practically oriented direction.

The paper is structured as follows: Firstly, we review the literature on knowledge transfer in the context of MNCs and internationalization processes of firms. The retrospective literature review reveals a theoretical development from almost complete neglect of the knowledge transfer as a process of its own to the current outspoken interest in knowledge transfer and its effects on MNC performance.

Secondly, we outline the conceptual model of the study and develop research hypotheses. Thirdly, the empirical analysis is reported, including methodology, presentation of sample data, results and discussion of statistical tests. Conclusions and managerial implications make up the latter part.

Literature Review on Knowledge Transfer in MNCs

The literature on intra-organizational knowledge transfer has proliferated over the last two decades and today a large body of literature exists (for an overview, see Argote 1999). We will therefore restrict ourselves to a review of MNC literature that includes knowledge transfer aspects. At least three distinct streams of literature that specifically deal with knowledge transfer in multinational companies (MNCs) can be identified. These are: (1) literature on the internationalization process of firms, (2) literature on factors that facilitate or impede knowledge transfer of MNCs, and (3) Management-oriented literature on the use of transfer mechanisms in MNCs. The three literature streams seem to be converging in these years, but at their outset in the 1970s significant differences prevailed in terms of their approach to knowledge transfer in MNCs.

Importance of Experiential Knowledge in the Internationalization Process

Knowledge plays a central role in the internationalization process theory that explains firms' incremental international expansion (Carlson 1975, Bilkey/Tesar 1977, Johanson/Vahlne 1977). Based on the behavioral theory of the firm (Cyert/March 1963, Aharoni 1966) the theory describes firms' international expansion as a trial-and-error-based learning process: "... international expansion is inhibited by the lack of knowledge about markets and such knowledge can mainly be acquired through experience from practical operations abroad" (Forsgren/Johanson 1992, p. 10). As they gain local market knowledge firms expand internationally through a series of gradual investments.

Following Penrose (1959) the internationalization process theory distinguishes between objective knowledge and experiential knowledge. Objective knowledge is explicit (e.g. market data, legislation, export technicalities) and can be traded in the market. A critical assumption of the theory is that objective knowledge is of minor importance in the internationalization process of firms. It is first of all the on-going acquisition of experiential knowledge that determines the gradual commitment in the internationalization process. Knowledge of the market, the clients, the problems and the opportunities abroad are acquired by operating in the foreign market. It is through interaction with specific clients and other market actors that firms accumulate experiential knowledge. Consequently, the problems and opportunities intrinsic to a certain market and specific customers will primarily be discovered by those who are working in that market, e.g. people in the sales subsidiary or some other front-line unit. The internationalization process theory sees the individuals as holders of knowledge and emphasizes the idiosyncratic nature of experiential knowledge. Referring to Penrose (1959) the internationalization process theorists maintain that "experience itself can never be transmitted, it produces a change – frequently a subtle change – in individuals and cannot be separated from them" (Johanson/Vahlne 1977, p. 30).

Furthermore, the possibility of transforming experiential knowledge into objective knowledge, i.e. the process through which tacit skills and knowledge are made explicit, is not recognized in the theory. Accordingly, the intra-organizational transfer of experiential knowledge from one affiliate to another can only take place through rotation of the individuals who possess the knowledge. But the transfer of knowledge is not only futile; it is also pointless to the extent that the crucial knowledge is market-specific: knowledge about how to do business in foreign market A is of little use in foreign market B.

Thus, three characteristics are intrinsic to the experiential knowledge deemed pivotal by the internationalization process theory: (1) it is acquired and possessed by individuals, (2) it is context-specific (market-specific), and (3) it is not codifiable. Taken together, these characteristics make the transfer of knowledge almost a non-issue in the internationalization process theory. In other words, there is limited scope for organizational learning in the theory and decision-making is almost absent in relation to knowledge management issues like articulation and transfer of knowledge.

The MNC as a Superior Vehicle for Knowledge Transfer

The path-breaking conceptual and empirical studies of Zander (1991), Kogut/Zander (1992, 1993), and Zander/Kogut (1995) completely reverse this view by focusing on capabilities of knowledge transfer in MNCs. The very reason why MNCs exist is that they are efficient vehicles for creating and transferring knowledge across borders (Kogut/Zander 1993). In particular the capabilities of transferring tacit knowledge across borders distinguish the MNCs from the purely domestic firms. To a certain extent tacit knowledge can be codified, i.e. transformed into explicit knowledge. Codification of tacit knowledge facilitates the transfer process, but at the same time increases the risk of uncontrolled dissemination of firm-specific, proprietary knowledge. Thus, a trade-off exists between, on the one hand, incurred costs of communication and, on the other hand, assumed risk of knowledge dissemination, i.e. making the knowledge more susceptible to competitors' imitation. The internalization of business transactions holds the potential of changing this codification trade-off. First, as Kogut/Zander (1993) point out, internalization enables efficient transfer of tacit knowledge. Secondly, as Hedlund (1994) argues, internalization facilitates the knowledge codification process: "To a large extent [organizations] are 'articulation machines', built around codified practices and deriving some of their competitive advantages from clever, unique articulation." (Hedlund 1994, p. 76). The insights of Kogut, Zander, and Hedlund pull in the direction of making knowledge creation, knowledge characteristics and codification of (tacit) knowledge the central issues. Still, the knowledge *management* focus of these scholars is the decision of codification of strategic knowledge – rather than the managerial task of finding the proper fit between knowledge characteristics and transfer mechanism. Implicitly, knowledge characteristics and transfer mechanisms are supposedly interrelated to the extent that the two variables are inseparable.

More recently, several scholars have brought attention to various organizational or environmental factors that facilitate, or impede, the transfer of knowledge across (multinational) organizations.

Teece (1977) found that the principal factors determining the transfer of knowledge are the degree of previous experience of transferring knowledge of firms, the cost of transfer, the age of the technology, and the number of firms using similar technology. Davidson/McFetridge (1985) found that transfer to unaffiliated firms is promoted if the firms have transferred knowledge in past. The development of knowledge transfer routines demands repetition that again requires standardization of the transfer process. Kogut/Zander (1992) found that firms with experience of knowledge transfer developed efficient procedures for codifying and transferring tacit knowledge. Another finding was that over a period of time firm-specific knowledge becomes less tacit and more codifiable. Simonin (1999) found that experience with particular partner firms eases subsequent transfer of marketing knowledge to these partners. He also found that general experience in knowledge transfer was an important facilitator.

Szulanski (1996) explored 'internal stickiness' of knowledge, i.e., factors that impede the intra-firm transfer of knowledge. He identified two sets of factors that impede the internal transfer of knowledge: motivational factors and knowledge-related factors. The former is related to the motivation of the subsidiary manager(s) to devote the necessary time and resources for conducting the transfer. The latter stem from the tacit, context-specific and ambiguous nature of certain knowledge. Furthermore, Szulanski points out that motivation to acquire and receive knowledge is important since new knowledge may disrupt current organizational practices and working routines. According to Szulanski (1996) knowledge acquisition and reception may require substantial investments in time and effort.

Transfer of knowledge is influenced by the socio-cultural and institutional distance between the foreign country and the home country of the MNC (Adler 1995). Knowledge in firms is contingent on their socio-cultural environment (Hofstede 1984): what is appropriate knowledge in one country may not suit the needs of firms in other countries. In turn, this may cause problems to the knowledge transfer process. Factors such as different language, business culture, and institutional framework make up a 'psychic distance' as perceived by the MNC manager (Johanson/Vahlne 1977). As the psychic distance between nations increases it is more difficult for firms to acquire knowledge from abroad (Mowery et al. 1996). Thus, a clash between national cultures may jeopardize the international transfer of knowledge. Furthermore, several studies suggest that geographical proximity is positively associated with knowledge transfer (Galbraith 1990, Lester/McCabe 1993, Epple et al. 1996).

Knowledge Transfer Mechanism

In contrast to the positive theories of MNCs the management-oriented MNC literature is dominated by studies of knowledge transfer mechanisms rather than knowledge characteristics and knowledge codification. In a seminal study Keegan (1974) seeded an interest for the knowledge transfer media used by MNC executives. Keegan addressed the question of MNC-managers' information sources in terms of transfer mechanisms. In his study of information sources utilized by headquarters executives in multinational companies Keegan found that written media (documentary sources such as reports and letters) were of much less importance than oral communication, including face-to-face communication. In a more recent study of managers' use of communication media in 14 multinational companies de Meyer (1991) found that face-to-face communication made up an important part of oral communication, and the emergence of new telecommunication technology did not seem to have changed this. Thus, telephone conversations, tele- and videoconferencing, etc., complements – but does not substitute for – face-to-face communication. Ghoshal et al. (1994) found that informal networking activities – such as direct contact among managers through joint work in teams, task forces, etc. – were the main determinants of knowledge flows in MNCs. In their influential contribution to the field of multinational management Bartlett/Ghoshal (1989) outline different knowledge transfer mechanisms used by MNCs in their pursuit of 'transnational strategies'.

Conceptual Model and Development of Hypotheses

The conceptual model of the study seeks to establish the relationships between: (A) the characteristics of the internationalization knowledge as acquired by the MNC, (B) the mechanisms, or media, employed by the MNC in order to transfer the acquired internationalization knowledge across the organization, and (C) the performance implications to the knowledge transfer operation and the subsequent knowledge application in the MNC, see Figure 1.

Figure 1. Conceptual Model of the Study (with Indication of Hypotheses)

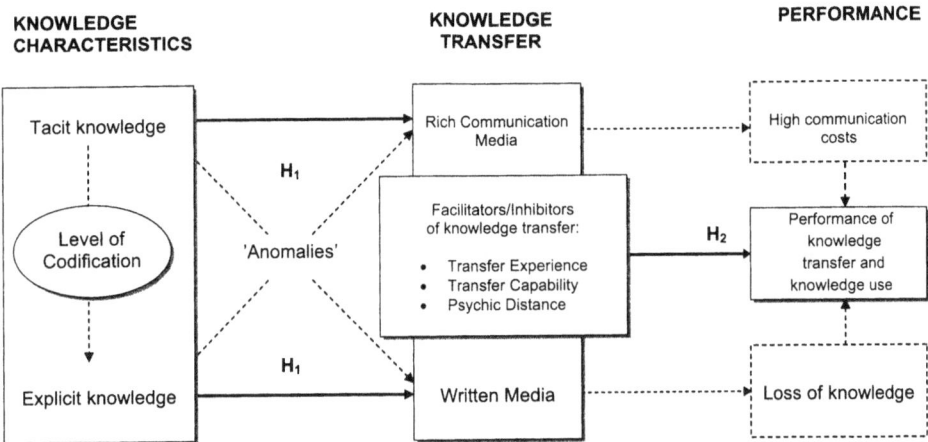

Knowledge Characteristics Prior to Transfer

According to the conceptual model the internationalization knowledge acquired by a firm – in casu an MNC – can be categorized as either being tacit or explicit (Polanyi 1966, Nonaka/Takeuchi 1995). Tacit knowledge is hard to articulate with formal language since it is embedded in individual experience and involves intangible factors such as personal beliefs, perspectives and value systems (Nonaka/Takeuchi 1995). In contrast, explicit knowledge can be articulated in formal language (grammatical statements, mathematical expressions, specifications, etc.). This dichotomized categorization of knowledge is obviously an overt simplification inasmuch as most knowledge is not completely tacit or 100% explicit, but somewhere in-between the two extremes, and will often consists of inseparable components with different characteristics. Furthermore, prior to its intra-organizational transfer some tacit knowledge may be subject to a partial or full conversion into explicit knowledge, i.e. the MNC that creates and/or acquires the internationalization knowledge engages in a process of 'codification' or 'articulation'.

The Knowledge Transfer Process

Firms can transfer knowledge across countries through a variety of different modes. For reasons of simplification our conceptual model only identifies two basically different mechanisms of knowledge transfer: 'Rich communication media' and 'written media'. These two transfer mechanisms constitute two extremes that presumably, in practice, rarely occur in pure forms. It is more likely that in most cases will the actual transfer of internationalization knowledge – the focal knowledge of this study – include both face-to-face communication and written media (Håkanson 2000).

Rich communication media comprise face-to-face communication, informal interaction, and team based mechanisms (Daft/Lengel 1986). This will require individual or team level visits, sharing of experience and face-to-face interaction or socialization (Nonaka/Takeuchi 1995). Face-to-face interaction between individuals facilitates transfer of knowledge that is experienced-based, and permits interactive communication, questioning, flexibility, and adaptation (Daft/Huber 1987, Bresman et al. 1999). Almeida/Kogut (1996) show that transfer of people allow exploitation of experiential and tacit knowledge in new locations. Rich communication media also allow transfer of knowledge that the sender may be unaware of or is unable to express in a written media. Rich communications media are also suitable when partners need to adapt new, joint business practices. These adaptations may concern, for example, international differences in culture, laws, and business practices. Rich communication media are also more suitable for transferring 'holistic' type of knowledge, i.e. knowledge that requires facial expression and trust-creation between those who transmit knowledge and those who receive it (Huber 1991, Sharma 1998). However, transfer of knowledge through rich communication media is costly. Face-to-face communication is made difficult due to the involved travel costs, to dissimilar organizational cultures, and to language differences.

On the other extreme, knowledge can be transferred by written media, involving transfer based on manuals, data base development, written instructions, and blueprints. In comparison with rich communication media, manuals and other written media are less costly transfer mechanisms because limited individual level interaction is required and because the marginal costs of replicating written media are low. Accordingly, large companies, such as most MNCs, can achieve economies of scale when using written media. However, the more tacit and context-specific the acquired knowledge, the less efficient is the use of written media.

On the face of it, the choice of transfer mechanism is closely related to the characteristics of the particular knowledge. We would expect 'rich communication media' to be the first choice of mechanism when the predominantly tacit knowledge is to be transferred across the organization, and 'written media' to be preferred as carrying mainly explicit knowledge.

However, we submit that the choice of transfer mechanism is not completely given by the characteristics of the knowledge in a predetermined way. As indicated in Figure 1 'anomalies' may occur, i.e. explicit knowledge is transferred by use of rich communication media and tacit knowledge through written media. We consider the characteristics of knowledge and the transfer mechanism to be two logically separable issues. This approach contrasts the line of thinking in which the very characteristics of knowledge is defined by its eligibility to transfer from individual to individual and across organizations, see for example Johanson/ Vahlne (1977) and Grant (1996). Instead we follow the line of Hedlund/Nonaka (1993) who distinguish between the storage of knowledge (as a stock), the transfer of knowledge (as a flow), and the transformation of knowledge (as interactions). In the same vein, we propose to logically disentangle the knowledge codification decision and the choice of transfer mechanism as two separate issues both open to managerial discretion. This line of thinking leads us to the formulation of the following hypothesis:

Hypothesis 1. Internationalization knowledge that is tacit/explicit when acquired will be transferred across the MNC organization through rich communication media/written media.

As indicated in Figure 1 different factors may facilitate or impede the knowledge transfer process in the MNC organization. Thus, the ease by which knowledge transfer is carried out is to some extent contingent on e.g. the specific organizational configuration of the MNC. From the literature review (subsection 2.) we can extract at least three different factors. Two factors, 'transfer experience' and 'transfer capability' are related to the MNC configuration and affect the knowledge transfer process in a positive way. A third factor, 'psychic distance' is a mix of organizational and environmental subsets and is supposed to impede the knowledge transfer process of MNCs. Therefore, we need to control for these variables when testing for the performance implications of the fit between knowledge characteristics and transfer mechanism.

The Performance of MNC Knowledge Transfer

The performance of knowledge transfer is contingent on internal and external factors that facilitate or inhibit the knowledge transfer process, such as transfer experience, transfer capability, and psychic distance. The facilitators and inhibitors represent situational characteristics usually exogenous to the management of the MNC organization. In most instances, the opportunity to control or manipulate these factors is, at best, limited and indirect. In contrast, MNC managers are themselves responsible for the effectuation of a proper fit between knowledge characteristics and transfer mechanisms, and this fit has performance implications as well.

Potentially, the knowledge transfer costs can be substantial. In Teece's seminal study (1977) of knowledge transfer in relation to international projects he estimated the transfer costs to vary from 2 per cent to 59 per cent of the total project costs. The costs involved are, first of all, derived from the efforts to codify and teaching complex knowledge to recipient MNC units (Kogut/Zander 1993). It is indeed likely that the difference between a successful and unsuccessful knowledge transfer is measurable on the financial bottom line of the MNC units involved in the transfer. Bresman et al. (1999) argue that even though financial performance – for example revenue from jointly developed products – is a result of knowledge transfer, successful knowledge transfer is such an important prerequisite for satisfactory financial performance that it qualifies as a dependent variable in its own right.

Hence, we posit that an important success criterion of MNC knowledge transfer is the right fit between the characteristics of the acquired internationalization knowledge and the knowledge transfer mechanism used by the MNC.

Explicit knowledge is transferred most efficiently through written media, such as manuals and blueprints, because it will save the unnecessary communication costs associated with face-to-face communication. However, the use of written media for knowledge that is inherently tacit is likely to involve loss of knowledge. This is because not all knowledge in firms can be expressed in symbols and text. In their study of Disney Inc, Branen/Wilson (1996) found that Disney Inc in its internationalization process was unable to replicate its knowledge elsewhere. Due to the historical nature of the knowledge accumulation process the firm was not fully aware of all its knowledge. Hansen et al. (1999) submit that an important aspect of knowledge management is to find the right degree of codification and choose the proper knowledge transfer medium. Loss of strategic knowledge may be a result of 'exaggerated use' of written media. Garnished with anecdotal evidence the authors argue that sometimes firms do make unsuitable 'fits' with concomitant adverse performance consequences. Furthermore, as pointed out by Kogut/Zander (1993), codification and use of written media also increases the risk of dissemination of strategic, firm-specific knowledge to competitors. The potential knowledge loss when using written media is indicated by the dotted line in the lower, right-hand corner of Figure 1.

The knowledge loss – both internally and externally – is minimized when rich communication media are used. This transfer mechanism, however, incurs high communication costs. These costs are related to international travelling, rotation of personnel, meetings, etc. – confer the dotted line in the upper, right-hand corner of Figure 1. Therefore, MNCs should only use rich communication media with care, i.e. only when the internationalization knowledge is inherently tacit. The 'right fit' is between inherently tacit knowledge and rich communication media; a 'misfit' appears when more or less explicit internationalization knowledge is transferred by use of rich communication media – involving 'unnecessarily' high communication cost.

Hence, a trade-off between loss of knowledge on the one hand and high communication costs on the other hand confronts the MNC manager. Choosing the appropriate transfer mechanism is important if the MNC is to transfer knowledge efficiently. Therefore, we can formulate the following, second hypothesis:

Hypothesis 2. Performance of transfer is maximized when tacit internationalization knowledge is transferred across the MNC organization through rich communication media and explicit knowledge by written media.

Figure 2 illustrates, in a simple two-by-two matrix, the logic of the hypothesis on 'fits' and 'misfits' between knowledge characteristics and the transfer mechanisms.

Figure 2. Performance (Mis)fit Between Knowledge Characteristics and Knowledge Transfer Mechanisms

KNOWLEDGE CHARACTERISTICS ▶ TRANSFER MECHANISM ▼	Tacit	Explicit
Rich communication media	FIT	MISFIT (High communication costs)
Written media	MISFIT (Knowledge loss)	FIT

Empirical Analysis

Data

The data of the study were gathered through a mail survey carried out in Denmark. The database 'CD-Direct' was used to identify Danish firms with (1) international operations, (2) more than 20 employees. Firms complying with these two criteria were supposed to be involved in some transfer of internationalization knowledge. The Danish population of such firms comprised 723 units that varied greatly in terms of size, industry (both manufacturing and service firms were included), and geographical location of their international operations. In August 1998 the questionnaire was sent out to identifiable company informants – primarily managing directors – in the 723 firms. Most questionnaires were completed by the managing director or another top executive. A reminder was mailed one month after the initial mailing. Upon this follow-up procedure the number of replies reached 246, corresponding to a 34 per cent response rate. For various reasons (e.g. the closing-down of foreign business activities) a number of returned questionnaires were not usable. After exclusion of incomplete questionnaires a total of 198 replies – making up a net response rate of 27.4 per cent – was usable for data processing. A test was conducted to check the sample for non-response bias. Regarding size and number of foreign subsidiaries no statistically significant differences between respondents and non-respondents were found.

An average profile of the firms in the sample is shown in Table 1. The average turnover of the sample firms was DKK 238,000,000 (equivalent to US $ 28,000,000). The average number of employees was 192 including personnel in Denmark and abroad. But as reflected by the standard deviations in Table 1 the

Table 1. Characteristics of the Sample (n = 198)

Company characteristics (1998)	Mean	Standard deviation
Total turnover (million DKK) – % of sales abroad	238 (US $ 28 million) 42.9	488 (US $ 57 million) 31.2
Total number of employees – % employed overseas	192 14	419 23
Number of foreign countries in which the company operates	18	17
Years of export experience	21	18

variation in terms of firm size is considerable. One seventh of the personnel was employed outside Denmark and almost one half of the average turnover is generated outside the home country.

The average firm is fairly internationalized and possesses considerable experience in conducting foreign operations (21 years). However, the sample includes also a group of 'novice' exporters.

Operationalization of Variables

The identified company informants, i.e. mostly the managing directors, were asked to select one recent international business assignment, such as the entry of a new foreign market or a considerable expansion of an exiting international business. The respondent should consider the chosen business assignment to be important for the continued international expansion of the firm. Furthermore, the selected business assignment should, preferably, be well underway; that is, the company should already be involved in business in the foreign location. Given this focus, the company informants were asked to indicate the amount and character of the internationalization knowledge required for the particular business assignment.

Following Erikson et al. (1997) internationalization knowledge is of three different kinds: Institutional knowledge on the host country, knowledge on counterparts in the host country and organizational knowledge on managing foreign operations. All three kinds of internationalization knowledge are required to conduct foreign activities. Furthermore, each of these three kinds of internationalization knowledge is divided into 6–7 items – or, as we label them, knowledge components. The characteristics of the internationalization knowledge as acquired and the knowledge transfer mechanisms were then assessed for the twenty internationalization knowledge components. The knowledge components are listed in Table 2. Altogether the twenty components make up internationalization knowledge of firms.

The *characteristics of knowledge* were measured by asking the company informants to indicate for the individual internationalization knowledge component to what extent the knowledge needed for the particular assignment was acquired through own, practical experience or via purchase of external expertise. Thereby, the respondents indicated tacitness or explicitness, respectively, of the acquired internationalization knowledge. Furthermore, for each knowledge component the company informant was asked to indicate the characteristics of knowledge on a 7-point Likert scale. The Likert scale went from 1 (= own practical experience) to 7 (= purchase of external expertise).

Table 2. Correlation Between Knowledge Characteristics and Transfer Mechanisms for Various Internationalization Knowledge Components

Internationalization Knowledge Components		Knowledge Characteristics Tacit–Explicit Mean	Transfer Mechanism Rich–Written Mean	Correlation Coefficients
Institutional knowledge about host country in terms of ...	1. Technology standards	2.54	3.50	–0.10
	2. Laws on products and quality standards	3.19	3.86	0.02
	3. Business legislation	3.63	3.41	0.16**
	4. Financial practice and currency rules	3.17	3.42	0.22***
	5. Business culture	2.43	2.35	0.15**
	6. Infrastructure	2.80	2.73	0.22***
	7. Structure of industry	2.86	2.77	0.22***
Business knowledge about ...	8. Customers in Denmark	2.12	2.66	0.30***
	9. Customers abroad	2.35	2.84	0.34***
	10. Suppliers in Denmark	2.39	2.72	0.46***
	11. Suppliers abroad	2.54	2.85	0.35***
	12. International organizations	3.32	3.20	0.36***
	13. Authorities abroad	3.82	3.40	0.33***
General internationalization knowledge about ...	14. Human resource management abroad	2.48	2.57	0.40***
	15. Financing abroad	3.48	3.29	0.39***
	16. Development & adaptation of products	2.18	2.93	0.27***
	17. Development & adaptation of production	2.36	2.98	0.19***
	18. Making business with new customers	2.15	2.59	0.23***
	19. Making business on new markets	2.37	2.61	0.32***
	20. Collaboration with other companies	2.61	2.72	0.41***

Note: ***, ** and * indicates 1%, 5% and 10% level of significance, respectively.

The applied *mechanism of knowledge transfer* was measured in a similar way by asking the company informants to indicate to what extent internationalization knowledge for the particular foreign assignment was transferred across the organization through daily face-to-face communication (proxy for 'rich communication media') or via company manuals, reports, or other written media. For each of the twenty internationalization knowledge components the respondents were asked to give their indication on a 7-point Likert scale going from 1 (= daily face-to-face communication) to 7 (= company manuals, reports or other written media).

The *performance of the knowledge transfer* was measured as the company informant's perception of the overall satisfaction with the particular foreign assignment on a 7-point Likert scale (ranging from 1 = no gains, to 7 = substantial gains). The assumption is that this perceptual performance variable captures the various dimensions of performance (discussed in the sub-section 3.3), including knowledge loss and high communication costs.

Furthermore, three control variables are included in the model reflecting facilitators and deterrents of knowledge transfer that have been identified in the literature (see sub-section 2.). The three control variables are: (1) transfer experience (measured on a 7-point Likert scale as international experience of adapting products to foreign markets), (2) transfer capability (measured on a 7-point Likert scale as level of routines for modification of business procedures to fit foreign market conditions), and (3) psychic distance (measured on a 7-point Likert scale as the perception of distance to the foreign location of the business assignment in question).

Two additional control variables are included: (4) the characteristics – when acquired – of the particular internationalization knowledge, and (5) the mechanism of transferring the particular knowledge.

Results

Descriptive data on the variables and a correlation matrix is shown in an appendix.

The *Hypothesis 1* is proposing a relationship between the characteristics of the internationalization knowledge as acquired and the applied transfer mechanism. Tacit internationalization knowledge is hypothesized to be transferred mainly through rich communication media and explicit internationalization knowledge mainly by written media. The tests of *Hypothesis 1* is conducted by estimating the correlation coefficients of the variation between, on the one hand, knowledge characteristics of the particular internationalization knowledge component (i.e. tacitness versus explicitness) and, on the other hand, the mechanism used for transferring this particular internationalization knowledge component (i.e. rich communication media versus written media). Following the hypothesis the correlation coefficients are expected to be significantly positive. The coefficients are shown in Table 2 (last column). Eighteen out of the twenty coefficients are, as expected, significantly positive. All in all, this gives strong support for the hypothesis saying that internationalization knowledge acquired as tacit knowledge will be transferred mainly by rich communication media, while explicit internationalization knowledge is transferred primarily through written media.

However, the coefficients vary from 0.15 to 0.46 indicating that the relationships between knowledge characteristics and transfer mechanism are far from being unambiguous. In other words, the mechanism of knowledge transfer is not exclusively given by the characteristics of the internationalization knowledge in a pre-determined way. Although there is an association between the characteristics of the knowledge and the transfer mechanism as expected, a substantial number of company managers did indicate unorthodox combinations of knowledge characteristics and transfer mechanisms: either they transferred tacit knowledge by written media or they transferred explicit knowledge through rich communication media. In order to further examine this relationship we split the characteristics of knowledge and the transfer mechanisms into two groups (values 1–3 and values 4–7 on the Likert scales). Then we look at the relationships for all the twenty internationalization knowledge components pertaining to the 198 sample firms (i.e. 20 × 198 = 3,960 relationships). We then divide all the relationships into a two-by-two matrix along the same lines as in Figure 2. This is done in Figure 3.

Figure 3. Distribution of Performance (Mis)fits of the Sample

KNOWLEDGE CHARACTERISTICS ▶ TRANSFER MECHANISM ▼	Tacit	Explicit
Rich communication media	1,307 (33.0 %)	630 (15.9 %)
Written media	721 (18.2 %)	1,303 (32.9 %)

As shown in Figure 3, most relationships follow the predicted pattern (quadrant 1 and 4). Of the 3,960 relationships in total 1,307 relationships follow the pattern proposed in *Hypothesis 1* (corresponding to 33 per cent of all relationships). Thus, tacit internationalization knowledge is transferred mainly through rich communication media. 1,303 relationships (32.9 per cent) follow the pattern predicted in *Hypothesis 1* (explicit internationalization knowledge is mainly transferred by written media). This means that two thirds of the relationships follow the predicted dominant pattern. Still, there is a substantial proportion – one third – of the relationships that follows different patterns. In 721 relationships (corresponding to 18.2 per cent) the tacit internationalization knowledge is transferred by written media, and in 630 cases the explicit internationalization knowledge is transferred by rich communication media. All in all, these figures confirm *Hypothesis 1* in so far as the hypothesis also predict a significant number of 'exceptions' to the general rule of fit between knowledge characteristics and transfer mechanisms. Still, a strong reservation should be kept in mind as regards the observation of seemingly tacit internationalization knowledge being transferred through written media. Our empirical research design does not take into account the possibility of codification of tacit internationalization knowledge prior to transfer. In other words, since we did not investigate to what extent the firms carried out transformation of tacit knowledge a great deal of the 721 observations may in fact be explicit – and not tacit – internationalization knowledge transferred through written media. Because of this shortcoming in our research design we may very well overestimate the number of 'misfits'.

Our variable for characteristics of knowledge is constructed so low values indicate tacit knowledge while high values indicate the characteristics of explicit knowledge. Similarly, the variables of transfer mechanism are indicating rich communication media for low values and written media for high values. In the case of 'fits' as discussed above both values will either be low (tacit knowledge transferred by rich communication media) or high (explicit knowledge transferred by written media). So, for the product of the two variables the fit combinations are expected to lie in both ends of the scale, while the non-fit combinations are expected to lie in-between. Therefore, following *Hypothesis 1* on the performance fit we expect a U-shaped relationship between 'performance' on the one side and the interaction term of knowledge characteristics and transfer mechanism on the other side. In order to test this we apply the following model:

Performance = f (knowledge, transfer mechanism, (knowledge * transfer mechanism)^2, controls)

Hence, the model includes the interaction term of the characteristics of internationalization knowledge and the transfer mechanism in first and second order.

Following *Hypothesis 2* we expect the interaction term of first order to be significantly *negative*. Conversely, the interaction term of second order is expected to be significantly *positive*. This indicates that performance will increase both in the low and high ends of the scale – the intervals of observed combinations where the characteristics of knowledge and the transfer mechanisms fit together.

The model was conducted for the twenty knowledge components and with the performance variable – twenty different models in total. However, Table 3 shows the results where all the twenty knowledge components are added together into one single variable (with Cronbach alpha = 0.89 for knowledge characteristics and Cronbach alpha = 0.92 for transfer mechanisms). Table 3 only includes the

Table 3. Regression Analysis of the Hypothesized Model

	Performance
Intercept	2.68***
	(0.86)
Knowledge Characteristics * Transfer Mechanism	−0.39**
	(0.19)
(Knowledge Characteristics * Transfer Mechanism)^2	0.15**
	(0.07)
Transfer Experience	0.68*
	(0.35)
Transfer Capability	0.01**
	(0.005)
Psychic Distance	−0.07*
	(0.04)
Knowledge Characteristics as Acquired (Tacit – Explicit)	0.59*
	(0.31)
Transfer Mechanism	0.14**
(Rich Communication Media – Written Media)	(0.008)
F-value	3.20***
N	198
R-square	11.1%

***, **, and * indicates 1%, 5% and 10% level of significance, respectively

results of a regression analysis where all the twenty knowledge components are collapsed into one single variable. More rigorous analyses were conducted for all the twenty knowledge components, but the results are not shown. Furthermore, as the dependent variable is measured on a 7 point Likert scale and there is some controversy on whether this can be interpreted as interval data (see for example Nunnally 1978) we have also conducted a logistic regression model (prog logistic) with ordinal responses (SAS 1991). The results turned out to be almost identical with the ones obtained by use of the ordinary regression model. The results of the alternative regression model confirm the reliability of our model.

As can be seen in Table 3, the interaction term of first order is significantly negative and that of second order is significantly positive (both on 5% significance level). The same picture holds when looking at the similar regression analyses for the individual knowledge components.

All control variables appeared to affect performance significantly (on 5 and 10 per cent levels). Transfer experience, transfer capability and psychic distance came out with the expected signs. Somewhat surprisingly, however, the characteristics of knowledge and the transfer mechanism did not only appear to have an effect on performance in interaction, but also as independent variables. On a 10 per cent significance level performance is associated in a positive way with explicit internationalization knowledge and written media.

As significant problem with this test might be that the data has a self-selection bias in the sense that managers are aware of the performance implications of their choices. This is violating the assumption (in the regression analysis) that the dependent variable (performance) should not be determined by the same factors as the independent variable (choice of transfer mechanism). In order to correct for this self-selection bias we have run the Heckman two stage regression procedure (Heckman 1979). The results turn out to be very similar with the first order effect of the interaction between knowledge characteristics and transfer mechanism being significantly negative and the second order effect being positively significant (as in the OLS-model).

Conclusions and Managerial Implications

For a long time theories on the existence and growth of MNCs and on the internationalization process of firms either assumed an almost frictionless intra-organizational knowledge transfer process, or considered the crucial internationalization knowledge to be extremely context-specific, thereby making the transfer process more or less futile. Hence, the knowledge transfer process was hardly an issue in the early versions of these theories. Since then, IB scholars have – inspired by organizational learning literature – gradually adopted a less deterministic and more sophisticated view on the knowledge transfer processes of MNCs: Transfer of knowledge within the multinational organization is neither frictionless or futile and requires a great deal of managerial discretion.

In this study we have examined the choice of mechanisms for transferring internationalization knowledge across multinational organizations. In a somewhat simplified decision matrix we would – on the face of it – expect tacit internationalization knowledge to be transferred through rich communication media and explicit knowledge through written media. Empirical evidence of Danish MNCs shows that most – but far from all – transfers of internationalization knowledge follow the expected pattern. Hence, up to one third of the observed combinations may be described as mismatches of knowledge characteristics and transfer mechanisms. The data indicate that to some extent are these mismatches associated with impaired performance as perceived by the MNC managers involved in the foreign business assignment. These findings send a warning signal to MNC managers to show a great deal of vigilance in their choice of knowledge transfer mechanisms.[1]

Appendix Correlation matrix

	1	2	3	4	5	6	7	8
1 Performance	1.00							
2 Characteristics of Knowledge (C)	−0.04	1.00						
3 Transfer Mechanism (T)	0.05	0.31***	1.00					
4 C * T	0.0003	0.78***	0.79***	1.00				
5 C * T^2	0.03	0.72***	0.72***	0.96***	1.00			
6 Transfer Experience	0.21***	−0.10	0.14**	0.03	0.04	1.00		
7 Transfer Capability	0.23***	−0.18**	0.08	−0.08	−0.11	0.24***	1.00	
8 Psychic Distance	−0.13*	0.08	−0.05	−0.0001	−0.01	−0.02	−0.06	1.00
Mean	5.26	2.71	2.97	8.36	89.6	5.40	5.67	3.58
Standard Deviation	1.26	0.93	1.07	4.46	86.5	1.32	1.64	2.21

Note: ***,**, and * indicates 1%, 5% and 10% level of significance, respectively

Endnote

1 The authors would like to thank Peter Buckley, Ivo Zander and Udo Zander for their valuable comments and suggestions to an earlier version of the paper.

References

Adler, N., *International Dimensions of Organizational Behaviour*, 2nd edition, Boston: PWS Kent 1995.
Aharoni, Y., *The Foreign Investment Decision Process*, Boston: Harward Business School 1966.
Almeida, P./Kogut, B., The Exploration of Technological Diversity and the Geographic Localization of Innovation, *Small Business Economics*, 9, 1996, pp. 21–31.
Argote, L., *Organizational Learning: Creating, Retaining and Transferring Knowledge*, Boston: Kluwer Academic Publishers 1999.
Bartlett, C. A./Ghoshal, S., *Managing Across Borders: The Transnational Solution*, Boston: Harvard Business School Press 1989.
Bilkey, W. J./Tesar, G., The Export Behaviour of Smaller Sized Wisconsin Manufacturing Firms, *Journal of International Business Studies*, 8, 1, 1977, pp. 93–98.
Branen, M./Wilson, J., Recontextualization and Internationalization: Lessons in Transcultural Materialism from the Walt Disney Company, *CEMS Business Review*, 3, March 1996.
Bresman, H./Birkinshaw, J./Nobel, R., Knowledge Transfer in International Acquisitions, *Journal of International Business Studies*, 30, 3, 1999, pp. 439–462.
Carlson, S., *How Foreign is Foreign Trade? A Problem in International Business Research*, Uppsala: Uppsala University Press 1975.
Cyert, R. D./March, J. G., *A Behavioural Theory of the Firm*, Englewood Cliffs, NJ: Prentice-Hall 1963.
Daft, R. L./Lengel, R. H., Organizational Information Requirements, Media Richness and Structural Design, *Management Science*, 32, 5, 1986, pp. 554–572.
Daft R. L./Huber. G. P., How Organizations Learn: A Communication Framework, *Research in Sociology of Organizations*, 5, 1987, pp. 1–36.
Davidson, W. H./McFetridge, D. G., Key Characteristics in the Choice of International Technology Transfer Mode, *Journal of International Business Studies*, 16, 2, 1985, pp. 5–21.
de Meyer, A., Tech Talk: How Managers Are Stimulating Global R&D Communication, *Sloan Management Review*, 32, Spring 1991, pp. 49–58.
Epple, D./Argote, L./Murphy, K., An Empirical Investigation of the Micro Structure of Knowledge Acquisition and Transfer through Learning by Doing, *Operations Research*, 44, 1996, pp. 77–86.
Eriksson, K./Johanson, J./Majgård, A./Sharma, D., Experiential Knowledge and Cost in the Internationalization Process, *Journal of International Business Studies*, 28, 2, 1997, pp. 337–360.
Forsgren, M./Johanson, J., Managing Internationalization in Business Networks, in Forsgren, M./Johanson, J. (eds), *Managing Networks in International Business*, Philadelphia: Gordon and Breach 1992, pp. 1–16.
Galbraith, C. S., Transferring Core Manufacturing Technologies in High Technology Firms, *California Management Review*, 32, 4, 1990, pp. 56–70.
Ghoshal, S./Korine, H./Szulanski, G., Interunit Communication in Multinational Corporations, *Management Science*, 40, 1, 1994, pp. 96–111.
Grant, R. M., Toward a Knowledge-based Theory of the Firm, *Strategic Management Journal*, 17, Special Issue 1996, pp. 109–122.
Gupta, A. K./Govindarajan, V., Knowledge Flows and the Structure of Control Within Multinational corporations, *Academy of Management Review*, 16, 1991, pp. 768–792.
Håkanson, L., From Tacit Knowledge to Scientific Theory: The Power and Logic of Articulation, *Competitive Paper* presented at the EIBA 26th Annual Conference in Maastricht, December 10–12, 2000.
Hansen, M./Nohria, N./Tierney, T., What's Your Strategy for Managing Knowledge?, *Harvard Business Review*, 77, March–April 1999, pp. 106–116.
Heckman, J. J., Sample Selection Bias as a Specification Error, *Econometrica*, 47, January 1979, pp. 153–161.
Hedlund, G., The Hypermodern MNC – A Heterarchy?, *Human Resource Management*, 25, 1, 1986, pp. 9–36.

Hedlund, G., A Model of Knowledge Management and the N-Form Corporation, *Strategic Management Journal*, 15, 2, 1994, pp. 73–90.
Hedlund, G./Nonaka, I., Models of Knowledge Management in the West and Japan, in Lorange, P./Chakravarthy, B./Roos, J./Van de Ven, A. (eds), *Implementing Strategic Processes: Change, learning and co-operation*, London: Blackwell 1993.
Hofstede, G., *Culture's Consequences: International Differences in Work Related Values*, Beverly Hills, CA: Sage Publications 1984.
Huber, G. P., Organizational Learning: The Contributing Processes and the Literature, *Organization Science*, 2, 1, 1991, pp. 88–115.
Johanson, J./Vahlne, J.-E., The Internationalization Process of the Firm – A Model of Knowledge Development and Increasing Foreign Market Commitments, *Journal of International Business Studies*, 8, 1, 1977, pp. 23–32.
Keegan, W. J., Multinational Scanning: A study of the Information Sources Utilized by Headquarters Executives in Multinational Companies, *Administrative Science Quarterly*, 19, 3, 1974, pp. 411–421.
Kogut, B./Zander, U., Knowledge of the Firm, Combinative Capabilities, and the Replication of Technology, *Organization Science*, 3, 3, 1992, pp. 383–397.
Kogut, B./Zander, U., Knowledge of the Firm and the Evolutionary Theory of the Multinational Corporation, *Journal of International Business Studies*, 24, 4, 1993, pp. 625–646.
Lester, R. K./McCabe, M. J., The Effect of Industrial Structure on Learning by Doing in Nuclear power Plant Operation, *The Rand Journal of Economics*, 24, 1993, pp. 418–438.
Mowery, D. C./Oxley, J. E./Silverman, B. S., Strategic Alliances and Inter-firm Knowledge Transfer, *Strategic Management Journal*, 17, 1996, pp. 77–91.
Nonaka, I./Takeuchi, H., *The Knowledge-Creating Company*, Oxford: Oxford University Press 1995.
Nunnally, J., *Psychometric Theory*, NY: McGraw-Hill 1978.
Penrose, E., *The Theory of the Growth of the Firm*, London: Basil Blackwell 1959.
Polanyi, M., *The Tacit Dimension*, Garden City, NY: Doubleday 1966.
SAS, *SAS/STAT User's Guide, Release 6.03 Edition*, Cary, NC: SAS Institute Inc. 1991.
Sharma, D., A Model for Governance in International Strategic Alliances, *Journal of Business & Industrial Marketing*, 13, 6, 1998, pp. 511–528.
Simonin, B. L., Transfer of Marketing Know-how in International Strategic Alliances: An Empirical Investigation of the Role and Antecedents of Knowledge Ambiguity, *Journal of International Business Studies*, 30, 3, 1999, pp. 463–490.
Szulanski, G., Exploring Internal Stickiness: Impediments to the Transfer of Best Practice within the Firm, *Strategic Management Journal*, 17, 1996, pp. 27–43.
Teece, D. J., Technology Transfer by Multinational Firms: The Resource Cost of Transferring Technological Know-how, *Economic Journal*, 87, 1977, pp. 242–261.
Zander, U., *Exploiting a Technological Edge: Voluntary and Involuntary Dissemination of Technology*, Doctoral dissertation, Stockholm: Institute of International Business 1991.
Zander, U./Kogut, B., Knowledge and the Speed of the Transfer and Imitation of Organizational Capabilities, *Organization Science*, 6, 1, 1995, pp. 76–92.

Jiatao Li/Oded Shenkar

Knowledge Search and Governance Choice: International Joint Ventures in the People's Republic of China[1]

Abstract

- This paper longitudinally examines knowledge search and governance choice in China-based international joint ventures from transaction costs and knowledge-based perspectives, complementing recent studies of IJV learning in other transitional economy contexts.

- The knowledge-governance link is tested from a local partner perspective in a transitional economy *from intention to formation*, using data on ninety IJVs over the 1988–1998 period.

Key Results

- Both the intentions to form equity ventures and their eventual formation are predicted by the Chinese firms' search for tacit knowledge, high knowledge base, and limited knowledge overlap with foreign partners. *Intentions* to form equity ventures are also predicted by a low knowledge base, producing a U-shaped effect that is not replicated at the formation stage. Implications for theory development are delineated.

Authors

Jiatao Li, Associate Professor, Department of Management of Organizations, Hong Kong University of Science and Technology, Hong Kong.

Oded Shenkar, Ford Motor Company Professor of Global Business Management, Fisher College of Business, Ohio State University, Columbus, OH, USA.

Jiatao Li/Oded Shenkar

Introduction

The choice of mechanisms by which firms learn and accumulate new skills and capabilities is a fundamental issue in strategic management (Teece/Pisano/Shuen 1997). The knowledge-based theory of the firm focuses on knowledge as a key competitive asset and views the firm as a repository of specialized knowledge (Conner/Prahalad 1996, Kogut/Zander 1992). When knowledge is tacit and/or organizationally embedded, it is difficult to acquire and cannot be effectively transferred via markets or fully specified in a contractual fashion (Argote/Ingram 2000, Badaracco 1991).

Cooperative ventures differ in their ability to facilitate knowledge transfer across firm boundaries (Mowery/Oxley/Silverman 1996, Teece/Pisano 1994). The equity joint venture (EJV), legally and administratively independent from the parent firms, is considered superior to the non-equity joint venture (NEJV) as a vehicle for the transfer of tacit knowledge because of its ability to replicate the organization of the parent firms (Kogut 1988). In contrast, the more market-like NEJV, which includes contractual joint ventures and technology transfer agreements that do not involve equity sharing, does not accord an opportunity for organizational replication and hence does not facilitate tacit knowledge transfer (Osborn/Baughn 1990).

The nature of knowledge, however, is not the only determinant of governance choice in knowledge transfer (Pisano 1989, Lane/Salk/Lyles 2001). Knowledge search is also driven by the general or partner-specific absorptive capacity (Cohen/Levinthal 1990, Lane/Lubatkin 1998). From a knowledge-based perspective, the governance mode is chosen to facilitate knowledge absorption under these circumstances. From the transaction costs perspective, governance choice will reflect cost and hazard considerations, e.g., the potential for opportunism on the part of transacting parties (Williamson 1985).

In this paper, a model is developed to explain the choice of governance modes for international joint ventures (IJVs). Drawing on transaction costs and knowledge-based theories of the firm, hypotheses regarding modal choices for knowledge transfer are developed along three theory streams, namely, the nature of the knowledge, the knowledge base of the recipients, and the knowledge overlap between partners. Rather than following the customary use of formations as proxy for strategic intentions (Tallman/Shenkar 1994), this study longitudinally examines the 1988 preferences of Chinese firms and the China-based ventures they eventually formed with foreign partners up to 1998. While the IJV literature has generally treated the local partners as passive providers of relief from local customs and regulations (Yan/Gray 1994), we will examine Chinese partners as the focal firms in this study.

The study makes several contributions to the literature. First, it offers a test of knowledge-governance links from a local partner perspective in a transitional economy *from intention to formation*. To the best of our knowledge, it is the first longitudinal study of this kind in transitional economies and possibly in the IJV literature as a whole. The longitudinal nature of this study represents not only an empirical contribution, for the gaps revealed between intentions and formations offer key insights and hence venues for theory development which are now delineated in the paper. Second, the study combines transaction costs and knowledge-based perspectives on IJVs to develop the governance implications of learning and knowledge transfer in IJVs in China, thus complementing recent studies of IJV learning in other transitional economy contexts (e.g., Lane/Salk/Lyles 2001). Finally, this study has both theoretical (e.g., exploring the interface between transaction costs and absorptive capacity) and practical (e.g., understanding the preferences of local firms can help the MNE prepare for negotiations) repercussions.

Theory and Hypotheses

The nature of knowledge can be positioned along a continuum ranging from explicit to tacit. While explicit knowledge can be codified and programmed (Nonaka 1994), tacit knowledge is experiential and non-programmable, rooted in action and in an idiosyncratic context (Penrose 1959, Polanyi 1966, Nelson/Winter 1982). Embedded in a firm's context, tacit knowledge is unique and inimitable, and thus of greater strategic value (Barney 1991). Because it cannot be represented as a set of easily communicated rules and blueprints, tacit knowledge cannot be readily packaged and transmitted via contractual channels and is difficult to acquire, analyze, and disseminate (Dietrich 1994, Teece 1981). A virtual replication of the organization in which it is embedded is necessary if such knowledge is to be effectively transmitted (Kogut 1988, Conner/Prahalad 1996, p. 485).

More than other IJV modes, the EJV offers a reliable vehicle for tacit and embedded knowledge transfer between partners. From a transaction costs perspective, the hierarchical nature of the EJV permits the handling of contingencies which are likely to arise when such knowledge is transferred and implemented (Teece 1986). The EJV also tends to create synergetic effects leading to "common benefits" (Davies 1977, Khanna/Gulati/Nohria 1998). From a learning perspective, prolonged co-habitation of managerial and technical personnel from the foreign and local firms creates interactive learning opportunities within a mentoring context (Gulati 1995). The cohabitation permits behavioral processes that are conducive to knowledge transfer, e.g., continuous observation allowing for vicarious learning and symbolic storage of appropriate behavior underlying the acquisition of complex knowledge (Wood/Bandura 1989).

In transitional economies, the knowledge learned from foreign parents tends to relate to skills in management, marketing, and decision-making (Lane/Salk/Lyles 2001, Shenkar/Li 1999). In a post hoc analysis, Lane et al. (2001) examined the content of knowledge learned by the Hungarian-based JVs between 1993 and 1996. They found a significant increase in the learning of the more tacit forms of knowledge such as managerial techniques and marketing expertise over the study period. Shenkar and Li (1999) used similar categories for learning in another transitional economy (China) and suggested that learning management skills entails highly tacit, socially embedded knowledge. The more tacit the knowledge, the more difficult it is to transfer and to assimilate it because of its social nature and causal ambiguity. This is especially true in transitional economies where learning new managerial skills requires cognitive and behavioral change (Child/Markoczy 1993, Shenkar/Li 1999, Lane/Salk/Lyles 2001). Therefore,

Hypothesis 1. When seeking knowledge transfer from IJV partners, local firms in transitional economies are more likely to choose an EJV over a NEJV when the knowledge is tacit.

From a knowledge perspective, a firm's knowledge base represents its "absorptive capacity", namely its ability to recognize the value of new external information, assimilate it, and apply it to commercial ends (Cohen/Levinthal 1990, p. 128, Lane/Salk/Lyles 2001). It is what makes the firm an effective "repository of embedded knowledge" (Badaracco 1991). From this perspective, having a limited knowledge base will curtail the absorptive capacity of the recipient company, triggering difficulties in absorbing knowledge from others (Ellis 1965). This includes the knowledge to be absorbed from IJV partners, which may well be the primary reason for forming the venture in the first place (e.g., Kogut 1988). In this logic, a firm with a substantial knowledge base will opt for an EJV because it is convinced that it will be in a position to benefit from the learning opportunities embedded in this mode.

From a transaction costs perspective, the argument is more complex. Broadly speaking, the absorptive capacity argument is focused on the perspective of the knowledge recipient in an IJV setting and hence is mostly concerned with how to develop knowledge resources via effective transfer. In contrast, transaction costs theory is more concerned with how to defend existing knowledge resources from the opportunism of others, in this case, the potential partners. Such defenses are not logically triggered unless the focal firm has become a nontrivial knowledge owner, by accumulating a substantial knowledge base. As the knowledge owner, local firms will opt for an EJV as a way of providing "mutual hostage" protection of rights that would be otherwise difficult to defend (Williamson 1975). Superior monitoring and creation of incentives for the partners to support common rather than individual benefit add to the advantage of an EJV for a knowledge owner (Hennart 1988, Khanna/Gulati/Nohria 1998).

In transitional economies, the knowledge contributed by local partners tends to be embedded in the local environment (e.g., knowing how to adapt the technology to local conditions) (Inkpen/Beamish 1997, Luo/Shenkar/Nyaw 2001). Under an EJV, local partners can protect some of this embedded knowledge while learning from the foreign parent (see *Hypothesis 3* on low knowledge overlap). Also, because of incentives provided to EJVs in China, this mode accords better access to government sources of knowledge (e.g., research centers).

IJVs within transitional economies are not well represented by Hamel's (1991) "learning race" metaphor, rather, they are collaborations which foster competitive advantages by using the joint venture organization to create, store, and apply knowledge (Grant/Baden-Fuller 1995, Lane/Salk/Lyles 2001). Transferring knowledge between organizations is always difficult (Szulanski 1996), but differences between firms in developed and transitional economies add to the challenge. Understanding and assimilating complex organizational knowledge requires the active engagement of both parties as well as certain structural and cognitive preconditions. Theory suggests that forming a separate equity-based IJV organization will facilitate learning by providing the expectation of a stable, long-term relationship which allows trust and knowledge sharing to develop (Beamish/Banks 1987, Lane/Salk/Lyles 2001). Therefore,

Hypothesis 2. When seeking knowledge transfer from IJV partners, local firms in transitional economies are more likely to choose an EJV over a NEJV when they have a high knowledge base.

Learning from a partner in an IJV setting is a dyadic property pertaining to the development of relation-specific assets (Lane/Lubatkin 1998). The ability of a recipient firm to untangle and assimilate knowledge is a function of whether or not it has overlapping knowledge bases with its "teacher". The relationship between overlapping knowledge and partner-specific absorptive capacity is explicitly argued by Dyer and Singh (1998). Overlapping knowledge base allows collaborating firms to systematically identify valuable know-how in each other and transfer it across organizational boundaries, via inter-firm routines and social interactions.

Several empirical studies confirmed that knowledge overlap between partners facilitates partner learning and knowledge transfer (Lane/Salk/Lyles 2001, Mowery/Oxley/Silverman 1996, Szulanski 1996). However, previous studies have not examined the impact of knowledge overlap between the partners regarding governance choice. From a knowledge perspective, limited overlap between a local/recipient firm and its partner shifts the learning burden to the governance form. The interactive learning and cohabitation provided by an EJV structure can compensate for the limited inter-party exchange by creating internal overlap within the venture's boundaries, establishing the interface necessary for knowledge transfer. An EJV is hence preferred from this perspective. From a transaction costs perspective, a low level of knowledge overlap increases uncertainty regarding partner behavior because the firm is less likely to be able to decipher the partner's actions (Williamson 1975). Uncertainty favors an EJV because it pre-empts the incorporation of contingencies into a contract. It also necessitates more protection for the transacting parties in the form of monitoring and access to independent financial information. Furthermore, the local partner is likely to prefer an EJV under low overlap because the embedded nature of its own knowledge requires multiple channels for diffusion. Therefore,

Hypothesis 3. When seeking knowledge transfer from IJV partners, local firms in transitional economies are more likely to choose an EJV over a NEJV when the knowledge overlap between partners is low.

Research Setting and Method

Research Site, Sample and Procedure

Explosive growth in the number of IJVs in China – from five in 1979 to hundreds of thousands today – presents a challenging opportunity for the study of IJVs in transitional economies (Pearson 1991). It is typical of such economies that local firms seek new technology, capital, and management and marketing skills from foreign partners. Lagging behind developed country standards, such firms nevertheless possess reasonable capabilities in using intermediate technologies, enjoying modest success in manufacturing some export-quality goods and benefiting from superior understanding of local markets and their institutions (Child 1994, Simon 1988).

The study was conducted in Shanghai, China's leading manufacturing base and home to almost 10 percent of all China-based IJVs in 1988 (*China Statistical Yearbook* 1998). The study was conducted in two phases. Phase I utilized a survey data set first collected in March 1988 from 90 proposed IJV projects seeking foreign partners. In Phase II, an event-history data set was developed in 1998, tracking the actual formation and governance mode of the 90 proposed IJV projects over the 1988–98 period. This paper reports the results of analysis based on both phases.

Phase I: Project Solicitations

Survey data were obtained from project listings of local firms seeking foreign partners, published by the Foreign Investment Development Agency (FIDA) in Shanghai (1988). Information on ninety IJV projects initiated by eighty firms was made available to prospective foreign partners seeking China-based IJVs. FIDA designed the questionnaire, which it passed on to the industrial bureaus in the city for distribution to individual firms. The questionnaires were filled out by the Managing Director (or his/her designee) of each firm that expressed interest in promoting its capabilities and requirements to prospective foreign investors. The senior author conducted site visits in 1994–95, in which he interviewed FIDA officials, the representatives of the Chemical Industries and the Electric and Electronics Industries Bureaus, and executives of about 1/3 of the firms. The visit confirmed that the firms provided genuine disclosure of their preferred IJV governance mode and a realistic assessment of their contributions to the proposed IJV.

The questionnaire covered the following items: (a) the nature of the proposed IJV project; (b) the IJV mode preferred by the local firm, i.e. an EJV or one of several NEJV forms; (c) the types of knowledge to be transferred from the foreign partner, i.e. management, marketing and/or technological know-how; (d) the contributions the local partners could make in those three areas; (e) the estimated number of employees for the IJV; and (f) whether the local parent was a state-owned firm or a collective/township enterprise. Preferences regarding foreign partner origin were not solicited in the original survey.

Phase II: Actual Formations

A follow-up survey was conducted in 1998 to develop event-histories of actual IJV formation and governance choice of the proposed IJVs over the 1988–98 period. We tracked the 90 proposed projects with secondary data sources such as directories of Shanghai-based IJVs, phone directories, and information from our 1994–95 field interview records of 30 firms. We then conducted telephone interviews with all sample firms to confirm the status of the proposed IJV project, the governance mode adopted, nationality of the foreign partners, and the types of knowledge transferred. Of the original 90 projects, 10 projects had been solicited by firms that were no longer in existence (four went bankrupt and six were closed during the study period). Interviews with their supervising government bureaus confirmed that their closure was the result of state restructuring or poor operations, and was not IJV related. Of the remaining 80, phone interviews were conducted with the General Manager or other senior managers having information regarding the related projects. Among those, 34 (43 percent) project solicitations resulted in actual IJV formations, including 29 EJVs and 5 NEJVs.[2] The remaining 46 solicitations did not yield an IJV throughout the study period and were treated as right-censored. The 80 projects form the sample for the event-history analysis.

Models and Dependent Variables

Phase I: Logistic Models on EJV Preferences

Among the 90 proposed IJV projects, 53 (59 percent) indicated seeking EJVs only, 11 (12 percent) indicated seeking NEJVs only. 26 IJVs (29 percent, from 22 firms) did not indicate preference for an EJV or a NEJV. The dependent variable, the preferred governance mode of an IJV, was coded as an ordinal response variable, with JV = 3 if the local partner preferred an EJV, JV = 2 if no preference in JV structure, and JV = 1 for a NEJV.

An ordinal logistic regression model was used to examine the propensity of local firms to seek an EJV rather than a NEJV. The model was estimated with the maximum likelihood method:

$$P[JV] = 1 \Big/ \left[1 + \exp\left(-\sum_{j=1}^{k} B_j X_j\right)\right].$$

Where $P[JV]$ is the probability that an EJV is sought and X_j is the vector of explanatory variables in this study, including the nature of knowledge to be transferred, the knowledge base of the local partner, the knowledge overlap between partners, and control variables such as IJV size, local parent firm size, state ownership, and an industry dummy variable.

Phase II: Event-history Analysis of Actual Formations

An ordinal logistic regression model was also used to examine the actual selection of EJV governance mode upon IJV formation.[3] The dependent variable for the actual formation sample was coded as an ordinal response variable, with JV = 3 if the local partner selected an EJV mode, JV = 2 if there was no JV formation during the study period, and JV = 1 for a NEJV formation.

Independent and Control Variables

Nature of Knowledge

In the absence of a continuous measure, three binary variables were used to indicate whether a local firm was seeking the transfer of management, marketing, or technology know-how from a foreign partner. For example, binary variable Management is coded as "1" if a local firm was seeking the transfer of management skills from a foreign partner, and "0" otherwise. Following Lane et al. (2001) and Shenkar and Li (1999), management and marketing skills were taken to represent tacit or embedded knowledge. In contrast, technology can be typically codified and is less imprinted in organizational idiosyncrasies and routines than are marketing and especially management. This is particularly true for Chinese firms, which tend to have a narrower view of technology than Western companies (Pearson 1991).

Knowledge Base

Two recent empirical studies have examined the types of knowledge and learning in IJVs in transitional economies (Lane/Salk/Lyles 2001, Luo 1999). Lane et al. (2001) use a survey questionnaire to measure knowledge transfer from foreign parents for Hungary-based IJVs in five areas: managerial techniques; marketing expertise; technological expertise; product development; and manufacturing process. In another study, Luo (1999) examines knowledge of foreign parents in four areas including organizational capabilities, marketing knowledge, technological skills, and environmental familiarity for IJVs in China.

Consistent with these empirical studies, we use the contributions of local partners in three areas (i.e., management, marketing, and technology) as a proxy for the knowledge base of the local partners. The local partners' contributions to the IJV were measured as binary variables, namely whether or not local firms were able to contribute their knowledge, in each of the areas above, to the venture. Those contributions were summed up to create a 0 to 3 index (3 = highest), taken to represent the local partner's knowledge base. While our measure of local partner knowledge base is constrained by the data, it can, nonetheless, serve as an indicator of the general absorptive capacity of the local partners (e.g., Luo 1999). Future research is clearly needed in collecting more fine-grained measures of the local partner knowledge base.

Knowledge Overlap

Drawing on the partner-specific absorptive capacity argument, we examine the knowledge overlap between local and foreign partners as a predictor of IJV governance form. Knowledge overlap is measured by inter-partner similarities in each of the three knowledge realms we discussed above.

An overlap was judged when a local partner sought knowledge transfer in an area in which it already possessed knowledge. For instance, the overlap was coded as "1" if a local firm sought the transfer of marketing skills from the foreign partner when it already possessed marketing knowledge and "0", otherwise. The three overlaps were then aggregated to form a knowledge overlap index ranging from 0 to 3. A score of 3 indicates that the local firm has knowledge overlaps in all three areas with a potential partner. For the IJVs, assimilating foreign parent knowledge is a sense making process whereby the IJV connects the new knowledge to its existing knowledge. Therefore, the relevance of the student firm's basic knowledge to the teacher firm's knowledge base will be positively associated with the interorganizational learning (Luo/Shenkar/Nyaw 2001).

Control Variables

Based on theory and literature review, five control variables have been added to the models: IJV size, local parent firm size, state ownership, single or multiple ventures, and an industry dummy variable. Penrose (1959) as well as Osborn and Baughn (1990) suggest that the size of the IJV and the size of parent firms are important determinants of the governance structure of alliances. IJV and local parent firm size were measured by the number of employees (in thousands).

The ownership structure of local partners, such as state ownership, may affect the choice of the IJV structure because state-owned firms face different institutional pressures from non-state firms (Child 1994). State-ownership is coded as "1" for state-owned firms, and "0" for non-state (e.g., collective, township) firms. Multiple alliances increase the relative scope of inter-firm cooperation and could affect the tendency to extract common versus private benefits (Khanna et al. 1998). There is also evidence that repeated alliances between two partners are less likely to be equity-based as a result of emerging inter-firm trust (Gulati 1995).[4] The variable is coded as "1" if the local firm was seeking multiple IJVs and as "0" for a single IJV.

Finally, given that industry conditions may alter the preferences for IJV mode (Harrigan 1988, Hitt/Ireland/Goryunov 1988), it is prudent to control for potential industry level effects. The previous studies show that foreign firms are more likely to internalize their operations in the overseas markets in industries with high advertising intensity (e.g., Gatignon/Anderson 1988, Pan/Tse 2000). The rationale is that firms need to protect their brands, which are the outcomes of their investment in brand building through advertising (Osborn/Baughn 1990, Pan/Tse 2000). Thus, firms in industries with high advertising intensity, such as consumer industries, are more likely to adopt an EJV mode. Therefore, we coded dummy variables for two sectors: consumer goods and industrial goods (Osborn/Baughn 1990). Other industry level analyses were pre-empted by sample size.

Results

Table 1 reports the descriptive statistics and correlation matrix for all variables for intention data. Among the 90 proposed IJVs, the majority was seeking EJVs. About one third sought the transfer of management skills, and over half sought the transfer of marketing skills or technology, respectively. The majority of local partners were able to contribute to the IJV in at least one knowledge area, thus possessing a basic level of general absorptive capacity. In about half of the cases, local partners overlapped with foreign partners in the areas where they sought knowledge transfer. Seventy four percent of the sample firms were state-owned, and 23 percent of the IJVs were from local firms seeking multiple ventures simultaneously. About two-thirds of the IJV projects were in consumer industries.

Table 2 reports the descriptive statistics for the sample of 80 IJV projects where event-history data on actual IJV formation were available. Of these 80 proposed ventures, 34 formed IJVs and the remaining 46 did not form IJVs during the study period. The majority of local firms were able to contribute to the IJV in at least one knowledge area. In 40 percent of the cases, local partners overlapped with foreign partners in the areas where they sought knowledge transfer.

Table 1. Descriptive Statistics and Correlation Matrix: Intentions

Variables	Means	s.d.	Minimum	Maximum	1	2	3	4	5	6	7	8	9	10
1. Joint venture	2.48	0.69	1	3	1.0									
2. Seek management	0.33	0.47	0	1	0.16	1.0								
3. Seek marketing	0.54	0.50	0	1	0.11	0.50*	1.0							
4. Seek technology	0.58	0.50	0	1	−0.07	0.56*	0.80*	1.0						
5. Knowledge overlap	0.98	1.27	0	3	−0.01	0.73*	0.67*	0.64*	1.0					
6. Knowledge base	1.36	1.35	0	3	−0.02	0.51*	0.59*	0.53*	0.84*	1.0				
7. IJV size	0.27	0.25	0.009	1.8	−0.06	0.08	−0.04	−0.02	0.06	0.06	1.0			
8. State-ownership	0.74	0.44	0	1	−0.22*	0.25*	−0.08	0.12	0.19	0.08	0.10	1.0		
9. Multiple venture	0.23	0.43	0	1	−0.47*	0.11	0.19	0.26*	0.07	0.03	−0.13	0.32*	1.0	
10. Consumer goods	0.69	0.47	0	1	0.26*	−0.03	−0.18	−0.14	−0.09	−0.09	0.01	−0.06	−0.25*	1.0
11. Local parent size	1.95	4.89	0.04	35	0.02	0.02	−0.04	0.13	−0.07	−0.12	−0.01	0.19	−0.02	0.12

Note: *$p < 0.05$; N = 90

Table 2. Descriptive Statistics and Correlation Matrix: Actual Formation

Variables	Means	s.d.	Minimum	Maximum	1	2	3	4	5	6	7	8	9	10
1. Equity joint venture	2.30	0.58	1	3	1.0									
2. Seek management	0.36	0.48	0	1	0.15	1.0								
3. Seek marketing	0.55	0.50	0	1	–0.05	0.53*	1.0							
4. Seek technology	0.56	0.50	0	1	–0.02	0.61*	0.87*	1.0						
5. Knowledge overlap	1.03	1.29	0	3	–0.09	0.73*	0.68*	0.71*	1.0					
6. Knowledge base	1.36	1.36	0	3	–0.10	0.53*	0.58*	0.61*	0.86*	1.0				
7. IJV size	0.27	0.26	0.009	1.8	0.12	0.07	–0.04	–0.01	0.07	0.07	1.0			
8. State-ownership	0.78	0.42	0	1	0.07	0.22	–0.01	0.13	0.20	0.12	0.07	1.0		
9. Multiple venture	0.24	0.43	0	1	–0.14	0.13	0.27*	0.26*	0.10	0.09	–0.16	0.30*	1.0	
10. Consumer goods	0.69	0.47	0	1	0.12	0.00	–0.18	–0.16	–0.05	–0.06	0.01	–0.04	–0.26*	1.0
11. Local parent size	1.99	5.16	0.08	35	0.23*	0.01	–0.03	0.12	–0.07	–0.11	–0.02	0.17	–0.05	0.14

Note: $*p < 0.05$; N = 80

Table 3 reports the results of the data analysis.[5] Models 1–4 report the logistic regression estimates where the dependent variable was the preference of an EJV mode for the IJV. Models 5–7 report the results of logistic regression estimates for the actual formation sample, where the dependent variable was the selection of EJV structure selection upon formation. Overall, the models were fairly robust, as indicated by their –2 log likelihood(s) and associated chi-squares.

For the logistic regression analysis of EJV modal intentions, several interesting results emerge. First, the EJV was the preferred mode for local firms seeking transfer of tacit knowledge (i.e., marketing and management skills), supporting the first *Hypothesis 1*. The NEJV was preferred when seeking the transfer of technology, shown by the negative effect of technology transfer on the preference of EJV in Models 1–4 in Table 3. Second, *Hypothesis 2* is supported with a high knowledge base predicting an EJV. However, a low knowledge base also predicts an EJV choice. In other words, a local partner's knowledge base shows a curvilinear effect on its preference for EJV structure: a negative first-order but a positive second-order effect on EJV structure preference (Model 4). The inflection point for knowledge base is 1.29, well within the observed data range (just below the mean of 1.36). Finally, the intention results show that a limited knowledge overlap between partners increases the propensity of local firms to seek an EJV, supporting the *hypothesis* on partner-specific absorptive capacity (*Hypothesis 3*).

The findings of the event-history analysis of EJV formation over the 1988–1998 period are reported in Models 5–7. The results show that tacit knowledge (e.g., management) has a positive effect on the actual selection of EJV mode, confirming H1. A local partner's knowledge base has a positive effect on the selection of the EJV mode upon formation, confirming *Hypothesis 2*. In a departure from the intention results, actual formations show no curvilinear effect.

Table 3. Selection of Equity Joint Ventures

	Preferences for Equity JV (1988) Logistic Regression Estimation				Propensity to Form Equity JV (1988–98) Logistic Regression Estimation		
Variables	Model 1	Model 2	Model 3	Model 4	Model 5	Model 6	Model 7
Intercept 1	3.84***	3.74***	3.74***	3.35***	2.43***	2.24**	2.41**
	(1.0)	(1.02)	(1.03)	(1.03)	(0.92)	(0.93)	(0.96)
Intercept 2	1.18	0.74	0.74	0.18	−1.40*	−1.62*	−1.47*
	(0.86)	(0.84)	(0.86)	(0.87)	(0.81)	(0.85)	(0.87)
IJV size	−1.30	−1.19	−1.19	−1.29	0.93	0.90	0.97
	(0.94)	(0.95)	(0.95)	(0.97)	(0.96)	(0.95)	(0.95)
Local parent size	0.07	0.04	0.04	0.05	0.48*	0.50*	0.50**
	(0.08)	(0.07)	(0.08)	(0.07)	(0.25)	(0.26)	(0.25)
State-ownership	−1.13	−0.72	−0.72	−0.02	0.08	0.13	−0.10
	(0.78)	(0.76)	(0.76)	(0.81)	(0.72)	(0.73)	(0.77)
Multiple venture	−2.15***	−2.55***	−2.55***	−3.16***	−1.06	−1.10	−0.95
	(0.65)	(0.71)	(0.71)	(0.79)	(0.70)	(0.71)	(0.73)
Consumer goods	1.11**	1.19**	1.19**	1.46**	−0.12	−0.15	−0.21
	(0.55)	(0.56)	(0.57)	(0.60)	(0.56)	(0.57)	(0.57)
Knowledge sought							
Management	1.49**	2.65***	2.65***	2.13**	2.71***	2.98**	3.25***
	(0.68)	(0.89)	(0.93)	(0.98)	(0.93)	(0.99)	(1.03)
Marketing	2.44**	3.72***	3.72***	5.40***	0.64	0.83	0.60
	(1.09)	(1.26)	(1.26)	(1.54)	(1.13)	(1.16)	(1.20)
Technology	−2.82***	−2.89**	−2.89***	−2.98***	−0.30	−0.49	−0.68
	(1.09)	(1.14)	(1.14)	(1.20)	(1.16)	(1.19)	(1.23)
Knowledge overlap		−0.93**	−0.93*	−1.72**	−1.03***	−1.43***	−1.26**
		(0.40)	(0.56)	(0.72)	(0.38)	(0.56)	(0.59)
Knowledge base			0.001	−2.84**		0.36*	1.33
			(0.37)	(1.24)		(0.20)	(1.10)
Knowledge base²				1.10**			−0.37
				(0.46)			(0.42)
−2 log likelihood	112.1	105.9	105.9	99.8	110.3	109.3	108.5
Chi-square	42.6***	48.8***	48.8***	54.9***	39.8***	42.1***	43.7***

Note: ***$p < 0.01$; **$p < 0.05$; *$p < 0.1$; Standard errors are in parentheses.

Similar to intention data results, formation data supports *Hypothesis 3*, with low knowledge overlap predicting an EJV.

The results also show the effects of several control variables. Local firms prefer an EJV for projects in consumer industries and a NEJV when searching for multiple ventures. For actually established IJVs, large parent firms increase the likelihood of opting for an EJV. IJV size, however, does not show effects in all models.

Discussion

A central assumption in the IJV literature is that the EJV is the vehicle of choice for the transfer of tacit knowledge (*Hypothesis 1*). This assumption, consistent with both transaction costs and knowledge-based views of the firm, is supported in this study for both the intention and the actual IJV formation data. To our best knowledge, this is the first time that this assumption is confirmed not only for actual formations but also at the level of strategic intentions, solidifying support for the relationship between knowledge type and governance.

Also supportive across both intentions and formations are the results for *Hypothesis 3*. In line with the original hypothesis, limited knowledge overlap among the partners predicts an EJV. The fact that the results from intentions and formations are similar suggests, from a transaction costs perspective, that foreign partners share the preferences of Chinese firms and opt for an EJV as a way of protection from the uncertainty entailed in the operation of a party with different skills. From a knowledge-based perspective, the formation results may reflect a belief on the part of the foreign partner that it is more capable of developing relation-specific assets which will allow it to beat its partner in the "race to learn" (Dyer/Singh 1998, Hamel 1991, Williamson 1985).

Most interesting are the divergent results obtained for intentions and formations in testing *Hypothesis 2*. The intention results show a U-shaped effect of knowledge base that is not replicated for formation models. For local partners, an EJV is desirable not only when one has a significant knowledge base (as initially hypothesized), but also when it lacks such a base altogether. This latter finding can be explained in that the local firm who lacks a knowledge base is seeking an EJV in the hope that it will compensate for its own knowledge deficiency. These local firms, not IJV experienced and not knowledgeable about the manufacturing process and the product, apparently believed that the co-habitation with a foreign firm would be sufficient to generate knowledge diffusion. In contrast, local firms with some knowledge base were more realistic about their ability to absorb knowledge by virtue of governance alone.

By the time the IJV is formed, a low knowledge base is no longer an EJV predictor however. Assuming that the intention-to-formation change is the result of a foreign partner bargaining for its preferences, this implies that the foreign partner is less interested in establishing an EJV when the local partner has little to offer in terms of its own knowledge. This partner is typically viewed to sustain rents from its knowledge and is regarded as only being interested in the local partner's government contacts, understanding of the local market, and so forth. The results in this study suggest that the foreign firm may be looking for a local partner with sufficient professional skills to enable effective learning. This implies that local partner learning may not be viewed by the foreign parent so much as a threat, but rather as a prerequisite for the IJV's efficient operations without which the interests of the foreign investor may be seriously harmed. This seems to support an organizational learning approach which emphasizes the positive aspects of learning, largely taking on a knowledge recipient perspective, over a transaction costs perspective which largely represents a knowledge owner perspective. However, other results in this paper suggest some convergence of the two perspectives.

The differences between intention and formation data on the control variables can largely be explained as a bargaining outcome (Yan/Gray 1994). As Barnett, Greve and Park (1994) argue, large size protects firms from the process of selection, in this case enabling the local partners to implement their desired governance mode. When seeking to form multiple IJVs, Chinese partners are likely to prefer NEJVs–a result consistent with previous studies (e.g., Gulati 1995). The result is also consistent with our field interviews with several companies seeking foreign partners for multiple ventures. The interviews suggested that the managers were concerned about the fact that forming multiple EJVs will drain the limited financial and managerial resources of the Chinese parent.

Finally, the focus on consumer (vis-à-vis industrial) goods has an impact on modal intentions but not on actual formations. One explanation is that consumer goods involve tacit market knowledge in the eyes of a recipient but not on the part of a sophisticated foreign player. Another explanation is that foreign parents command a clear advantage in the industrial sector, which includes capital goods with more complex technology, and their bargaining power could have counterbalanced the Chinese preference for EJVs. As previous studies have generally found that firms in industries of high advertising intensity favor an equity mode over a non-equity mode (e.g., Pan/Tse 2000), further studies are needed to clarify the industry effects.

Limitations and Future Research

Special circumstances pertaining to the present study affect but do not necessarily challenge the generalizability of the findings. For example, Koza and Lewin (1998) argue that absorptive capacity will have its greatest impact in alliances seeking explorative knowledge, suggesting generalizability of the argument to transitional economies. The sample's restriction to manufacturing actually provides a tougher test for the theory. In contrast to extractive industries, where the bargaining power of the host country is initially low but tends to increase with the rising cost of disengagement, in manufacturing industries the bargaining position of the host government is the greatest at the outset. This implies that the gap uncovered between intentions and formations regarding knowledge base might be even more pronounced in extractive industries.

In addition, while the Chinese government may have influenced IJV mode choice by expressing approval and offering incentives that favor EJVs, it did so precisely because it viewed the EJV mode as more effective for the transfer of tacit knowledge. And while China's market attractiveness increased between 1988 and 1998 that enhanced the government's bargaining power, the results suggest a considerable impact of foreign partner preferences. Taken as a whole, country-specific circumstances should be considered among other "externalities which influence the value of the strategic assets to the parties" (Kogut 1988, p. 321).

The present study provides an additional impetus to adopt longitudinal research design in IJV research. The different results obtained for intentions and for actual formations underline the dynamic nature of IJV systems. Extending longitudinal designs further into the IJV life cycle will allow for the testing of additional yet unproven predictions. For instance, Dymsza (1988) noted that in IJVs between developed and developing country partners, the latter's contribution is likely to become less important over time. Similarly, Mowery et al. (1996) suggests that partner-specific absorptive capacity among alliance partners may increase over the course of collaboration as a result of organizational learning and technology transfer within the venture.

Finally, while this study provides a glimpse of foreign partner intentions as extrapolated from the gap between local partner intentions and actual formations, a natural extension would be to collect data from foreign partners directly, preferably while controlling for nationality. Such expansion of research scope should complete the view of IJVs as the dynamic, multipartite systems.

Endnotes

1. We thank Tim Devinney, Anne Tsui, Steven White, and editors (Torben Pedersen and Volker Mahnke) and reviewers of the special issue for comments and suggestions, and Abbie Hui for research assistance. We gratefully acknowledge support from Hong Kong RGC Competitive Earmarked Grant (HKUST6198/98H) and Wei-Lun Foundation.
2. We have also collected information on the nationality of the foreign partners. The 29 EJVs include foreign partners from 10 countries: Hong Kong (9 EJVs), USA (7), Germany (4), Japan (3), Taiwan (3), and one each from Belgium, France and Thailand. The five NEJVs include two from Hong Kong, and one each from Japan, Taiwan, and USA. The IJV literature has shown that the nationality of foreign partners affects IJV governance mode choice (e.g., Pan/Tse 2000, Luo/Shenkar/Nyaw 2001). Our limited sample size, however, precludes the exploration of foreign partner nationality in the statistical analysis.
3. We have also run Cox (1972) proportional hazard regression models, with similar results as those for multinomial logistic regressions reported in Table 3.
4. Because we also examine the intentions, we cannot measure the repeated alliances between two partners. Therefore, we have included "seeking multiple jv" as a control variable.
5. To address the issue of high correlation between some variables and possible multicolleniarity, we have run multiple models where we enter each of the variables separately into the models. The results are consistent with those reported in Table 3. The results of these additional regression models can be obtained from the authors.

References

Argote, L./Ingram, P., Knowledge Transfer: A Basis for Competitive Advantage in Firms, *Organizational Behavior and Human Decision Process*, 82, 1, 2000, pp. 150–169.

Badaracco, J. L., *The Knowledge Link*, Boston: Harvard Business School Press 1991.

Barnett, W. P./Greve, H. R./Park, D. Y., An Evolutionary Model of Organizational Performance, *Strategic Management Journal*, 15, 1994, pp. 11–28.

Barney, J., Firm Resources and Sustained Competitive Advantage, *Journal of Management*, 17, 1, 1991, pp. 99–120.

Beamish, P. W./Banks, J. C., Equity Joint Ventures and the Theory of the Multinational Enterprise, *Journal of International Business Studies*, 18, 1987, pp. 1–16.

Child, J., *Management in China during the Age of Reform*, Cambridge: Cambridge University Press 1994.

Child, J./Markoczy, L., Host Country Managerial Behavior and Learning in Chinese and Hungarian Joint Ventures, *Journal of Management Studies*, 30, 4, 1993, pp. 611–631.

China Statistical Yearbook, Beijing: China Statistics Press 1998.

Cohen, W./Levinthal, D. A., Absorptive Capability: A New Perspective on Learning and Innovation, *Administrative Science Quarterly*, 35, 1990, pp. 128–152.

Conner, K. R./Prahalad, C. K., A Resource-Based Theory of the Firm: Knowledge Versus Opportunism, *Organization Science*, 7, 5, 1996, pp. 477–501.

Cox, D. R., Regression Models and Life Tables, *Journal of the Royal Statistics Society*, Series B 34, 1972, pp. 187–220.

Davies, H., Technology Transfer Through Commercial Transactions, *Journal of Industrial Economics*, 26, 2, 1977, pp. 161–175.

Dietrich, M., *Transaction Cost Economics and Beyond: Towards a New Economics of the Firm*, London: Routledge 1994.

Dyer, J. H./Singh, H., The Relational View: Cooperative Strategy and Sources of Interorganizational Competitive Advantage, *Academy of Management Review*, 23, 4, 1998, pp. 660–679.

Dymsza, W. A., Successes and Failures of Joint Ventures in Developing Countries: Lessons From Experience, in Contractor, F./Lorange, P. (eds.), *Cooperative Strategies in International Business*, Lexington, MA: Lexington Books 1988, pp. 403–424.

Ellis, H. C., *The Transfer of Learning*, NY: Macmillan 1965.

Gatignon, H./Anderson, E., The Multinational Corporations' Degree of Control over Foreign Subsidiaries: An Empirical Test of a Transaction Cost Explanation, *Journal of Law, Economics and Organization*, 4, 2, 1988, pp. 305–336.

Grant, R. M./Baden-Fuller, C., A Knowledge-Based Theory of Inter-Firm Collaboration, *Academy of Management Best Paper Proceedings*, 1995, pp. 17–21.

Gulati, R., Does Familiarity Breed Trust? The Implications of Repeated Ties for Contractual Choice in Alliances, *Academy of Management Journal*, 38, 1995, pp. 85–112.

Hamel, G., Competition for Competence and Inter-Partner Learning within International Strategic Alliances, *Strategic Management Journal*, 12, 1991, pp. 83–103.

Harrigan, K. R., Joint Ventures and Competitive Strategy, *Strategic Management Journal*, 9, 1988, pp. 141–158.

Hennart, J.-F., A Transaction Costs Theory of Equity Joint Ventures, *Strategic Management Journal*, 9, 1988, pp. 361–374.

Hitt, M./Ireland, D./Goryunov, I., The Context of Innovation: Investment in R&D and Firm Performance, in Gattiker, E./Larwood, L. (eds.), *Managing Technological Development: Strategic and Human Resource Issues*, New York: de Gruyter 1988, pp. 73–92.

Inkpen, A./Beamish, P. W., Knowledge, Bargaining Power, and the Instability of International Joint Ventures, *Academy of Management Review*, 22, 1, 1997, pp. 177–202.

Khanna, T./Gulati, R./Nohria, N., The Dynamics of Learning Alliances: Competition, Cooperation, and Relative Scope, *Strategic Management Journal*, 19, 1998, pp. 193–210.

Kogut, B., Joint Ventures: Theoretical and Empirical Perspectives, *Strategic Management Journal*, 9, 1988, pp. 319–332.

Kogut, B./Zander, U., Knowledge of the Firm, Combinative Capabilities, and the Replication of Technology, *Organization Science*, 3, 1992, pp. 383–397.

Koza, M. B./Lewin, A. Y., The Co-Evolution of Strategic Alliances, *Organization Science*, 9, 3, 1998, pp. 255–264.

Lane, P. J./Lubatkin, M., Relative Absorptive Capacity and Inter-Organizational Learning, *Strategic Management Journal*, 19, 1998, pp. 461–477.

Lane, P. J./Salk, J. E./Lyles, M. A., Absorptive Capacity, Learning, and Performance in International Joint Ventures, *Strategic Management Journal*, 22, 12, 2001, pp. 1139–1161.

Luo, Y., Dimensions of Knowledge: Comparing Asian and Western MNEs in China, *Asia Pacific Journal of Management*, 16, 1999, pp. 75–93.

Luo, Y./Shenkar, O./Nyaw, M. K., A Dual Parent Perspective on Control and Performance in International Joint Ventures: Lessons From a Developing Economy, *Journal of International Business Studies*, 32, 1, 2001, pp. 41–58.

Mowery, D. C./Oxley, J. E./Silverman, B. S., Strategic Alliances and Inter-Firm Knowledge Transfer, *Strategic Management Journal*, 17, Winter Special Issue 1996, pp. 77–91.

Nelson, R. R./Winter, S., *An Evolutionary Theory of Economic Change*, Cambridge, MA: Harvard University Press 1982.

Nonaka, I., A Dynamic Theory of Organizational Knowledge Creation, *Organizational Science*, 5, 1, 1994, pp. 14–37.

Osborn, R. N./Baughn, C. C., Forms of Inter-Organizational Governance for Multinational Alliances, *Academy of Management Journal*, 33, 3, 1990, pp. 503–519.

Pan, Y./Tse, D. K., The Hierarchical Model of Market Entry Modes, *Journal of International Business Studies*, 31, 4, 2000, pp. 535–554.

Pearson, M. M., *Joint Ventures in the People's Republic of China*, Princeton, NJ: Princeton University Press 1991.

Penrose, E. T., *The Theory of the Growth of the Firm*, Oxford: Basil Blackwell 1959.

Pisano, G. P., Using Equity Participation to Support Exchange: Evidence from the Biotechnology Industry, *Journal of Law, Economics, and Organization*, 5, 1, 1989, pp. 109–126.

Polanyi, M., *The Tacit Dimension*, Garden City, NY: Doubleday 1966.

Shenkar, O./Li, J. T., Knowledge Search in International Cooperative Ventures, *Organization Science*, 10, 2, 1999, pp. 134–143.

Simon, D. F., *Technological Innovation in China: The Case of Shanghai Semiconductor Industry*, Cambridge, MA: Ballinger 1988.

Szulanski, G., Exploring Internal Stickiness: Impediments to the Transfer of Best Practice Within the Firm, *Strategic Management Journal*, 17, Winter Special Issue 1996, pp. 27–43.

Tallman, S. B./Shenkar, O., A Managerial Decision Model of International Cooperative Venture Formation, *Journal of International Business Studies*, 30, 1994, pp. 299–315.

Teece, D. J., Multinational Enterprise: Market Failure and Market Power Considerations, *Sloan Management Review*, 22, 1981, pp. 3–17.

Teece, D. J., Profiting from Technological Innovation: Implications for Integration, Collaboration, Licensing and Public Policy, *Research Policy*, 15, 1986, pp. 285–305.

Teece, D. J./Pisano, G., The Dynamic Capabilities and Strategic Management, *Industrial and Corporate Change*, 3, 1994, pp. 537–556.

Teece, D. J./Pisano, G./Shuen, A., Dynamic Capabilities and Strategic Management, *Strategic Management Journal*, 18, 7, 1997, pp. 509–533.

Williamson, O. E., *Markets and Hierarchies: Analysis and Antitrust Implications*, New York: Free Press 1975.

Williamson, O. E., *The Economic Institutions of Capitalism*, New York: Free Press 1985.

Wood, R./Bandura, A., Social Cognitive Theory of Organizational Management, *Academy of Management Review*, 14, 3, 1989, pp. 361–384.

Yan, A./Gray, B., Bargaining Power, Management Control and Performance in United States-China Joint Ventures: A Comparative Case Study, *Academy of Management Journal*, 37, 6, 1994, pp. 1478–1517.

mir *Edition*

Tobias Specker

Postmerger – Management in den ost- und mitteleuropäischen Transformationsstaaten

2002, XX, 431 pages, Br., € 64,– (approx. US $ 58.–)
ISBN 3-409-12010-6

Since the beginning of the transformation process in the Middle and Eastern European countries, German companies have put a special emphasis on entering these markets via corporate acquisitions. Tobias Specker analyses the critical issue of postmerger management with a specific focus on the particular transformation context. His theoretical reflections are supported by results of an explorative study of various German companies.

The book is addressed to lecturers and students of international management. Consultants and managers will also receive valuable information.

Betriebswirtschaftlicher Verlag Dr. Th. Gabler GmbH, Abraham-Lincoln-Str. 46, 65189 Wiesbaden

Management
International Review
© Gabler Verlag 2003

Marjorie A. Lyles/Georg von Krogh/John Harald Aadne

Knowledge Acquisition and Knowledge Enablers in International Joint Ventures and their Foreign Parents[1]

Abstract

- This study addresses Enablers that facilitate the acquisition of knowledge by international joint ventures (IJVs) from their foreign parents. Enablers are important factors influencing the foreign parents' sharing of knowledge with the IJV. We also posited that Enablers such as Knowledge Acquisition (KA) Capacity, Interaction Climate within the IJV, and Performance are important Enablers for the IJVs' acquisition of knowledge.

Key Results

- A model was tested using data on 176 IJVs in Hungary collected during 1996. We find that the foreign parents' Knowledge Sharing Commitment, Influence in Decision-Making, and Ownership Control predict high KA IJVs, whereas Trust and business Relatedness between the IJV and its foreign parent did not. We also find that the IJV's Interaction Climate and Performance predict high KA, whereas Knowledge Acquisition Capacity (including Absorptive Capacity) did not.

Authors

Marjorie A. Lyles, Professor of International Strategic Management, American United Life Chair, Indiana University Kelley School of Business, Indianapolis, IN, USA.
Georg von Krogh, Professor of Management, Institute of Management, University of St. Gallen, St. Gallen, Switzerland.
John Harald Aadne, Accenture, Oslo, Norway.

Introduction

Knowledge management has become essential for ensuring the competitiveness of firms (Nonaka/Takeuchi 1995), by enabling knowledge creation, acquisition, and dissemination within and between firms (von Krogh/Ichijo/Nonaka 2000). A growing body of theoretical and empirical work explores the relationship between knowledge and inter-organizational cooperation (Lyles/Salk 1996), but only a few studies address the organizational mechanisms enabling knowledge acquisition in the context of inter-firm collaboration. For the purpose of this paper, enablers for Knowledge Acquisition (KA) include: a particular climate for cooperation within or between firms; organizational mechanisms that enhance receptivity; the type of control exercised in the cooperation; and the intent to learn from partners.

Generally, international joint ventures (IJVs) involve the acquisition of knowledge about industry and market conditions, technology, cultural contexts, and new management approaches (Anand/Delios 1997). Yet empirical research examining Knowledge Acquisition (KA) in IJVs is still in its infancy. Furthermore, little work aims at identifying those IJVs that are particularly good at Knowledge Acquisition in order to assess the Enablers involved. In this paper we will fill part of this gap by comparing IJVs in terms of what we call "High" and "Low" Knowledge Acquirers in IJVs. We consider the specific process and context of KA from the foreign partners in IJVs by drawing on existing literature.

A Model of Knowledge Acquisition and Enablers

Frequently, foreign parents use IJVs to overcome the liability of foreignness by utilizing the partner's networks, market knowledge, and other supporting resources (Reuer/Leiblien 2000). The IJV also can be a springboard for further commitment and in this sense, the IJV can be important for developing economic activity in transition economies.

In this paper, *knowledge* refers to the embodied know-how of organizational members, and *knowledge acquisition* (KA) refers to the knowledge that is transferred from the parent firm to the IJV. The ability of a firm to learn from another is determined by the relative characteristics of the two firms, particularly the relationship between their Enablers for Knowledge Acquisition (Lane/Salk/Lyles 2001). Given our IJV focus, and the context of IJV activity, in this section we define and distinguish between Foreign Parent Enablers and IJV Enablers that facilitate the acquisition of new knowledge as shown in Figure 1.

Figure 1.

FOREIGN PARENT ENABLERS

Knowledge Sharing Commitment
(measured by)
Training
Job Rotation

Trust
(measured by)
Level of Trust
Degree of Conflict between Parents

Control
(measured by)
Ownership
Influence in Decision Making

Relatedness
(measured by)
Degree of Relatedness

JOINT VENTURE ENABLERS

Knowledge Acquisition Capacity
(measured by)
Absorptive Capacity
Receptivity

Interaction Climate Within IJVs
(measured by)
Informal Communication
Conflict within IJV

Performance
(measured by)
Industry Comparison

Foreign Parent Enablers

Foreign Parent Enablers are conditions that facilitate the sharing of the foreign parents' knowledge and technology. For the most part, all IJVs require some knowledge transfer from the foreign parent, either in terms of managerial, technological, and/or administrative activities. Of particular importance are the foreign parent's willingness and ability to assume the role of a teacher and its underlying motives for sharing knowledge (Hennart/Roehl/Zietlow 1999).

Knowledge Sharing Commitment

Several authors argue that cooperative relationships are characterized by various degrees of knowledge and resource sharing (Hedlund/Nonaka 1993), but few studies explain the outcome in terms of KA. Whereas learning intent secures the internalization of new knowledge, Knowledge Sharing Commitment has an opposite focus: to bestow new knowledge and technology. This type of commitment is part of the foreign partner's desire to contribute technology, management, and expertise.

The literature on KM identifies helping behavior as important to Knowledge Sharing Commitment, such as training a novice for a new task (von Krogh/Ichijo/Nonaka 2000). It is manifested in at least two ways. First, the foreign partner can engage in extensive training of IJV managers. Lyles and Salk (1996) found empirical support for the linkage between training by a foreign parent and Knowledge Acquisition in IJVs.

Second, designing job rotation programs for local employees can be helpful. Research suggests that job rotation enables the internal transfer of knowledge (Hedlund/Nonaka 1993). We expect Job Rotation between the IJV and the foreign partner, to improve the local IJV's KA in management, technology, and market related areas, and also to realize potential benefits from using existing technologies of the foreign parent.

Hypothesis 1A. Higher degree of Knowledge Sharing Commitment by the foreign parent will increase the probability of being a high knowledge acquisition IJV.

Hypothesis 1B. Job Rotation will increase the probability of being a high knowledge acquisition IJV.

Trust

Trust between the partners and KA can impact the success of cooperative relationships and KA (Lane/Salk/ Lyles 2001). Lack of Trust often causes a serious breakdown in the value creation process; a suspicious attitude towards local partners could be detrimental for KA and Performance.

Several authors have found evidence that Trust positively impacts KA in IJVs (Hyder/Ghauri 2000) and strategic alliances in general (Wathne/Roos/von Krogh 1996). Trust contributes to an atmosphere of openness and free exchange of knowledge, because the parents do not feel that protective measures are necessary to prevent opportunistic behavior (Larson et al. 1998).

Conflict is a concept highly related to the lack of trust (Smith 2000). Conflict inhibits the development of norms of fair exchange and reciprocal trust necessary to support an enduring IJV relationship (Shenkar/Zeira 1992). Disagreement over goals is often a pervasive conflict issue in IJVs (Shenkar/Zeira 1992) and has been reported as a major cause for failures of IJVs.

Hypothesis 2. Higher level of Trust will increase the probability of being a high knowledge acquisition IJV.

Control

The effect of Control on knowledge acquisition in IJVs has received limited attention, with some notable exceptions (Tiemessen et al. 1997). Control mechanisms are essential for coordinating activities, allocating resources, and achieving strategic objectives in IJVs. We define Control based on two aspects: as the extent of the foreign parent's equity position or Ownership and the Influence In Decision Making in the IJV (Steensma/Lyles 2001).

First, the KM literature generally acknowledges equity positions as an Enabler of KA (Das/Teng 2000). The importance of the size of the equity position is a contested issue; Dasgupta and Teng (1998) argue that a 50/50 position is best in situations of contractual incompleteness. This is typically characteristic in IJVs because unintended learning on behalf of the local partner is difficult, if not impossible to control completely (Hamel 1991). Empirical results presented by Lyles and Salk (1996) indicate a linkage between 50/50 Ownership and high KA.

Second, Mjoen and Tallman (1997) argue that equity position alone represents a rather narrow definition of Control for IJVs. In IJVs, an important function of Control is to avoid "inert-knowledge" (Renkl 1996) in which foreign parent knowledge is either under-used or -acquired. The foreign partner can "activate" KA by influencing decisions in those areas where knowledge is of relevance to the IJV. Thus, the degree of Control, here defined as Influence In Decision Making and equity position or Ownership, will have a positive impact on Knowledge Acquisition.

Hypothesis 3. The increase of foreign partner Control will increase the probability of the IJV being a high knowledge acquisition IJV.

Relatedness

Prahalad and Bettis (1986) argue that firms have difficulties acquiring the new knowledge needed to succeed in new industries and businesses. Similarly, the more related the knowledge bases of two firms, the easier it should be for two organizations to learn from each other (Hedlund 1994). Relatedness should also impact how the two organizations approach critical issues in knowledge sharing and acquisition, and higher Relatedness should lead to a reduced level of noise in knowledge sharing and acquisition. A related IJV may in general receive more attention from the foreign parent, and both substantial parent-IJV interaction and larger commitment of resources can be expected. Higher Business Relatedness between IJV and foreign partner should therefore lead to more opportunities of mutual gains for the IJV and its foreign parent, from knowledge acquisition.

Hypothesis 4. Relatedness between the IJV's business area and the foreign partner's business activities will increase the probability of being a high knowledge acquisition IJV.

International Joint Venture Enablers

Of particular importance is the IJV's Capacity to acquire new knowledge, to assimilate and to disseminate it.

Knowledge Acquisition Capacity

The IJV's capacity for KA will be influenced by two factors: Absorptive Capacity and Receptivity. First, the IJV's Absorptive Capacity influences the effectiveness of its inter-partner learning (Sen/Egelhof 2000). Drawing on cognitive psychology, Cohen and Levinthal (1990) propose that the more an organization knows about a particular technology, discipline, or research, and the higher the effort, the more it can absorb new, related knowledge.

Lyles and Salk (1996) identify two characteristics of IJV's with a positive impact on Absorptive Capacity: flexibility and creativity. Flexible, non-bureaucratic, non-hierarchical organizations are thought to have a positive association with Absorptive Capacity. In such IJVs, employees form temporary groups, project teams, or communities of practice to accommodate new knowledge (Davenport/Prusak 1998). Often interdisciplinary, these groups are generally more open to new stimuli and knowledge from the outside; they work more creatively in combining new and existing knowledge. Whereas the IJV might have capacity to absorb new knowledge, it must also have Receptivity to this knowledge. Hamel (1991) and Larson, et al. (1998) argue that the commitment of all parties involved influences the Receptivity to the knowledge.

Hypothesis 5. High Knowledge Acquirer JVs have a higher degrees of Absorptive Capacity and Receptivity than low knowledge Acquirer JVs.

Interaction Climate within IJV

Whereas KA capacity highlights the potential to absorb and receive knowledge, it says little about the interaction climate for internal dissemination of knowledge. Whereas the IJV might identify key formal communication channels, train R&D personnel, and have a long-term commitment to stay in business, the actual widespread acquisition of new knowledge often depends on social interaction (Cohen/Prusak 2001). Unless there is a climate that encourages informal interaction and sharing of knowledge, new learning and new understandings may not take place in IJVs.

Makhija and Ganesh (1997) and Nahapiet and Ghoshal (1997) argue that through social networking, valuable tacit knowledge is shared in the organization. The reputations transmitted through informal channels also decreases the time and efforts needed to locate experts (Szulanski 1996). When the Interaction Climate is good, experts develop informal but normative ties to other members. They derive utility from social approval and from following a social norm of sharing knowledge with others (von Krogh 2002).

Hypothesis 6. More Interaction within the IJV will increase the probability of being a high knowledge acquisition IJV.

Performance

Lyles and Salk (1996) found that high KA IJVs performed significantly better than Low Acquisition IJVs but made no attempt to outline causal direction between the two constructs. It could be argued that KA leads to higher Performance of the IJV (Tsang 2000). Some authors argue the reverse, that IJV Performance, as compared to that of other firms within its industry, and its long-term orientation are important for keeping the IJV focused on its objectives of learning from the foreign parent (Hamel 1991). We have chosen the latter view.

Hypothesis 7. Better than industry average performance of the IJV will increase the probability of being a high knowledge acquisition IJV.

Methodology

Hungarian Context

The *Wall Street Journal* (September 27, 1999) cites Hungary as one of five countries to be noted for successfully undertaking transformation and becoming integrated into the world economy. While Hungary started the transitional process early and proceeded through a more gradual approach than many other transitional economies, it still suffered through the problems of privatization and of establishing a commercial legal system. It exhibited characteristics such as an informal economy, inaccurate reporting, slow decision-making, little market knowledge and an economic slowdown from 1988–1995. For these reasons, Hungary in the 1990's represents an ideal natural laboratory for the study of knowledge transfer to IJVs in transitional economies. Its somewhat longer history of tolerance for market conditions suggests that the experiences of Hungarian IJVs in the 1990's may presage what is in store for firms in other transitional economies.

Sample Selection

The IJVs comprise a stratified, representative sample in terms of industries and the countries of origin of the foreign partners (see Steensma/ Lyles 2000). The sample was based on statistics from the Hungarian Central Statistical office and the data were collected in 1996. We were able to control for IJV size, age and type. The IJVs were primarily formed between 1989 and 1991. Thus, our sample consists of a total of 176 small/medium sized IJVs with an average employee size of 72 employees. The informants were the presidents, general managers or managers. The response rate was close to 44%. It is possible that the sample is somewhat biased in the direction of better performing IJVs. We suspect that the worst performing IJVs were less willing to agree to an interview. Only IJVs with complete data were included in the analysis.

Variables

The definitions of the variables used to test our propositions are given below. For those measures comprising scales constructed from multiple questionnaire items, consistency was assessed using Cronbach's Alpha. The constructs are in Appendix 1 and as follows:

Knowledge Acquisition was the dependent variable. This scale was designed to assess KA from the foreign parent across a variety of areas including product development and knowledge about foreign cultures and is based on the scale used by Lyles/Salk (1996). *High Knowledge Acquirers* are those firms that scored at least one deviation above the mean. *Low Knowledge Acquirers* are those firms that scored at least one deviation below the mean. After the sample was classified, there were 36 High and 35 Low Knowledge Acquirers.

Foreign Parent Enablers

Seven variables operationalize Foreign Parent Enablers. The *KNOWLEDGE SHARING COMMITMENT* Enabler includes the two variables of *Training* and *Job Rotation* from the IJV to the foreign parent. The Enabler *TRUST* was operationalized through two variables, which are *Level of Trust*, which measures the level of trust between the parent firms, and *Degree of Conflict between the Parents*. *CONTROL*, as an Enabler, is measured by two variables: *Ownership*, which categorizes the IJVs as Dominant Foreign Parent, a 50/50 shared management JV, or Dominant Domestic Parent; and foreign parent *Influence in Decision-Making*, which is the total percentage of relative influence of the foreign parent in decision-making compared to the influence of the local parent and the JV management. The Enabler *RELATEDNESS* is the similarity between the IJV and foreign parent business areas.

IJV Enablers

Five variables operationalize the IJV Enablers. *KNOWLEDGE ACQUISITION CAPACITY*, as an Enabler, is measured by: *Absorptive Capacity*, based on the scale developed by Lyles and Salk (1966), and *Receptivity*, demonstrating the motivation to learn due to the expectation that the IJV will be in business for a long period of time. *INTERACTION WITHIN THE IJV*, as an Enabler, is measured by two variables: *Informal Communication* and *Conflict within the IJV*. The final Enabler, *PERFORMANCE*, is measured by the *Industry Comparison* of the joint venture's performance as opposed to other firms in its industry.

Data Analysis

Because we are interested in testing the differences between the groups of High and Low Knowledge Acquirers, the hypotheses were tested using 3 logistic regression analyses. The first model represents the degree to which the Foreign Parent Enablers correctly predict the High Knowledge Acquirers versus the Low Knowledge Acquirers. The second model tests the degree to which the IJV Enablers correctly predict the High Knowledge Acquirers versus the Low Knowledge Acquirers. We also used a Chi-Square analysis to test the difference between High and Low Knowledge Acquirers and Ownership type. The third model is another analysis done on the combined factors. The correlations between the variables were evaluated using Pearson's correlation statistics. All but one of the pair-wise correlations were below 0.5. Thus, only one correlation between the variables (Table 1) was above an acceptable level. The correlation between the two measures of Conflict is high, indicating a strong relationship between Conflict between the Parents and Conflict between the IJV and the foreign parent. Since these two measures were used independently in the two models tested, it was decided that multicollinearity was not considered a problem for the overall analysis.

Following Podsakoff and Organ (1986), we used the Harman's one-factor test to examine the extent of common method bias in our data. A principal components factor analysis reveals that there are 6 factors with eigenvalues greater than 1.0 which together account for 64% of the total variance. The presence of several distinct factors combined with the relatively low amount of variance explained by the first factor (only 19%) indicates that our data does not suffer from common method variance (Podsakoff/Organ 1986).

Results

Table 1 presents the means, standard deviations, and Pearson partial order correlations among the variables used in the regression analysis. All variables exhibit reasonable normality. Knowledge acquired shows significant and positive relationships with Relatedness, Training, Foreign Parent Influence, Job Rotation, Absorptive Capacity, Receptivity, and Performance. The relationships between Relatedness, Training, and Foreign Parent Influence in Decision Making with Knowledge Acquired are the strongest but each still only predicts about 5% to 6% of Knowledge Acquired.

The IJVs were identified based on their Knowledge Acquisition scores as High Knowledge Acquirers, Normal Knowledge Acquirers, or Low Knowledge Acquirers. Only the High Knowledge Acquirers, those IJVs that scored at least one deviation about the average (n = 36), and Low Knowledge Acquirers, those IJVs that scored at least one deviation below the norm (n = 35), were included for the additional analysis. Only those cases with no missing data were included.

Results from Foreign Parent Enablers

Model 1 shows the logistic regression of the ability of Foreign Parent Enablers to distinguish between High and Low Knowledge Acquirer IJVs. The model is significant and our results indicate two Enabler variables have a relationship

Table 1. Correlations

Variable	Mean	Std. Dev.	1	2	3	4	5	6	7	8	9	10	11
1. Knowledge Acquired	13.86	5.6											
2. Trust	4.08	1.07	0.11										
3. Relatedness	1.53	0.5	0.24**	−0.08									
4. Conflict between Parents	5.13	2.85	0.07	0.44***	0.11								
5. Training	2.28	1.28	0.29***	−0.02	0.13	0.03							
6. Foreign Parent Influence	21.58	28.51	0.30***	−0.03	0.33**	0.07	0.23**						
7. Job Rotation	1.17	0.37	0.22***	0.02	0.06	0.02	0.13	0.23***					
8. Absorptive Capacity	8.34	1.69	0.19*	0.32***	−0.03	−0.25**	−0.01	−0.14	−0.02				
9. Conflict betw. JV and Parent	3.08	1.71	0.06	−0.30***	0.07	0.70***	0.09	0.02	−0.01	−0.21**			
10. Receptivity	4.38	1.11	0.17*	0.17*	0.05	−0.18*	−0.10	0.25**	0.06	0.20**	−0.22**		
11. Informal Communication	3.59	1.15	0.14	0.14	−0.11	−0.15*	0.03	−0.09	−0.02	0.25**	−0.07	0.12	
12. Performance	3.81	0.86	0.20*	0.19*	0.03	−0.13	0.05	0.13	0.14	0.21**	−0.07	0.33**	0.03

Note: *** < 0.01; ** < 0.1; * < 0.5

Table 2. Logistic Regression Analyses for Knowledge Enablers

VARIABLES	MODEL 1 β	MODEL 2 β	MODEL 3 β
Trust			
Trust Between IJV's Parents	0.21		0.17
Conflict Between Parents	−0.01		1.48
Knowledge Sharing Commitment			
Training by Foreign Parent	0.50**		1.50**
Job Rotation	1.30		6.44*
Control			
Influence in Decision Making	0.08*		0.29
Relatedness			
Relatedness of IJV & Foreign Parent	1.02		2.86†
Knowledge Acquisition Capacity			
Absorptive Capacity		0.05	−0.42
Receptivity		0.44	2.37†
Interaction within IJV			
Informal Communication		0.70**	2.94**
Conflict between IJV and parents		0.41*	−2.05
Performance			
Industry Comparison		0.91**	2.02**
Chi Squared	32.19	19.59	60.12
Sig	0.001	0.01	0.001
d.f.	6	6	12
Low Knowledge Achievers			
Percent Observed Correct	88.46%	68.57%	92.31%
High Knowledge Achievers			
Percent Observed Correct	84.85%	80.56%	93.94%
Overall	86.44%	74.65%	93.22%

Note: † $p < 0.10$; * $p < 0.05$; ** $p < 0.01$; *** $p < 0.001$

Table 3. Foreign Parent Enablers: Cross Tab Test of Learning Categories and Ownership

Classification Table for Knowledge Acquisition Categories

	Domestic Dominant	Ownership Foreign Dominant	Shared	Total
Learning Categories				
High	10	19	7	36
Low	18	14	3	35
Total	28	33	10	71

Chi square = 4.63; d.f. 2; sig. = 0.09

between Foreign Parent Knowledge Enablers and KA categories, i.e. High- versus Low Knowledge Acquirers. 86% was correctly predicted by this model.

The significant predictors are Training (sig. = 0.06) and foreign parent Influence in Decision Making (sig. = 0.02). We find the Knowledge Sharing Commitment Enabler of the foreign parent, as evidenced by the Training variable, and the Control Enabler, as evidenced by the Influence in Decision Making variable, to have a positive relationship with predicting High Knowledge Acquirers. This analysis supports *Hypotheses 1* and *3*, but does not support *Hypotheses 2* and *4*.

Table 3 presents a Cross-tabulation of the Knowledge Acquisition Categories and Ownership and is also significant. The results indicate that of the shared ownership IJVs, 70% are High Knowledge Acquirers. In IJVs that are Foreign Dominant IJVs, 60% are High Knowledge Acquirers. Approximately 50% of the Low Knowledge Acquirers are IJVs in which the Domestic Partner has Dominant equity position. This supports *Hypothesis 3*.

Results from IJV Enablers

Model 2 shows the logistic regression testing the Joint Venture Enablers' ability to distinguish between High Knowledge Acquirer IJVs from Low Knowledge Acquirer IJVs. The model is significant (Chi square = 19.59; sig. = 0.01). It indicates that the IJV Knowledge Enablers Model were able to correctly classify 74.65% of the IJVs.

The significant IJV Enabler variables were Conflict between the IJV and Parents (sig. = 0.071), Informal Communication (sig. = 0.021), and Performance (sig. = 0.022). *Hypothesis 6* and *7* are supported, while *Hypotheses 5* is not.

Model 3 shows the results of utilizing both sets of Enablers to predict High Knowledge Acquirers. In this model, 93.22% of the IJVs are correctly classified and Chi square = 60.12 (sig. = 0.001). The variables that are significant at a 0.10 level are Job Rotation, Relatedness, Training, Informal Communication, Performance, and Receptivity.

Discussion

Our objective was to identify those Enablers that facilitate KA by the IJV. Contrary to prior research and our predictions, overall levels of Trust, Parent Conflict, and Absorptive Capacity did not significantly predict Knowledge Acquisition by the IJV. However, Training by the foreign parent, Influence in Decision-Making, Informal Communication, Conflict within the IJV, and Ownership were significant at the 0.10 level. For the combined model (Model 3) Job Rotation, Training, Relatedness, Receptivity, Informal Communication and Performance were significant.

Looking more closely at Foreign Parent Enablers, we found that *Knowledge Sharing Commitment by the foreign partner predicts a High-Knowledge Acquisition IJV*. We show that there is strong support for Training as an Enabler for KA. This result confirms previous findings of Lyles and Salk (1996) and Zhang and Goffin (1999). In fact, of the two ways of showing Knowledge Sharing Commitment, Training might be more effective in an IJV setting than Job Rotation. The purpose of Job Rotation is to break with work specialization to provide more generalized skills and improved dialogue across functional boundaries (Lindbeck/ Snower 2000). Job Rotation might be more appropriate for KA in settings where a certain level of specialization and expertise has already been reached. Given that the IJV has great potential for acquiring functional expertise and knowledge, as our results show, Training might be more effective than Job Rotation for Knowledge Acquisition.

We find that *foreign parent Influence in Decision-Making predicts High Knowledge Acquisition*. This result confirms the propositions made in the KM literature, i.e. appropriate control mechanisms are necessary for KA (Nonaka/ Takeuchi 1995). Influence in Decision-Making facilitates the foreign partner's encouragement of KA in those areas where the IJV could benefit. Future studies might address the types of decisions influenced as these impact on both Knowledge Acquisition and Control. Shared IJV equity-ownership (50/50) also predicts a High Knowledge Acquisition. Our findings clearly support that KA is enabled by Ownership (Lyles/Salk 1996).

Against expectations, *Level of Trust and Level of Conflict did not predict High Knowledge Acquirers*. Our findings contrast the general consensus in the KM literature, that high Trust is needed between parties in order to foster and encourage KA (Davenport/Prusak 1998). KA between foreign partners and IJVs is highly complex, and, counter to the findings by Hyder and Ghauri (2000), this study finds that shared Ownership and Influence in Decision-Making outweighs the importance of a trusting relationship between the partners. In general, "familiarity may breed trust" (Gulati 1995), but transitional economies like Hungary, offer limited prior experience between the foreign and the local partners. Control helps to resolve issues relating to the future direction of the IJV and to reduce opportunism by the domestic parent once the knowledge is transferred (Steensma/Lyles 2000).

Contrary to expectations, *Relatedness did not predict high KA*. We speculated, along with other authors (Lane et al. 2001) that the more related the businesses, the easier it should be for the IJV to acquire knowledge. However, Relatedness does not seem to warrant a strong emphasis. Our results support Inkpen and Dinur's (2000) call for future studies of KA in IJVs and Relatedness.

With regard to IJV Enablers, *a higher quality of the Interaction Climate within the IJV and its Performance predict high KA*. Informal communication was significant in predicting the High Knowledge Acquirers both in the IJV Enabler model and in the combined model. This result supports several arguments in both the KM and IJV literature that Informal Communication enables Knowledge Acquisition. Strong Informal Communication will help to translate skills and knowledge from the foreign parent to the IJV; increase the speed with which knowledge can be transferred; allow an interactive and iterative discussion on the value of knowledge; help to identify and encourage sharing by experts with tacit knowledge; and clarify the utilization of knowledge from experts. Likewise, Conflict between the IJV and parents was significant in explaining Low Knowledge Acquisition IJVs (sig. = 0.071).

An important omission from our study, as well as from much of the KM theory, is the systematic examination of the antecedents of a high quality Interaction Climate, and more research is needed on this topic. Future research might also examine in what ways Informal Communication affects the types of IJV learning, and learning rates as well (Miner/Mezias 1996). It should also address the reduction of ambiguity in task performance through learning between the foreign parent and the IJV.

We find that *IJV's Performance predicts Knowledge Acquisition*. This result supports the premise that high performing IJVs learn more easily from their foreign parents than low performing IJVs. High performance may make the IJV more open to new ideas from the foreign parent and drive knowledge acquisition towards its strategic objectives (Arino/de la Torre 1998). Poor Performance frequently leads to the foreign partner being reluctant to continue knowledge sharing with the IJV.

Contrary to expectations, *Knowledge Acquisition Capacity did not predict a High Knowledge Acquirer.* We measured KA by the Enabler variables Absorptive Capacity and Receptivity, and our results contradict those of recent studies (Lyles/Salk 1996). When the High- and Low Knowledge Acquirers were compared on Absorptive Capacity, there is a significant difference between the two groups (T = 2.39; sig. = 0.03). However, Absorptive Capacity did not enter as an important variable for predicting the High Knowledge Acquirers. A possible explanation might be that Absorptive Capacity is a term relative to industry or level of specialization. We speculate that in rapidly changing economies, where IJV managers might be eager to learn while paying less attention to specialization in the search and use of knowledge, where IJV managers track down and use sources of knowledge more broadly, Absorptive Capacity could be a less effective predictor of *relative* KA performance. Perhaps the general "eagerness to learn," rather than a passive "capacity to learn," is a better predictor of effective KA behavior. The "eagerness to learn" predictor finds tentative support in Maruyama (1996) who presents five micro-level case studies of human resource practices in Western-Hungarian IJVs.

Conclusion

This paper contributes to our understanding of knowledge management in IJVs, and in particular, those organizational mechanisms enabling IJVs to acquire knowledge from their foreign parents. At least three implications can be drawn from this study.

First, aligned with existing theory, the foreign parent's Commitment to Share Knowledge with the IJV, the foreign parent's Influence in Decision Making of the IJV, as well as Ownership Control all predict High KA in IJVs. Future research should attempt to test whether or not these results hold for other empirical settings, such as other transitional economies. We did not find that high levels of Trust between IJV and the foreign parent, low degree of Conflict among the partners, and high degree of Business Relatedness between the IJV and the foreign parent predicted High KA IJVs. We suggest that in transitional economies, Trust cannot be assumed ex-ante between the parties, and Ownership Control will be the likely mechanism used by the foreign parent to avoid opportunism and unwanted spillover of knowledge associated with the IJV. We suggest that future research should examine how different types and levels of control relate to different forms of decision-making influence. It would also be useful to explore the relationship between levels of Trust, types and levels of Control, and KA in IJVs, across various empirical settings.

Second, we found that Interaction Climate within the IJV as well as high IJV Performance would predict High KA IJVs. Future research should explore Interaction Climate and seek to identify the antecedents of a high-quality Interaction Climate. Against expectations of conventional theory, we found that KA Capacity, including Absorptive Capacity, was not a predictor of High A IJVs. This might result from the empirical setting of this study and/or the diminishing relative importance of the Absorptive Capacity concept in predicting KA. Our results suggest that future research on KA in IJVs needs a stronger emphasis on the *processes* of KA with a focus on the social dynamics of such activities.

Third, a managerial implication of this study is that foreign parent managers who are engaged in setting up or managing relationships to IJVs should examine their firm's overall Commitment to Sharing Knowledge with the IJV. Training programs have proven to be particularly effective in fostering such KA, and it might be worthwhile examining what type and forms of training programs are available and how they differ with respect to the impact on KA. Furthermore, management should also consider various ways in which knowledge sharing by the partner and KA by the IJV can be fostered by Ownership Control and Decision Making Influence. However, as Trust is gained over time, the need for preserving Control should be reexamined.

Appendix 1. Variable Items

Knowledge Acquired (5 Items, alpha = 0.84) (Lyles/Salk 1996):
To what extent have you learned from your foreign parent:
1. New technological expertise;
2. New marketing expertise;
3. Product development;
4. Managerial techniques;
5. Manufacturing/Production Processes

Conflict between the IJV and parent (3 items, alpha = 0.79):
1. To what extent have you had to deal with conflict over the original agreement?
2. To what extent have you had to deal with cultural misunderstandings?
3. To what extent have you had to deal with tensions between JV management and partners?

Training (1 Items):
To what extent has your foreign parent provided education and training of domestic managers?

Job Rotation (1 Items):
Has there been a process of job rotation from the IJV to the foreign parent? Where No = 1 and Yes = 2.

Level of Trust between Parents: How would you characterize the level of trust between the parent firms? Where 1 = low level of trust and 5 = high level of trust.

Conflict between the Parents (3 items, alpha = 0.78):
1. To what extent have you had to deal with conflict over the original agreement?
2. To what extent have you had to deal with mistrust among the parent firms?
3. To what extent have you had to deal with conflicting goals among the partners?

Ownership: *Dominant Foreign Parent; Dominant Domestic Parent; or Shared 50/50*

RELATEDNESS of IJV and Foreign Parent's Business is a single item (1= unrelated, 2 = related)

Foreign Parent Influence in Decision-making is the total percentage of relative influence of the foreign parent in financial decisions, product technology decisions, process technology, manufacturing, sales/marketing, management decisions, administrative support decisions, and pricing decisions as compared to the influence in decision making of the local parent and the JV management.

Absorptive Capacity (2 Items, alpha = 0.71): Indicate the extent to which you agree with the following statements as they describe your joint venture: The venture is flexible and continually adapting to change. And Creativity is encouraged in the JV.

Receptivity (Long Term Focus):
Whether the IJV will still be in operation in the next five years where 1 = do not know and 5 = Very Likely.

Informal communication:
The extent to which there is a lot of informal communication within the IJV where 1 = little and 5 = a lot.

Conflict within the IJV (2 Items, alpha = 0.71).
1. To what extent are there tensions between the JV management and the partners?
2. To what extent are there tensions between local and expatriate managers in the JV where 1= little and 5 = very much.

Performance: How would you would rate the JV's performance as compared to other firms in its industry where 1 = low and 5 = high performance.

Marjorie A. Lyles/Georg von Krogh/John Harald Aadne

Endnote

1 We would like to thank the Carnegie Bosch Institute, Indiana University, CIBER, U.S.A.I.D., and the Hungarian BBF Foundation for their assistance and funding. We are grateful to Kentora Nobeoka, Paul Carlile, and Fiona Murray for helpful comments.

References

Anand, J./Delios, A., Location Specificity and the Transferability of Downstream Assets to Foreign Subsidiaries, *Journal of International Business Studies*, 28, 3, 1997, pp. 579–603.
Arino, A./de la Torre, J., Learning from Failure: Towards an Evolutionary Model of Collaborative Ventures, *Organization Science*, 9, 3, 1998, pp. 306–325.
Cohen, M./Levinthal, D., Absorptive Capacity: A Perspective on Learning and Innovation, *Administrative Science Quarterly*, 35, 1990, pp. 128–152.
Cohen, D./Prusak, L., *In Good Company- How Social Capital Makes Organizations Work*, Boston: Harvard Business School Press 2001.
Das, T. K./Teng, B. S., Between Trust and Control: Developing Confidence in Partner Cooperation in Alliances, *Academy of Management Review*, 23, 3, 1998, pp. 491–512.
Dasgupta, S./Teng, B. S., Contractual Incompleteness and the Optimality of Equity Joint Ventures, *Journal of Economic Behavior and Organization*, 37, 4, 1998, pp. 391–413.
Davenport, T. H./Prusak, L., *Working Knowledge*, Boston: Harvard Business School Press 1998.
Gulati, R., Does Familiarity Breed Trust? The Implication of Repeated Ties for Contractual Choice in Alliances, *Academy of Management Journal*, 38, 1995, pp. 85–112.
Hamel, G., Competition for Competence and Interpartner Learning within International Strategic Alliances, *Strategic Management Journal*, 12, 1991, pp. 83–103.
Hedlund, G., A Model of Knowledge Management and the N-Form Corporation, *Strategic Management Journal*, 15, 1994, pp. 73–90.
Hedlund, G./Nonaka, I., Models of Knowledge Management in the West and Japan, in Lorange P., Chakravarthy B., Roos J. and Van de Ven A. (eds.), *Implementing Strategic Processes: Change, Learning and Co-operation*, London: Blackwell Business 1993.
Hennart, J.-F./Roehl, T./Zietlow, D. S., Trojan Horse or Workhorse? The Evolution of U. S.-Japanese Joint Ventures in the United States, *Strategic Management Journal*, 20, 1, 1999, pp. 15–30.
Hyder, A. S./Ghauri, P. N., Managing International Joint Venture Relationships – A Longitudinal Perspective, *Industrial Marketing Management*, 29, 3, 2000, pp. 205–218.
Inkpen, A./Dinur, A., Knowledge Management Processes and International Joint Ventures, *Organization Science*, 9, 4, 1998, pp. 454–468.
Inkpen, A. C., A Note on the Dynamics of Learning Alliances – Competition, Cooperation, and Relative Scope, *Strategic Management Journal*, 21, 7, 2000, pp. 775–779.
Lane, P./Salk, J./Lyles, M. A., Knowledge Acquisition and Performance in Transitional Economy International Joint Ventures, *Strategic Management Journal*, 22, 12, 2001, pp. 139–11620.
Larson, R./Bengtsson, L./Henrikson, K./Sparks, J., The Inter-organizational Learning Dilemma: Collective Knowledge Development in Strategic Alliances, *Organization Science*, 9, 3, 1998, pp. 285–305.
Lindbeck, A./Snower, D. J., Multitask Learning and the Reorganization of Work: From Tayloristic to Holistic Organization, *Journal of Labor Economics*, 18, 3, 2000, pp. 353–376.
Lyles, M. A./Salk, J. E., Knowledge Acquisition from Foreign Parents in International Joint Ventures: An Empirical Examination in the Hungarian Context, *Journal of International Business Studies*, Special Issue 1996, pp. 877–903.

Makhija, M. V./Ganesh, U., The Relationship between Control and Partner Learning in Learning-Related Joint Ventures, *Organization Science*, 8, 5, 1997, pp. 508–527.
Maruyama, M., Young Hungarian Managers in Foreign Joint Venture Firms, *Human Systems Management*, 15, 3, 1996, pp. 201–206.
Miner, A. S./Mezias, S. J., Ugly Duckling no More: Pasts and Futures of Organizational Learning Research, *Organization Science*, 7, 1, 1996, pp. 88–99.
Mjoen, H./Tallman, S., Control and Performance in International Joint Ventures, *Organization Science*, 8, 3, 1997, pp. 257–274.
Nahapiet, J./Ghoshal, S., Social Capital, Intellectual Capital, and the Creation of Value in Firms, *Academy of Management Best Paper Proceedings*, 1997, pp. 35–39.
Nonaka, I./Takeuchi, H., *The Knowledge-Creating Company*, New York: Oxford University Press 1995.
Podsakoff, P./Organ, D., Self-Reports in Organizational Research: Problems and Prospects, *Journal of Management*, 12, 4, 1986, pp. 531–544.
Prahalad, C. K./Bettis, R. A., The Dominant Logic: A New Linkage between Diversity and Performance, *Strategic Management Journal*, 7, 1986, pp. 485–501.
Renkl, A., Inert Knowledge: When What is Learned is not Used, *Psychologische Rundschau*, 47, 2, 1996, pp. 78–92.
Reuer, J. J./Leiblein, M. T., Downside Risk Implications of Multi-Nationality and International Joint Ventures, *Academy of Management Journal*, 43, 2, 2000, pp. 203–214.
Sen, F. K./Egelhof, W. G., Innovative Capabilities of a Firm and the Use of Technical Alliances, *IEEE Transactions on Engineering Management*, 47, 2, 2000, pp. 174–183.
Shenkar, O./Zeira, Y., Role Conflict and Role Ambiguity of Chief Executive Officers in International Joint Ventures, *Journal of International Business Studies*, 23, 1992, pp. 55–75.
Smith, M. R., On the Use of the Prisoners' Dilemma to Analyze the Relations between Employment Security, Trust, and Effort, *Review of Social Economy*, 58, 2, 2000, pp. 153–175.
Steensma, K./Lyles, M. A., Explaining IJV Survival in a Transitional Economy through Social Exchange and Knowledge-Based Perspectives, *Strategic Management Journal*, 21, 8, 2000, pp. 831–852.
Szulanski, G., Exploring Internal Stickiness: Impediments to the Transfer of Best Practice Within the Firm, *Strategic Management Journal*, 17, 1996, pp. 27–43.
Tiemessen, I./Lane, H. W./Crossan, M. M./Inkpen, A. C., Knowledge Management in International Joint Ventures, in Beamish, P. W./Killing, J. P. (eds.), *Cooperative Strategies: North American Perspectives*, San Francisco: The New Lexington Press 1997.
Tsang, E. W. K., Transaction Cost and Resource-Based Explanations of Joint Ventures: A Comparison and Synthesis, *Organization Studies*, 21, 1, 2000, pp. 215–242.
von Krogh, G., The Communal Resource and Information Systems, *Journal of Strategic Information Systems*, 11, 2, 2002, pp. 85–107.
von Krogh, G./Ichijo, K./Nonaka, I., *Enabling Knowledge Creation: How to Unlock the Mystery of Tacit Knowledge and Release the Power of Innovation*, New York: Oxford University Press 2000.
Wall Street Journal, September 27, 1999, p. 13.
Wathne, K./Roos, J./von Krogh, G., Towards a Theory of Knowledge Transfer in a Cooperative Context, in von Krogh. G./Roos, J. (eds.), *Managing Knowledge: Perspectives on Cooperation and Competition*, London: Sage Publications 1996.
Zhang, L. H./Goffin, Joint Venture Manufacturing in China: an Exploratory Investigation, *International Journal of Operations and Production Management*, 19, 5–6, 1999, pp. 474–490.

mir *Edition*

Jörg Frehse

International Service Competencies
Strategies for Success in the European Hotel Industry

2002, XXVI, 353 pages, pb., € 59,00 (approx. US $ 59,–)
ISBN 3-409-12349-0

European hotels, which tend to be individual businesses, have a hard time resisting the continued globalization pressure. In order to survive the fierce international competition, Europe's hotel business needs to offer their potential customers an added value that they do not receive from hotel chains. The author shows how European individual hotels can prevail by developing international service competencies.

The book is addressed to lecturers and students of economics, in particular in the field of management and tourism, as well as managers and consultants in the hotel and tourist industry.

Betriebswirtschaftlicher Verlag Dr. Th. Gabler GmbH, Abraham-Lincoln-Str. 46, 65189 Wiesbaden

Gabriel Szulanski/Robert J. Jensen/Tanya Lee

Adaptation of Know-how for Cross-border Transfer

Abstract

- A central tenet in various streams of literature is the need to attend to key factors in the environment when adapting organizational practices transferred across borders. More recently scholars have examined the need to focus on key factors of the practice itself.

- We explore the intersection of these two factors with an in-depth, five-year longitudinal study of the transfer of franchising know-how from the US to Israel.

Key Results

- The case exhibits two time periods, first giving more weight to the environment and then to the key factors in the practice itself.

- We conclude that undervaluing the complexity of the practice, even in a franchising context, may lead to ineffective knowledge transfer and poor local performance.

Authors

Gabriel Szulanski, Associate Professor, INSEAD, Asia Campus, Department of Strategy, Singapore.
Robert J. Jensen, Ph.D. Candidate, Wharton School, University of Pennsylvania, Department of Management, Philadelphia, PA, USA.
Tanya Lee, Research Associate, Wharton School, University of Pennsylvania, Department of Management, Philadelphia, PA, USA.

Gabriel Szulanski/Robert J. Jensen/Tanya Lee

Adaptation of Know-how for Cross-border Transfer

The evolution of thought in the fields of organizational theory (Kostova 1999, Kostova/Zaheer 1999, Scott 2001), international business (Bartlett/Ghoshal 1989, Griffith/Hu/Ryans 2000, Nohria/Ghoshal 1997, Prahalad/Doz 1987), and marketing (Cui/Liu 2001, Yan 1994) seems to suggest that local environmental factors are a preeminent and crucial consideration for multinational organizations. It follows, then, that concerted attention to those factors is a primary task in the successful adaptation of assets transferred across borders. Adaptation to key features in the environment ensures fit between the asset being transferred and the environment, allowing the asset to be successfully deployed in the local context (Kostova/Roth 2002, Sorge 1991). Such an emphasis has direct and rather specific and unambiguous implications for practice.

An important subset of assets transferred by multinational corporations is knowledge in the form of organizational practices or routines (Nelson/Winter 1982). Recently scholars have begun to draw increasing attention not only to key factors in the environment but also to the importance of factors specific to the practice being transferred (Szulanski 1996), highlighting the fact that many practices are imperfectly understood, even though they are performed regularly and relatively reliably (Lippman/Rumelt 1982, Rivkin 2000). One major implication, of this viewpoint is that, due to imperfect understanding, as practices are altered or adapted key characteristics of those practice may be inadvertently altered or lost, rendering the practice inoperable. In other words, it may be necessary to underplay the assumed degree of understanding of the practice and temper the ambition of adaptation efforts. Such an emphasis may have implications for practices that run somewhat counter to some of the prior implications arising from an emphasis on attuning to environmental differences in the adaptation effort.

To date the literature has tended to focus on one set of factors or the other, environmental or practice specific, without examining both simultaneously. The paucity of studies examining the intersection of the two leads us to believe that an in-depth examination of specific instances of adaptation of organizational practices/knowledge in real settings can illuminate the relative importance of such factors and contribute toward a theory of adaptation of organizational practices.

We report in this paper the findings of a five year longitudinal investigation of the adaptation process of US franchising know-how in Israel. We observe two different epochs: one where a large weight is given to environmental factors and little, if any, weight is given to practice specific factors that would circumscribe adaptation efforts. The results are extremely poor. The second epoch is characterized by a concerted emphasis on practice specific factors to a point that implies neglect, or at least substantial underplay, of environmental factors.

We assess a variety of alternative explanations for the observed pattern of results and conclude that the most plausible explanation has to do with the need to respect the complexity of the practice and the tendency to overestimate the extent of understanding of the practice.

We use the rich detail uncovered during our in-depth investigation to suggest and analyze dimensions for a contingency framework and principles for improving the management of adaptation and opportunities for future research.

Method

Setting

General Setting

We explore adaptation in the context of a franchise organization. Franchise organizations are suitable for studying the particular questions raised in this paper in that they grow primarily by transferring knowledge to new geographic locations allowing us to more clearly observe the incidence of transfer and adaptation. They also tend to operate in the service sector at the level of the individual consumer so there are strong pressures for local adaptation. Furthermore franchise organizations operate across an arms length interface with their franchisees and cannot completely control how their franchisees receive and use the knowledge being transferred (Bradach 1998, Kaufmann/Eroglu 1998). This allows for greater variation in the level of standardization or adaptation at the local unit than one might find in company owned stores where the company can resort to fiat to enforce compliance with a particular set of practices (Williamson 1975).

Specific Setting: Mail Boxes Etc. in Israel

The specific setting of our study is the Mail Boxes Etc. (MBE) franchise system in Israel. MBE in the United States was first launched in 1980 in San Diego, California to fill a need for postal services. MBE specializes primarily in services for the small office and home office (S.O.H.O.) environments. These services include photocopying, color copying, packing and shipping, parcel and express courier, complete mailbox service, Internet access, and office and packing supplies. MBE quickly grew to 250 franchise outlets by 1986, when it went public, to over 1000 centers in 1990, and to over 4000 centers in 1999. After securing a strong foothold in the United States and building a strong foundation of experience, in 1989 MBE decided to sell master franchise licenses abroad. By 1999 MBE was operating in, or had licensing agreements, for nearly 60 countries, and had over 700 international outlets.

Early stage growth of a franchise network is assessed primarily by measuring the growth in the number of franchises sold and stores opened[1], as opposed to same store sales growth (Bradach 1998, Love 1986). Such growth in the number of franchises and stores is vital as it provides a revenue stream of franchise fee payments from the sale of new franchise units. That revenue funds the development of the central infrastructure that is necessary to support the growing network of stores until royalty payments from those centers are substantial (Bradach 1998).

Successful growth of the network depends not only on the master lincensee's (ML) ability to implement the business concept in functioning franchisee owned stores but also to manage the process of growing a network of such stores. MBE transfers knowledge to its MLs on both accounts. The implementation of the business concept into a functioning store is fairly well codified. Detailed manuals and multimedia materials exist to support the implementation of the different profit centers, which include packing and shipping, B&W and color copying services, and mailbox rentals, as well as the set of business skills that the franchisee needs in order to manage their store, such as up-selling and cross-selling techniques, store management, and accounting procedures. The above knowledge is transferred via training sessions and hands-on experience as well as through the manuals and multimedia materials. MBE corporate headquarters insures consistency by monitoring the training programs, offering standardized materials such as signage and store fixtures, helping with store design, and by utilizing a computer program to perform a comprehensive and standardized evaluation of the compliance of the store with MBE standards. Furthermore, the store unit is conceived in terms of mandatory and optional profit centers, with mandatory centers typically accounting for the lion share of the revenues. The nature and mix of profit centers is closely monitored and significant deviations are discouraged. With over 700 international stores, MBE has already acquired substantial experience with the implementation of the business concept in different markets.

Corporate knowledge on how to manage the process of building the network consists of training on how to train and support franchisees, including contract negotiations, vendor relationships, land acquisition strategies and support in the design of stores and the evaluation of franchisee compliance. Through corporate training and interaction with other MLs in the network, MLs are also socialized into the cultural norms that typify MBE's franchise organization.

The knowledge of how to manage the growth process, however, hinges primarily on a detailed blueprint of activities and expectations for the first year of operations (the '52 week' plan) specifying the recommended timing for the

Figure 1. Event Chart

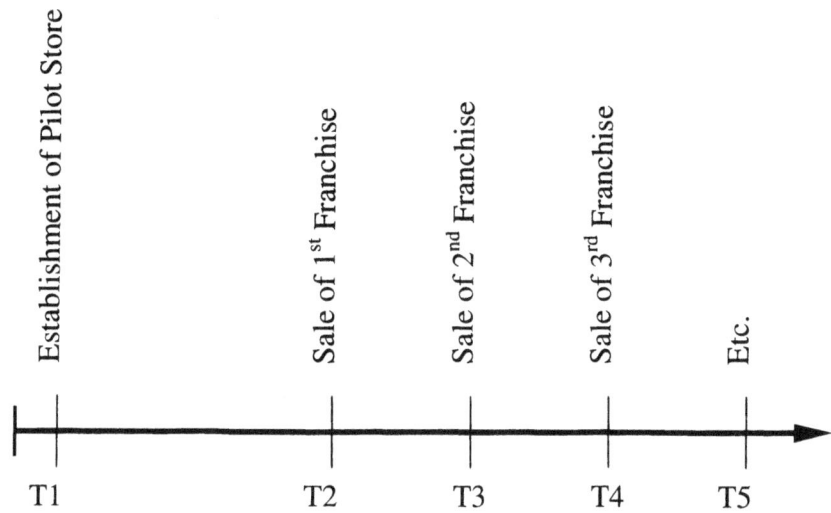

opening of the pilot store, for the selling of the first few franchise agreements, and for the subsequent opening of the corresponding franchise stores (see Figure 1). The blueprint also offers a detailed set of actions that are necessary to reach these key milestones including the timing of land searches, translation and formation of franchisee contracts, building and renovations, store openings, etc[2].

The underlying logic of the blueprint is that franchise sales should begin almost immediately after the pilot store is opened, even before the pilot store is fully functional and profitable. In this study we focus primarily on the extent to which the Israeli ML adheres to this blueprint. We interpret significant deviations from the blueprint as a rejection of the recommended logic for managing network growth.

The knowledge transferred to MLs contains a mixture of tacit and codified components. While compliance with the implementation of the business concept is relatively straightforward, what would constitute a deviation from the blueprint is harder to assess. Moreover, there is no theoretical model explicating the essential elements of the blueprint and insufficient empirical validation concerning the consequences that deviations from the blueprint would have for network growth. Of course strict compliance with the blueprint is often infeasible and small deviations from it, besides being necessary, are probably inconsequential. Yet, significant deviations may have noticeable consequences for the speed of growth. What constitutes a significant deviation, however, is ambiguous. For the purposes of this paper a major deviation is considered to be the omission or reordering of key milestones.

Gabriel Szulanski/Robert J. Jensen/Tanya Lee

Data Collection

Following Yin (1989) we employed an explanatory case study methodology. We employed case study methodology because we were examining a contemporaneous event in which the relevant actions could not be manipulated and where the causal links were too complex to effectively study with a survey only.

Data collection for this field investigation occurred primarily through a series of interviews with all of the relevant managers and employees at MBE headquarters and MBE Israel as well as extensive archival data gathering in both locations. After signing a confidentiality agreement we had complete access and cooperation in both locations. In all cases the interviews were semi-structured with an aim of uncovering the role of the ML and the process and difficulties of expanding a franchise network overseas, specifically the balance between copying headquarters' franchise system and adapting it to local needs.

The interviews with MBE headquarters occurred at MBE headquarters in San Diego, California. Those interviewed included the CEO of MBE, the Executive Vice President in charge of sales, the head of international operations, the head of international sales, the director of international franchise business development, and the international training director. We used these interviews to develop a thorough understanding of the MBE concept and the role MBE headquarters played in building the MBE network worldwide.

Following the interviews at MBE headquarters we also spent two weeks in July 1999 in Israel. These interviews included the CEO, COO, the director and assistant director of operations, the director of marketing, four franchise owners, and two suppliers. The CEO also completed a lengthy questionnaire as part of a wider, but connected study. Monthly e-mails and telephone conversations occurred prior to and following the on-site visits during the entire period of observation. The period of time tracked in the field investigation is 1995 to 1999. The data collection occurred in real time, mitigating the threat of retrospective bias. To minimize observer effects we were careful not to intervene and offered no opinions or suggestions to the participants. All interviews at both locations were taped and transcribed.

Our in-depth study of Israel represents our attempt to follow closely and provide a real time account of an actual instance of transfer. This in-depth probe is part of a broader investigation of the transfer of franchising knowledge across international borders at MBE. As part of that investigation, besides the interviews with management at corporate headquarters, we have interviewed and surveyed all MBE MLs. The broad familiarity with MBE's internationalization thus gained, allows us to appreciate the applicability to other MBE operations of lessons drawn from the Israeli experience. Furthermore, we discovered two characteristics that make Israel a particularly attractive site for an in-depth, longitudinal investigation of this nature.

First and foremost, Israel's demanding business conditions – which stem from high cost of capital, high fixed costs and rapid imitation of new business ideas – tend to accelerate the emergence of clear indications of the success or of the failure of an enterprise. Non-viable businesses become untenable after a short period of time. Secondly, Israel's population is culturally heterogeneous, a fact that provides a demanding ecology for any one social norm to survive. A stronger indication is necessary for a social norm to survive in Israel. Israelis are more averse to accept social norms than other cultures (Mann 1977). Thus we expected that norms – e.g., how to grow a network – that were suggested by the corporate office would be initially resisted by the Israeli ML and the effects of such a policy, if there are any, would be quickly detectable.

Data Reduction

Following Miles and Huberman (1984) we approached the data collection step with prior theoretical constructs, allowing us to reduce the data to comprehensible proportions. This is reflected in the use of semi-structured interviews where we specifically sought to understand decisions concerning adaptation or acceptance of standardized knowledge assets. We ensured validity of our understanding by confirming with the participants that our emerging understanding corresponded to their own.

MBE Israel and the Adaptation of Franchisor Knowledge Concerning Network Growth

Concerning the central issue of adapting knowledge at MBE Israel two clear time periods emerge, each defined by a distinct policy towards utilization of the parent's know how on managing the growth of a franchise network. We distinguish between a period of ex-ante adaptation, reflected in the omission and reordering of key blueprint milestones, and one of close adherence, reflected in close following of the recommended milestones. The first period spans from August 1995 to the end of 1997. The second period spans from 1998 to July 1999. Respondents unanimously pointed to a clear and specific event as the demarcation point.

Table 1 and Figure 2 give a quick synopsis of the findings from the case describing the growth experienced by the network during the two time periods.

Table 1. Adaptation of Knowledge Assets

	Period I 1995–1997	Period II 1998–1999
Knowledge Asset Adapted?	Alternative Logic Employed	Adhered to Corporate Logic
# New Stores Added	0	15

Figure 2. Growth of MBE in Israel

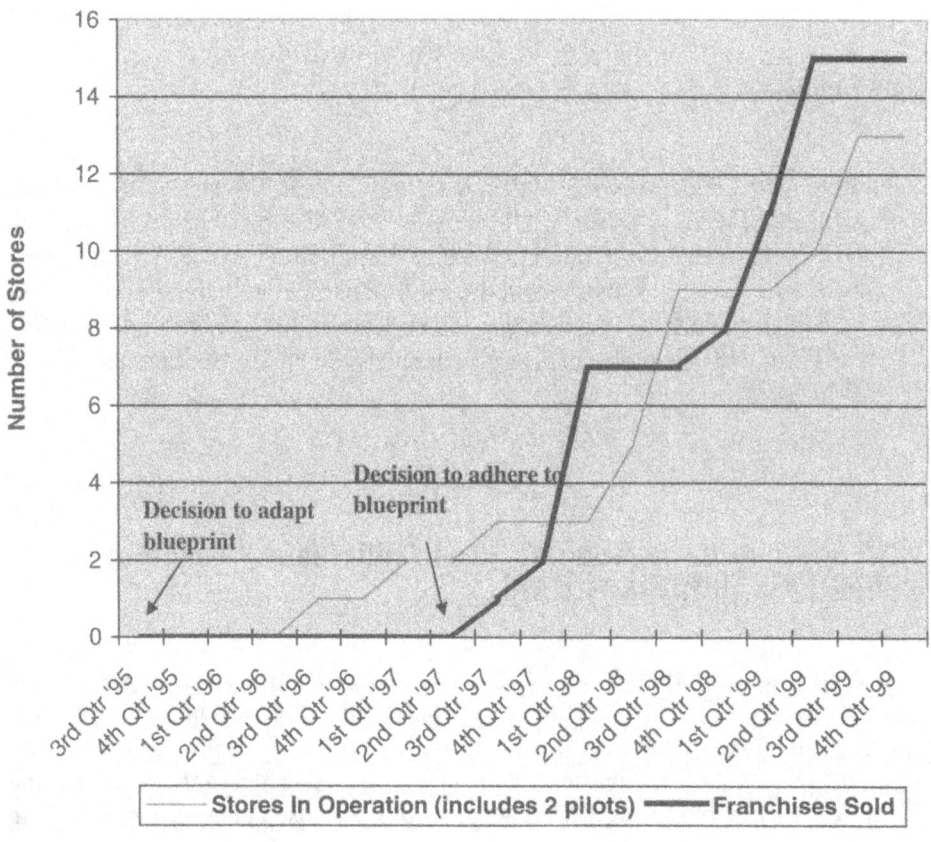

Albert Alhadef bought the rights to develop the MBE franchise network in Israel in August 1995. MBE, as they usually do, began the process of replicating their network in Israel with a series of intensive training sessions spanning several weeks. During these training sessions Albert was instructed in both building and operating a network and in establishing and operating a successful

MBE store. The training included in-depth field experience. MBE also aided Albert in the transfer of franchising knowledge by providing him with extensive manuals detailing the codified knowledge of both how to build and run a franchise network as well as an MBE store. Finally, MBE Headquarters introduced Albert to the global MBE network and gave him access to MLs in other countries that could serve as working examples and references in establishing the network in Israel. The attempt in the training, the written materials, and access to the network was to transfer a success-proven system that would work in many environments world-wide.

Next, Albert opened the pilot store (a model store run by the ML) in July 1996 and began focusing on building the pilot store and perfecting the sale of MBE services in Israel. From the beginning, Albert and the staff members that he hired believed that the MBE approach had to be substantially adapted if it were to be successful in Israel. Many of the business services being offered in the United States were not even defined or established in their small country. The word "mailbox" itself had no meaning and having the mailbox logo in the front of stores did little to attract customers. Albert was concerned that the fit of the MBE concept with the Israeli business reality was not sufficient to foster network growth.

This is why Albert and his partners were attracted by the flexibility of the MBE concept. They believed that not even MBE-USA understood the flexibility capabilities of what MBE could stand for in different settings. They understood this flexibility to mean that even on the local level, each franchisee could adapt to the special needs of their served area. By picking and choosing flexibly among the various components of the MBE concept, Albert and his associates believed they could create a market for MBE in Israel, possibly out-doing MBE's projections for network growth. The overriding tone during the entire period 1995 to late 1997 was focused on adaptation of the actual store to the local environment.

> "The MBE concept is so flexible that I don't think MBE home office has all the solutions. There's no way they can see all the needs of all the world and what is needed because the mission of MBE is that we will personalize a convenient business solution. There is no way you can think about all the system, what [services we] should give where. Each franchisee in each area in Israel also would have to adapt some of the things to these special areas without even consulting me or consulting USA. He will create his own area, own store to adapt it to this location." – Albert

Albert planned to overcome initial skepticism by developing a tangible and profitable MBE pilot store. Conceivably, proof of the fit between the business concept and the environment would drive network growth. This approach, however, violated the premises of the 52 week plan, as it omitted milestones outlined in the blueprint as well as the advice offered by various other MBE MLs from other countries[3]. According to the corporate know-how, network growth comes not from initial fit of the pilot store with the environment, but from synergies created by achieving critical mass in a growing network. In an attempt to adapt to the perceived characteristics of the local environment, marked by skepticism and suspicion of new franchising schemes, Albert abandoned the underlying logic of the blueprint and adapted the corporate know-how on managing network growth to fit his own conception of key success factors.

In a conscious attempt to increase the rate of growth Albert adapted the MBE system. His idea was that if he could perfect the pilot store and make it highly profitable he could use it as a primary means of attracting and convincing potential franchisees, dissolving their reluctance to invest in a new business concept. He explicitly hoped to out grow even the fastest growing MBE networks and to do MBE better than even those in the US could do it. This, of course, was a departure from the approach detailed by MBE headquarters. The philosophy during this period is captured in the following two quotations:

> "We don't go back to the US. We have our own knowledge here." – Ari
> "Ask US for help? It might be the proper way, but we have created our own experience." – Albert

According to MBE instructions and the experience of other international MLs, by the end of the first period, December 1997, Albert should have sold nearly 14 franchises and have over half as many stores already in operation. Instead he hadn't sold a single franchise yet and was still struggling to make the pilot store profitable. By focusing almost exclusively on the pilot store he had failed to reach all the remaining key milestones contained in the blueprint for the first 52 weeks. The result was not as he had intended. Instead of a perfectly functioning, highly profitable pilot store that could attract potential franchisees the pilot center wasn't even profitable and he had zero network growth. In fact, the pilot center did not become profitable until nearly half the final number of franchise units had been added to the network. Nor was the pilot center verging on breakeven at the end of 1997. Sales revenue growth had stalled and did not increase until critical mass in the network as a whole had been achieved. Finally, the growth following 1997 was not due to a perfected, Israeli version of the business concept (one well adapted to fit the Israeli market). First, the adapted model used in the pilot center had not achieved profitability. Second, the centers did not copy the pilot center model but each adapted the US model to match its own idiosyncratic local requirements. Clearly, the adaptation of the know-how on managing network growth did not produce the result that Albert had intended.

In December 1997 Albert decided to send one of his employees, Eitan, his COO, to an MBE International conference in Milan, Italy. Italy was one of the more successful MBE international networks with over 200 stores established in a period of 6 years. At that conference Eitan had an opportunity to see a successful network first hand. He returned to Israel with a clearer picture of how the network was supposed to grow and the benefits of close adherence to the blueprint.

> "The trip to Italy was a milestone for me, I think for all of us. I think Albert will agree with this milestone . . . December '97. It seems like every franchisor must . . . get to the point where you say, 'Okay, let's start listening to others and what they are doing.'" – Eitan

From December 1997 until the end of the period of observation Albert and his top managers shifted their policy from focusing on pilot store profitability to following the detailed blueprint that MBE had provided and attempting to meet each milestone. With a new focus and compliance with the MBE formula for managing network growth, the Israeli network grew from only the pilot store to two pilot stores plus 15 franchise outlets in two years. They were among the fastest growing young MBE networks at the time (growth often accelerates with age, but compared with other fairly new franchise networks they were now the second fastest growing ML in MBE history).

At first glance it might seem obvious that focusing on selling franchises would increase the size of the network. While this was the direct result of Albert's shift in thinking from adaptation to closer adherence to the knowledge assets it was not a shift in Albert's original intention. His intention from the beginning was to build a fast growing network. The shift, then, wasn't from a focus on growing the network, but from attempting to adapt the technique for growing the network to local conditions in order to achieve better than typical MBE growth rather than follow the pattern established by MBE. As he began to follow the pattern established by MBE he began to achieve the results that MBE had predicted he would when he first bought the rights to build the MBE network in Israel.

Interpretation

As Table 1 and Figure 2 both illustrate the shift in policy toward adapting the corporate know-how concerning managing network growth was strongly associated with a shift in the actual growth of the network. During the period of adaptation the Israeli network experienced zero growth. Following the shift toward utilization of the corporate know-how the network experienced high growth. There is, thus, a strong correlation between closely following the blueprint and network growth. To establish causality we now argue that this is the most plausible explanation.

In what follows, we enumerate and evaluate several alternative explanations. One alternative explanation is that the growth of MBE networks internationally is typically slow, because the brand is unknown and potential franchisees need time to familiarize themselves with the brand and evaluate its potential. In this scenario deviations, even significant ones, from the knowledge on how to manage network growth would be inconsequential. Many international MBE networks, however, including Italy, Australia, Japan, the UK, Mexico, and Venezuela, experienced quick, early growth, despite the lack of brand awareness (Figure 4 at the end of the paper graphs Italy and Australia's network growth).

Another potential explanation is that franchise network growth in Israel, not just MBE network growth, is typically slow. As mentioned earlier, however, Israel is a very demanding entrepreneurial business environment. The cost of capital and the high levels of fixed cost due to taxation make it a very unforgiving environment where in the best of cases, business concepts enjoy rapid but typically temporary success. Thus, in general, and evidence suggests that that is the case for franchising, business concepts do fail rapidly. It would be quite unusual for a typical franchise network growth process in Israel to fit the pattern of our data.

Another alternative explanation is that Albert's initial approach was correct and that adapting the method of network growth to the local environment by perfecting the pilot store before selling franchises was the main determinant of later growth. This, however, was not the case, because the pilot stores were never able to come close to breaking even until after there were many franchise stores in operation, in sufficient numbers to bring up the average revenue of all the stores in the network. In this case following the blueprint, rather than up front adaptation to the local environment, was the key to obtaining good results.

A similar explanation is that network growth in the second phase was fueled by a combination of adaptation and compliance with the know-how transferred from MBE headquarters. Rather than adherence to knowledge assets it was the mix of adherence and adaptation that produced the results. However, as operationalized, adaptation of the know-how involved the omission or reordering of key milestones contained in the blueprint. The shift in logic exhibited in the second phase required paying careful attention to the timing and ordering of such milestones. The two approaches thus are mutually exclusive and the growth, as argued in the previous paragraph, was not driven by the ordering of the approaches but rather by adherence to the know-how transferred by MBE headquarters.

Another potential explanation for our findings is the existence of a two year lag between demonstration of the MBE business and actual franchisee recruitment. However, this is not the case in MBE Israel with the average time from demonstration to franchise sale of less than four months during the period in question. A time lag of nearly two years between demonstration of the concept and sale of the franchise would be required if this were the cause of the pattern found in the data.

Finally, it could be argued that the pattern observed coincides with the business cycle in Israel. Concerning the economic climate of Israel we measured both economic indicators and average store revenue in the MBE Israel network to determine if an increase in economic growth was responsible for the increase in sales of new franchises during the second phase of the period of observation. GDP increased during the entire period of the study but at a decreasing rate during the second phase of the study. For the economic climate to have been the cause of the growth it should coincide, to some degree (although there may be a lag) with the pattern of network growth results. We find that the cross elasticity of store revenue to GDP is negligible for both periods. As the economic and cross elasticity indicators do not coincide with the pattern found in the data we can thus rule out this alternative explanation as well.

In sum, available evidence weakens the plausibility of each of the alternative explanations offered above. Unless we have omitted a major alternative explanation, our analysis, then, suggests that the interpretation concerning adaptation and adherence to standardized knowledge assets is likely to be the most plausible explanation for the pattern found in the data.

Discussion and Implications

Studies in the fields of organizational theory (Kostova/Roth 2002), international business, (Hannon/Huang/Jaw 1995), and marketing (Douglas/Wind 1987) have shown that sufficient attention must be paid to the key factors in the local environment if a transferred practice is to be successful (Griffith et al. 2000, Kirkman/Gibson/Shapiro 2001). The evidence from the MBE Israel experience suggests that attention also must be paid to the key factors in the practice itself. Successful adaptation of organizational practices, then, seems to require a sufficient understanding of the key factors of both the local environment and the practice being transferred. This gives rise to a framework where adapting at the intersection between deep understanding of both sets of factors predicts a potentially successful adaptation effort while adaptations undertaken with a shallow understanding of either or both factors will likely end in poor performance of the practice in the new locale (see Figure 3). This gives rise to two hypotheses:

Hypothesis 1. The lower the level of understanding of the receiver's environment the less successful the transferred practice will be.

Hypothesis 2. The lower the level of understanding of the practice the less successful the transferred practice will be.

Figure 3. Failure Sources in Adaptation

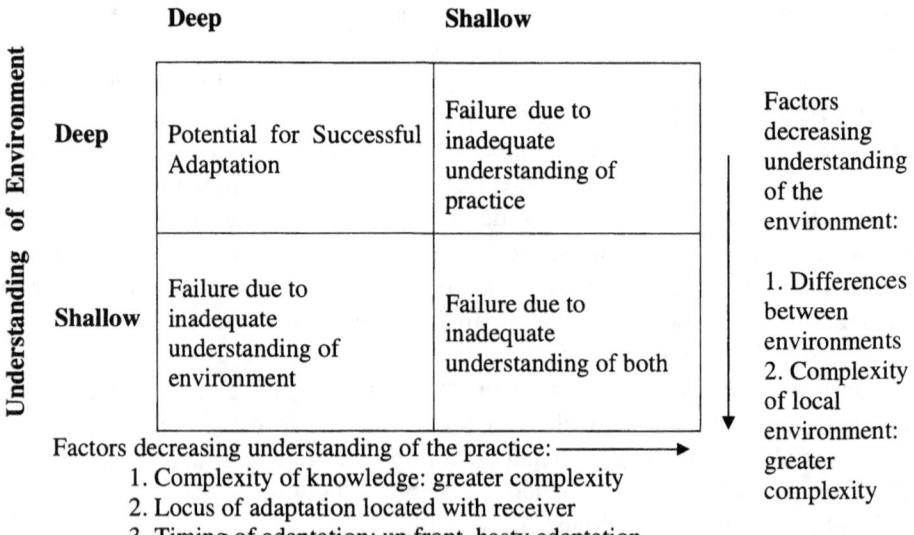

While not exhaustive, the case also illustrates five sets of factors, two environmental and three practice related, which may affect the depth of understanding. These factors are 1. differences between the source and recipient environment, 2. complexity of the environment, 3. complexity of the practice, 4. the locus of adaptation, and 5. the timing of adaptation.

Environmental Differences and Complexity

As argued earlier, the international business, marketing and institutional theory literatures are replete with assertions that markets and environments are different (Douglas/Wind 1987, Lemak/Arunthanes 1997, Scott 2001) and such differences must be taken into account if transferred practices are to be implemented successfully (Sorge 1991). Furthermore, institutional theorists posit that organizational practices are imbued with meaning and value that goes beyond the technical aspects of the routine (Kostova 1999, Selznick 1957). Because meaning is context sensitive and institutions can vary dramatically from one environment to another, differences between source and receiver institutions can lead to the source not understanding the key factors of the receiver's environment. Such a lack of understanding may lead to inadequate or inappropriate adaptation. In the case this is highlighted by Albert's assertion that Israel is a radically different market than the US and that because he understands the local market he is better suited to undertake the necessary adaptations.

Hypothesis 3. The greater the difference between source and receiver environment the less likely the source is to understand the key factors in the receiver's environment.

Environmental complexity may also result in a lack of adequate understanding as the key issues around which adaptation should occur may be ambiguous. One may expect that a receiver, given sufficient local experience, should have an adequate understanding of its environment. Such an assumption, however, may be unwarranted. First, the recipient, while embedded in a local context, is unfamiliar, by definition, with the practice being transferred and will likely be unaware of the exact nature of the interaction between the environment and the practice. Second, the recipient may be subject to superstitious (Levitt/March 1988) or myopic learning (Levinthal/March 1993), leading to a misunderstanding of the key environmental factors.

Hypothesis 4. The more complex the receiver environment the less likely the receiver is to understand its environment's key factors.

Knowledge Complexity

Organizational practices are often complex (Rivkin 2000) and causally ambiguous (Lippman/Rumelt 1982) and assuming simplicity during transfer may be detrimental to the performance of the practice at the recipient site. All other things being equal, tacit knowledge is often expected to pose significantly more problems for successful transfer and adaptation than codified knowledge (Nonaka/Takeuchi 1995). Thus, a transfer that involves a significant tacit component should be expected to require comparatively more attention to the knowledge factors if effective adaptation is to occur. Alternatively, when transferring a fairly explicit and codified practice more attention may be paid to fitting the practice to the key factors in the environment.

The current study, however, suggests that this characterization may be misleading in practice. Franchising is often considered to involve the transfer of fairly simple, highly codified organizational practices, often characterized as cookie cutter transfers (Bradach 1998). In such a context one would expect the factors of the knowledge to be well known, well understood, and, as a consequence, more easily altered in response to the need to fit the local environment. Accordingly, Albert's emphasis on the uniqueness of the Israeli environmental factors appears to be appropriate. However, as the rest of Albert's story illustrates, even highly codified practices may be insufficiently understood. A seemingly innocent neglect of the key factors in the practice in favor of the environmental factors resulted in substantially negative performance.

Hypothesis 5. Given a complex practice, lower levels of attention paid to the practice's key factors will result in poorer performance of the practice at the recipient site.

Locus of Adaptation

Another issue illustrated by the case is the locus of adaptation (Prahalad/Doz 1987). Does the adaptation occur at the source site, in the local context, or a combination of the two? If the knowledge is easily and well understood it seems reasonable that the adaptation could be attempted exclusively by the recipient. This may be desirable, from the recipient's point of view, because interaction with the source is often costly and time consuming. A higher estimation of the importance of the knowledge factor, however, would imply the need to increase the interaction with the source, despite the cost, possibly even bringing the source to the local environment in order to complete the adaptation in situ. Such a strategy would allow attention to both environmental and practice factors simultaneously.

Hypothesis 6. Adaptations undertaken by a source and receiver together will result in greater success of the transferred practice than adaptations undertaken solely by the receiver.

Timing of Adaptation

A third practice related issue is illustrated by generalizing beyond the bounds of MBE Israel. As mentioned earlier this case study is part of a larger study of MBE involving transfers of franchising know-how across borders. Specifically, we find that the weighting of environmental vs. practice factors during the adaptation process is a common occurrence in MBE. While a few ML[4] considered the environmental factors to be preeminent and adapted the practices before fully understanding them (with the same results as Albert), other's like the Italian Master Licensee gave considerably more weight to the practice factors and were reluctant to change something they didn't completely understand.

> "... Our system is very close to the US ... There was no point in buying a concept and then doing something else... We do it exactly like the US, not only in image but in business." *Italian Master Licensee*

Still other ML (Australia and Canada) realized the need to adapt in order to maximize the full potential of the practice in their local context but postponed adaptation because of uncertainty concerning the key factors in the MBE system including what could be safely changed and what would be problematic (see Figure 4 for a comparison of the growth of the Italian, Australian, and Canadian networks along with an unnamed network that followed Albert's strategy).

The strategy of Australia and Canada coincides with a more general trend among firms to postpone adaptation for a period until the practice is fully transferred and more completely understood by the recipient. Other firms employing the strategy of postponing adaptation include Xerox Europe, formerly Rank Xerox, and Great Harvest Bread Company. Xerox Europe requires recipient units to copy a practice exactly until the recipient unit is able to achieve the same results as the source unit (Financial Times 1997). Great Harvest Bread demands that franchisees follow established practices down to the letter for at least the first year of their contract (Great Harvest Bread 1999).

In the above examples it appears that adaptation activities do not occur at the beginning of the transfer. However, given that adaptation must occur and that there is a window of opportunity where adaptation is possible (Tyre/Orlikowski 1994), it likely cannot be deferred indefinitely. Little attention has been paid to this issue. Thus, while the case raises the issue and hints that delaying adaptation may enhance practice performance at the recipient site there is insufficient data to induce specific hypotheses.

The case for attending to key environmental factors has been made for some time. The literature has enumerated many factors and made repeated calls for academics and practitioners alike to respect the influence such factors have on transferred assets and practices (Bartlett/Ghoshal 1989, Kostova 1999, Prahalad/Doz 1987).

There is significantly less elaboration in the literature, however, of the key factors in organizational practices that must be attended to effectively manage an adaptation effort. Furthermore, the voices calling for attendance to such factors are fewer. However, as Albert's case illustrates failure to attend to such factors may be as, or possibly even more, detrimental than failure to attend to key environmental factors. Clearly, future research is much needed.

Figure 4. Network Growth

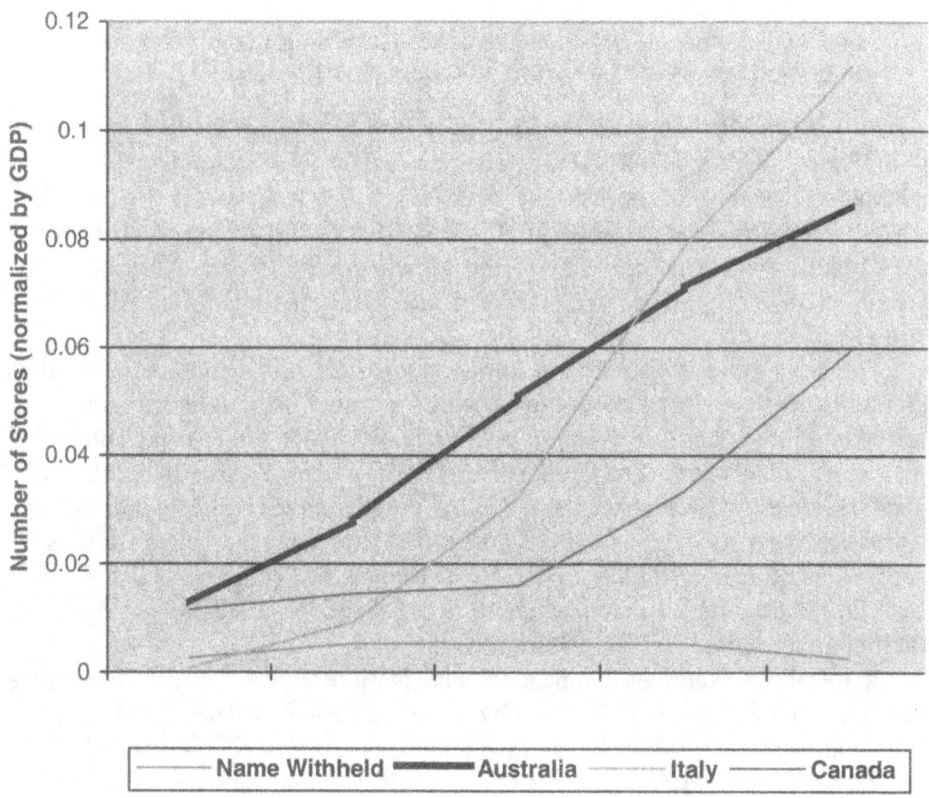

Endnotes

1 Bradach (1998) lists a few other key aspects including site selection, the ability to adapt the entire system, and, the subject of this paper, standardization versus local adaptation but he is clear that growth is the most important issue until the market begins to be saturated. Our case study takes place at the beginning of a network's lifespan, long before the market has become saturated.
2 Due to confidentiality reasons we cannot give exact details from the 52 week plan.
3 Some of the MLs have significant experience following the corporate guidelines for network growth. This experience accrued in multiple markets (Canada, Italy, the UK, Mexico, Venezuela, Australia). These ML networks experienced early and sustained network growth. In each there were varying degrees of adaptation of the business concept (though typically that adaptation was minor and occurred only after a substantial period of time). Other MBE international networks

adapted the business concept to a greater degree with varying degrees of success. Initial impressions imply that those MLs who adhered to the logic underlying the blueprint have had faster and more sustained growth than those who have not.

4 Names withheld for confidentiality purposes.

References

Bartlett, C. A./Ghoshal, S., *Managing Across Borders: The Transnational Solution*, Hutchinson: Business Books 1989.
Bradach, J. L., *Franchise Organizations*, Boston: Harvard Business School Press 1998.
Cui, G./Liu, Q., Executive Insights: Emerging Market Segments in a Transitional Economy: A Study of Urban Consumers in China, *Journal of International Marketing*, 9, 2001, pp. 84–106.
Douglas, S. P./Wind, Y., The Myth of Globalization, *Columbia Journal of World Business*, 22, 1987, pp. 19–29.
Financial Times, Xerox Makes Copies, 1997, p. 5.
Great Harvest Bread Co., Apprenticeship Agreement: 2, 1999, p. 2.
Griffith, D. A./Hu, M. Y./Ryans, J. K., Jr., Process Standardization across Intra and Inter-Cultural Relationships, *Journal of International Business Studies*, 31, 2000, pp. 303–324.
Hannon, J. M./Huang, I.-C./Jaw, B.-S., International Human Resource Strategy and Its Determinants: The Case of Subsidiaries in Taiwan, *Journal of International Business Studies*, 26, 1995, pp. 531.
Kaufmann, P. J./Eroglu, S., Standardization and Adaptation in Business Format Franchising, *Journal of Business Venturing*, 14, 1998, pp. 69–85.
Kirkman, B. L./Gibson, C. B./Shapiro, D. L., "Exporting" Teams: Enhancing the Implementation and Effectiveness of Work Teams in Global Affiliates, *Organizational Dynamics*, 30, 2001, pp. 12–29.
Kostova, T., Transnational Transfer of Strategic Organizational Practices: A Contextual Perspective, *Academy of Management Review*, 24, 1999, pp. 308–324.
Kostova, T./Roth, K., Adoption of an Organizational Practice by Subsidiaries of Multinational Corporations: Institutional and Relational Effects, *Academy of Management Journal*, 45, 2002, pp. 215–233.
Kostova, T./Zaheer, S., Organizational Legitimacy under Conditions of Complexity: The Case of the Multinational Enterprise, *Academy of Management Review*, 24, 1999, pp. 64–81.
Lemak, D. J./Arunthanes, W., Global Business Strategy: A Contingency Approach, *Multinational Business Review*, 5, 1997, pp. 26–37.
Levinthal, D. A./March, J. G., The Myopia of Learning, *Strategic Management Journal*, 14, 1993, pp. 95–112.
Levitt, B./March, J. G., Organizational Learning, *Annual Review of Sociology*, 1988, pp. 319–340.
Lippman, S. A./Rumelt, R. P., Uncertain Imitability: An Analysis of Interfirm Differences in Efficiency under Competition, *Bell Journal of Economics*, 13, 1982, pp. 418–438.
Love, J. F., *Mcdonald's: Behind the Arches*, New York: Bantam Books 1986.
Mann, L., The Effect of Stimulus Queues on Queue-Joining Behavior, *Journal of Personality and Social Psychology*, 35, 1977, pp. 437–442.
Miles, M. B./Huberman, A. M., *Qualitative Data Analysis: A Sourcebook of New Methods*, Newbury Park, CA: SAGE 1984.
Nelson, R./Winter, S., *An Evolutionary Theory of Economic Change*, Cambridge: Belknap Press 1982.
Nohria, N./Ghoshal, S., *The Differentiated Network*, San Francisco: Jossey-Bass Publishers 1997.
Nonaka, I./Takeuchi, H., *The Knowledge-Creating Company: How Japanese Companies Create the Dynamics of Innovation*, New York: Oxford University Press 1995.
Prahalad, C. K./Doz, Y. L., *The Multinational Mission: Balancing Local Demands and Global Vision*, New York: Free Press 1987.

Rivkin, J. W., Imitation of Complex Strategies, *Management Science*, 46, 2000, pp. 824–844.
Scott, W. R., *Institutions and Organizations*, Thousand Oaks, CA: Sage 2001.
Selznick, P., *Leadership in Administration: A Sociological Interpretation*, New York: Harper & Row 1957.
Sorge, A., Strategic Fit and the Societal Effect: Interpreting Cross-National Comparisons of Technology, Organization and Human Resources, *Organization Studies*, 12, 1991, pp. 161–190.
Szulanski, G., Exploring Internal Stickiness: Impediments to the Transfer of Best Practice within the Firm, *Strategic Management Journal*, 17, 1996, pp. 27–43.
Tyre, M. J./Orlikowski, W. J., Windows of Opportunity: Temporal Patterns of Technological Adaptation in Organization, *Organization Science*, 5, 1994, pp. 98–118.
Williamson, O. E., *Markets and Hierarchies: Analysis and Antitrust Implications*, New York: The Free Press 1975.
Yan, R., To Reach China's Consumers, Adapt to Guo Qing, *Harvard Business Review*, 1994, pp. 66–74.
Yin, R. K., *Case Study Research*, Newbury Park, CA: SAGE Publications Inc. 1989.

Alan M. Rugman/Alain Verbeke

Multinational Enterprises and Clusters: An Organizing Framework

Abstract

- The current literature on "diamond-based" clusters needs to incorporate international business theory concepts such as the flagship framework and the nature of subsidiary-specific advantages. This is because the traditional focus on domestic clusters, consistent with Porter's (1990) "diamond" framework largely neglects the value of trans-border multinational enterprise (MNE) activity.

Key Results

- The MNE is now simultaneously a knowledge generator and a knowledge seeker, and it is necessary to carefully identify the organizational characteristics of its involvement in localized or trans-border clusters. We develop a new two-stage framework that permits the classification of clusters and the identification of their organizational characteristics in terms of breadth of scope and dominant logic.

Authors

Alan M. Rugman, L. Leslie Waters Chair in International Business, Kelley School of Business, Indiana,University, Bloomington, IN, USA and Fellow, Templeton College, University of Oxford, Oxford, UK.
Alain Verbeke, Professor of International Business Strategy, McCaig Chair in Management, Haskayne School of Business, University of Calgary, Calgary, AB, Canada and Associate Fellow, Templeton College, University of Oxford, Oxford, UK.

Alan M. Rugman/Alain Verbeke

Introduction

This paper focuses on the interactions between the strategies of multinational enterprises (MNEs), particularly in the areas of knowledge generation and absorption, and the functioning of clusters. Here, the diamond concept is critical.

The diamond concept was introduced by Professor Michael Porter, in his influential book *The Competitive Advantage of Nations* in 1990, and further extended in his 1998 book, *On Competition*. The diamond of competitive advantage is viewed as instrumental to the creation of localized knowledge clusters, usually restricted to particular industries, which arise from the linkages among specific factor conditions, demand conditions, related and supporting industries and an idiosyncratic configuration of firm strategies, industry structure and extended rivalry. This framework has in some cases been useful in explaining why internationally successful industries from a particular nation became globally competitive, largely as an outcome of favorable local diamond determinants.

Recently, however, this observation has been complemented by two other important insights. First, in some cases firms appear to draw on the strengths of diamond determinants present in more than one nation, leading to the development of "double diamond" and even "multiple diamond" perspectives (Rugman/Verbeke 1993a, 1993b Rugman/van den Broeck/Verbeke 1995). Such perspectives appear especially useful when describing the functioning of firms from small open economies (Van Den Bulcke/Verbeke 2001). Second, foreign direct investment by multinational enterprises (MNEs) increasingly takes the form of knowledge seeking or strategic asset seeking investment, whereby the MNE attempts to augment its knowledge base through obtaining access to foreign pools of knowledge, i.e., by becoming a participant in various localized knowledge clusters simultaneously (Rugman/Verbeke 2001a).[1] We develop a conceptual framework that allows us to recognize the importance of MNEs in clusters and to differentiate among the possible roles of MNEs in cluster formation and functioning.

From Nation-based to Transborder Clusters

We define a cluster as a set of interconnected organizations characterized by a co-evolution (and related spill-over effects) of their economic trajectories, whether intended or emerging. Porter's (1990a) influential diamond of competitive advantage can be used as a tool to analyze the functioning of clusters. It builds upon the hypothesis that four localized, domestic parameters are instrumental to the co-evolution of firms and their joint international competitiveness, namely:

factor conditions, demand conditions, related and supporting industries, and firm strategy, structure and rivalry. Porter defines a cluster as "a geographically proximate group of interconnected companies and associated institutions in a particular field, linked by commonalities and complementarities" (Porter 1998, p. 199). Here, it is fundamentally conditions external to the individual firm that drive cluster functioning, with many forces and actors influencing the ultimate success of a cluster. These may include specialized and advanced production factors, sophisticated demand, cooperative linkages with firms in related and supporting industries and intense domestic rivalry, as exemplified by the cases of the Italian ceramic tile and footwear clusters.

Paradoxically, Porter advocates "leadership" at the company level, in particular to upgrade the "national diamond" system and even suggests in this context that many businessmen earn the title of "statesmen" because of their upgrading efforts, but fails to recognize the critical role of "core firms" in these clusters (Porter 1990b). On the contrary, intense domestic rivalry is viewed as the key to sustained innovation and upgrading, whereas an excessive role of one or a few firms in a domestic cluster, especially if stimulated by government policy, is viewed as conducive to the "national champion" syndrome, synonymous with structural inefficiency. Porter thus implicitly advocates the nurturing of "symmetrical" clusters with no single economic actor performing a dominant role.

As regards the potential contribution of international linkages to a cluster, although not entirely neglected by Porter, they are clearly viewed as secondary, see especially Porter (1998, pp. 252–253). Porter's relatively shallow treatment of the international components of these diamond determinants has been heavily criticized by international business and strategy scholars, most notably by Dunning (1993, 1997). More recently, Davis and Ellis (2000) have provided an impressive synthesis of some 80 scholarly studies which have attempted to extend, improve or otherwise critically assess the diamond (Porter 1990a).

A New Classification of Clusters

Building upon the above discussion, it would appear that Porter's work can be usefully extended by recognizing two elements. First, a cluster may be built around either one, or a few, "core" companies, i.e., firms that drive the cluster, or they may consist of several, more equal partners, with no particular firm performing a dominant role. In the first case, the cluster is "asymmetrical". Here, a core firm or cluster champion is critical: it can be defined as a company that takes on a leadership role in developing and sustaining the cluster, thereby intentionally fostering the co-evolution of the organizations involved and the creation of spill-over effects arising from this co-evolution. In the second case it can be called "symmetrical". Porter's diamond-based clusters, which supposedly thrive on internal competition within the cluster, are fundamentally of a symmetrical nature, as it is even argued that a lack of competition within the cluster and monopolization would seriously impede its potential to gain international competitiveness. A symmetrical cluster could be viewed in two ways. First, as a federation of equals, with no single actor taking the lead in cluster formation and exploitation but with a substantial calculative basis. Calculativeness implies that the organizations involved engage in a formal assessment of the private costs and benefits associated with participation in cluster formation and exploitation. Although these firms do not take on a leadership role, they try to affect cluster functioning to their benefit. Second, as an "organically growing" and primarily path-dependent cluster, perhaps with vastly different participants in terms of size or activities, but largely building upon a heritage of strong, socially embedded ties, which does not necessarily impede competition among cluster participants. Here, emerging, rather than deliberate cluster strategies in the Mintzbergian sense, prevail.

Porter's perspective appears particularly useful to explain the "organically growing" or "identity based" clusters. These emerge out of socially embedded relationships: "The existence of clusters suggests that much of a company's potential to achieve competitive advantage, both in operational effectiveness and in establishing a unique strategy, lies outside the company and even outside the industry" (Porter 1998, p. 255). Porter's view may be less appropriate to analyze more "calculative" clusters in which the participants engage in a formal, private cost-benefit calculus, which goes beyond simple cluster analysis. In the latter case, a "visible hand" may be important in achieving explicit (private) clustering objectives, in contrast to the more invisible hand characteristic of Porter's clusters, where "private sector roles in cluster upgrading can be found in all parts of the diamond" (Porter 1998, p. 257), which really implies that a multitude of uncoordinated actions ultimately contribute to cluster strengthening and spill over effects. In Porter's case, "cluster upgrading" through innovation, although viewed as instrumental to the sustainability of a cluster does not appear to result from a deliberate strategy in the Mintzbergian sense, but rather "emerges" from the separate and uncoordinated actions of various (groups of) cluster participants. Over time, routines are developed and a process of self-organization results, whereby a cluster structure arises that functions according to specific behavioral rules and that inhibits deviant, rule breaking behavior.

Such co-evolution (Koza/Lewin 1998) whereby diamond participants improve their resource positions because of the socially embedded network ties among them, may be characteristic of the initial stage in the life of many clusters, but it is limited by a lack of explicit efforts to achieve goal convergence. In fact, if an identity-based cluster is successful, it is reasonable to expect that at least some participants, especially MNEs, will try to replicate the characteristics of the cluster in other locations, including foreign ones. Here, a transition takes place from an organically growing to a calculative cluster and benefits may arise from the newly discovered causal linkages between specific cluster related activities and the resulting performance outcomes.

In contrast to Porter's case, an asymmetrical cluster assumes that some actors occupy "key positions" in the cluster. It is not the "identity" of the ties that is critical to cluster functioning but the purpose and the expected value added of these ties to the participants.

In theory, it could be argued that even a cluster orchestrated by a single "core" firm may contain "emerging" elements, i.e., a co-evolution of the cluster as a whole or a number of its participants, that was not anticipated or intentionally pursued by a "core" firm. In practice, the existence of a "core" firm, albeit possibly arising from coincidental "initial conditions" from both an institutional and technological perspective, implies almost by definition a cost/benefit calculus. Taking on the role of "core" firm requires the allocation of at least some resources to cluster formation that will likely be weighed against expected returns. A stronger calculativeness of the key actor(s) may weaken the cluster ties, especially if little or no resources are allocated to "identity building" because of uncertain returns on such investments. Yet, at the same time, this may also eliminate redundant ties and improve the cluster's ability to bridge "structural holes".

As noted by Hite and Hesterly (1999) in their insightful comparative analysis of identity-based and calculative clusters, albeit in the context of entrepreneurial companies, more calculativeness is a precondition to proactively manage a cluster, rather than to just accept the "constraints of path dependency". A calculative network is able to more effectively access new required resources and to deal with environmental uncertainties, even if in theory this may be at the expense of "social capital" creation. It also avoids implicit and explicit resistance to intentional management of the cluster, which can be expected from identity-based clusters, in which the roles of participants may largely result from "initial conditions", a particular sequence of historical events, or from chance. Saxenian's (1994) insightful description of both the Silicon Valley and Boston-Route 128 networks, respectively a more symmetrical and more asymmetrical cluster, highlights the importance of initial conditions and the danger of arguing that one cluster structure is necessarily always more effective than another one.

Nevertheless, it is important to recognize that the higher expected calculativeness associated with core firms in asymmetrical clusters results not solely from the time-dependent accumulation of capabilities in the cluster, and the related *ex post* need to properly exploit and nurture such capabilities, but also from the actual *ex ante* intent, (especially by the core firm itself) to optimize the generation and internalization of cluster spillover benefits accruing to the cluster participants. Competitive advantage usually results at least partly from purposive behavior, and not just from emerging external opportunities or co-evolution processes. Dyer and Singh (1998) have coined the term "relational rents" arising from idiosyncratic interfirm linkages and reflecting interorganizational competitive advantage.

A second issue is also important. A substantial body of conceptual and empirical research has demonstrated the impact of "transborder elements" on cluster functioning. More specifically, it appears that a "multiple diamond", rather than a "single diamond" cluster composition may be critical to cluster functioning and success. In this case, it is often the complementarity between the location-bound "strengths" of domestic diamond components and the non location-bound knowledge of the foreign components that leads to valuable new resource combinations. For example, foreign multinational enterprises may provide access to assets, skills and routines that may usefully complement the location-bound knowledge of domestic firms. Enright (1999) provides examples of the globalization of competitive advantage and the local dimensions of regional clusters.

Birkinshaw and Solvell's (2000) editing of a special issue of *International Studies of Management and Organization* entitled "Leading-edge Multinationals and Leading-edge Clusters" is representative for the new work on clusters characterized by transborder elements. Five key conclusions, especially relevant to the present paper, can be drawn from Birkinshaw and Solvell (2000).

First, MNEs appear especially prone to perform R&D investments in foreign locations with a strong technological activity, and this leads to a further strengthening of indigenous R&D activities, thus illustrating the co-evolution of domestic firms and foreign subsidiaries in host country clusters.

Second, there is an increase of knowledge seeking foreign direct investment (FDI) by MNEs. Here, foreign subsidiaries "specialize" in particular knowledge creating activities. This intra-firm specialization, and the related local embededness of know how, sometimes makes it difficult to achieve international innovation processes within the MNE, with subsequent knowledge diffusion to other affiliates.

Third, highly dynamic local clusters usually benefit from the presence of inward FDI; in contrast such virtuous cycles of co-evolution between indigenous and foreign cluster participants are much more uncertain in the case of weak or immature clusters, in which foreign firms typically limit the scope and depth of their cluster ties.

Fourth, the ability to attract FDI in an emerging cluster, especially by large MNEs with a high visibility, may signal at the international level that the cluster is credible; this may result in a foreign investment snowball effect benefiting the cluster.

Fifth, the argument that clusters dominated by foreign subsidiaries are likely to behave as satellites of the foreign parent companies, with little spill over effects accruing to indigenous cluster participants, is disproved by the facts. For

Multinational Enterprises and Clusters

Figure 1. A Classification of Clusters

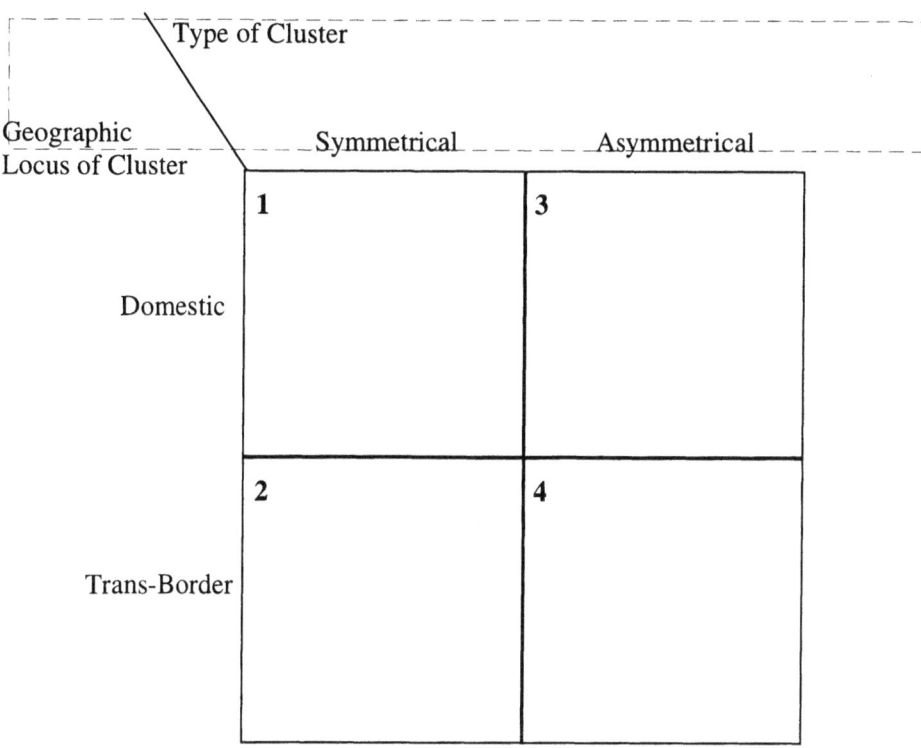

example, in the Hong Kong financial services cluster, subsidiaries of foreign MNEs perform the role of regional headquarters and have strong cluster ties among themselves and with local cluster participants.

The above analysis allows us to make a distinction among four types of clusters, as shown in Figure 1. The horizontal axis makes a distinction between symmetrical clusters and asymmetrical ones. The vertical axis distinguishes between domestic, i.e., single diamond based clusters, and transborder clusters characterized by an important foreign component, typically through the presence of MNEs.

Quadrant 1 represents the typical Porter based cluster, largely building upon domestic diamond components and without reliance on one or a few core firms. The domestic textile industry clusters in many countries can be positioned here, as can Porter's Italian ceramics cluster (Porter 1990b).

In quadrant 2, we find symmetrical, but transborder type clusters. This is typical for industries consisting of many small and medium sized firms facing the same "liability of foreignness". Such foreign threats (and opportunities) can lead to cluster responses in the form of establishing co-operative international cluster linkages. These can include: using new international distribution channels; developing international alliances that strengthen the domestic cluster; jointly sourcing valuable inputs through long-term contracts with suppliers, etc. The development of a marketing co-operative for small Chilean-based exporters of fresh fruit is one example. The New Zealand dairy co-operative is another (Cartwright 1993).

Quadrant 3 includes asymmetrical, domestic clusters characteristic for the industrial heritage of many "old economy" districts. Typically, one or a limited number of large companies represent the economic backbone of an entire geographic region, and largely determine the prosperity and health (or lack of it) of this area. Well known examples include the U. S. steel industry, segments of the chemical sector and other mature industries. Such industries may obviously be characterized by substantial trade and even foreign direct investment, but the actual development and absorption of new knowledge that would lead to firm-specific advantages (FSAs) remains a process largely dominated by domestic actors, without the creative involvement of foreign firms or organizations.

Finally, quadrant 4 represents the asymmetrical, transborder clusters of particular interest for this paper. Here, core firms engaged in purposive behavior to optimize the value added from clustering interactions, and international linkages are critical to the cluster's success. Examples occur in the flagship sectors analyzed by Rugman and D'Cruz (2000) i.e. in specialty chemicals, automobiles, telecom, etc. The next section describes the two key characteristics of such quadrant 4 clusters. This focus does not imply that transborder, core firm-based clusters are viewed as more effective than other types of clusters; rather there is a real need for a conceptual analysis that recognizes their existence and importance.

Key Characteristics of Transborder, Core Firm Based Clusters

The joint transaction cost and resource-based rationale for the existence of transborder, core firm based clusters has been provided elsewhere, and will not be repeated here, see Rugman and Verbeke (2003). In terms of Dunning's (1997) work, these clusters can be described through the use of the eclectic paradigm. As regards ownership advantages (O), they imply that the potential value embedded in inter-firm relationships, both domestic and foreign ones, must be taken into account as an important O component. In terms of location advantages (L), the focus is on linking interdependent assets and capabilities that are territorially embedded in a restricted geographic area, with valuable relationships located outside that area. Finally, as regards internalization advantages (I), the focus shifts from transactional advantages providing the rationale for the sustainability and growth of internal hierarchical coordination in well-established MNEs, to the capability of coordinating spatially dispersed activities not all under the MNE's control, and transferring knowledge across borders, but also across cluster participants. As argued by Dunning (1997), the above extension of the conventional eclectic paradigm allows us to understand why many MNEs, faced with market failure in areas such as innovation within the context of vertical contracting, prefer "voice" over "exit", in the spirit of Hirschman (1970). More specifically, they attempt to develop capabilities in cluster management, rather than revert to conventional internalization.

From a strategic management perspective, the two interesting key characteristics of a transborder cluster are first its open-ended nature in terms of geography, and second, the resulting, almost inherent limits to the public goods' nature of knowledge exchange within the cluster. The first point is important because clusters are usually associated with the concentration in geographic space of specialized economic activities. Here, spatial concentration is instrumental to agglomeration economies and to the development of "sticky places in slippery space" (Markusen 1996, Rugman/Verbeke 2001b). The key characteristic of transborder-clusters is, however, that they are by definition not confined to a narrowly defined geographic space. In other words, a "single diamond"-perspective needs to be replaced by a "double diamond" approach, whereby international relationships reinforce the competitiveness of the localized cluster. However, in contrast to conventional double (or multiple) diamonds, here the international linkages are not established merely through the inward and outward FDI strategies of individual firms leading to emerging spill-over effects to all cluster participants. Rather, spill-overs from international linkages arise either from a joint FDI approach of various localized cluster participants or from the intentional sharing of the benefits of international linkages with these partners (e.g., systemic, tacit knowledge on best practice manufacturing processes coming from foreign R&D activities.)

The second characteristic is equally important. In conventional Marshallian clusters, "untraded interdependencies" (Storper 1997) prevail, which implies that all cluster participants benefit from (quasi) free access to a shared, cluster-wide resource and knowledge base. This may be reinforced by a highly skilled, mobile pool of human resources. In addition, a shared set of relationships and routines, resulting from commonalities in the participants' organizational and technological trajectories, sometimes stimulated by government and community support mechanisms, may also be important. However, a critical feature of calculative clusters, dominated by a core firm, is selectivity. High calculativeness implies selectivity regarding (1) who should be considered "worthy" of participation in the cluster; (2) what resources and knowledge should be freely shared among cluster participants; and (3) what sets of relationships and routines should be reinforced. To put it in different words: selectivity implies to some extent intentional exclusion, even of economic actors located in the geographic heart of a cluster. Here, the creation of isolating mechanisms confers competitive advantage to "chosen" partners, not to all organizations that happen to be located in a particular geographic space.

This leads to an interesting paradox: core firm cluster formation depends upon the prior existence of identity-based cluster ties, but the core firm faces incentives to "re-engineer" the historically grown cluster relationships, so as to reduce the relative importance of social embeddedness for its "private club" of cluster participants. As a result, it can be expected that "private clubs", with idiosyncratic resource and knowledge bases, relationships and routines, similar to the Japanese Keiretsu, would be super-imposed on a broader, identity-based cluster in a well-defined geographic space. Tallmann and Jenkins (2002) provide a detailed case study of the British Motor Sport Valley, which closely resembles the transborder, core firm-based cluster type described above.

Given the above characteristics of transborder, core firm-based clusters, little has yet been said about their comparative benefits vis-à-vis other types of cross-border expansion. Here, the focus shifts from merely examining the MNE's role in the home country cluster to include the analysis of its functioning in host countries. A first important point is that the international "reach" of the core firm must be recognized by all home country cluster participants as instrumental to "leveraging" the set of multilateral interactions among them. Higher mutual gains should be achieved as compared to conventional internalization by all partners separately. This "leveraging" ability may firstly result from the size, slack resources and FSAs of the core firm(s). Second, the international character of the core firm, i.e., its presence in several locations, may reflect a proven ability to achieve effective governance when faced with very complex environments, i.e., transactional advantages (Dunning/Rugman 1985). Such ability may be particularly useful to all cluster participants, as cluster benefits fundamentally depend on the sharing of resources, knowledge, relationships and routines, both in a static and dynamic sense. The static case reflects the exploitation of relatively straightforward interorganizational complementarities, whereas the dynamic case implies interorganizational learning. Thus, accepting MNEs as lead partners in internationally linked clusters may simply be more efficient than international expansion through internalization by all network partners separately.

There are three possible reasons for this. First, routines related to daily operations may be performed more effectively because of the MNE's heritage of international intra-firm benchmarking and the diffusion of FSAs and best practices among production units and subsidiaries. Second, investment routines may have a tradition of being more informed, e.g., by inputs in the decision-making process originating from foreign sources. Third, adaptive routines in experienced MNEs may be more sophisticated than in other firms, because of the exogenously imposed requirement to take into account at times very divergent environmental changes in the various countries where the firm operates.

Paradoxically, what the MNE may lack most, when attempting to become an insider in foreign clusters, thereby providing the foundation for valuable knowledge transfer to the home country cluster participants, is access to identity driven ties in local, host country environments. Especially in the context of learning, an MNE may be unable to autonomously access and effectively utilize localized and idiosyncratic repositories of knowledge through either simple market contracts or acquisitions. This is especially troublesome when it is multilateral rather than independent, dyadic interactions that contribute relational value added. In other words, the MNE cannot just purchase resources or activities from specific actors in order to reap the expected benefits of clustering. One of the most powerful descriptions of such a situation is Westney's (1993) study on R&D subsidiaries of U. S. MNEs in Japan. These were "locked-out" of host country clusters, inter alia, because of their inability to hire and retain top scientists. This was, itself, a result of an insufficient understanding of the complex linkages prevailing in Japan among institutions such as universities and industrial organizations that hire scientific personnel.

In addition, the internalization of the activities themselves could eliminate the opportunity for learning altogether. This occurs if there is destruction of the complementary cognitive specialization and idiosyncratic resource bundles of the other host country cluster participants, as may happen when institutionalizing the core firm's routines across the newly internalized activities.

Perhaps most important to effective functioning in host country clusters is the MNE's reputation as core firm in localized clusters. A reputation for opportunistic behaviour may affect perceptions of the MNE's ability to appropriately perform a core firm role in other nations. The empirical evidence in this matter appears to largely support the more positive view on the distinctive, beneficial, role of FDI in the creation of host country clusters, and as a catalyst for economic development (Young/Hood/Peters 1994, Birkinshaw/Hood 2000, Hood/Young 1999, Enright 1999).

From Simple "Buyer Supplier"-Based to "Flagship" Based Clusters

The most extensively studied cluster linkages so far have been buyer-supplier linkages, which is not surprising, as even Porter (1998, p. 200) acknowledges that the identification of upstream or downstream linkages in the vertical chain of firms is usually the starting point for identifying cluster components. The study of hybrid, rather than conventional market driven relationships in vertical markets can be traced back to the seminal work of Blois (1972) on quasi-vertical integration. In the area of vertical linkages, enormous attention has been devoted to clusters in the automobile industry, with the Japanese automobile manufacturer Toyota regularly cited as the archetype of a successful core company. The value added of adopting such a core firm role becomes clear when, irrespective of dynamic learning effects, it appears that e.g. General Motors has had transaction costs related to procurement that were six times higher than Toyota's (Dyer 1996, Dyer/Singh 1998). Dyer and Nobeoka (2000) have provided what is probably the clearest and most comprehensive description of the Toyota driven supplier relationships to date. Their work builds upon a rich academic literature on the comparative value of interfirm relationships, especially as regards interorganizational knowledge creation and diffusion, including von Hippel (1988), Powell et al. (1996), etc.

The foundations of Toyota's success can be simply described as its superiority in "transferring productivity-enhancing knowledge" throughout the set of companies with which it is interconnected. The core firm's extreme calculativeness in creating learning routines is apparent and results from the simple fact that Toyota has most to gain from "public goods" that span the entire set of companies in its cluster. In the early stages of cluster formation in Japan, Toyota "heavily subsidized" the cluster, and interestingly, tried to engineer the creation of a fresh set of identity based ties, e.g. by promoting a "co-existence and co-prosperity" agenda with its suppliers. This is an important observation; it suggests that the adoption of a very long term perspective by the core firm in a calculative cluster may lead this firm to try to mimic the key characteristic of organically growing, identity based clusters. In practical terms, this ideology was given substance through four elements. First, a supplier association that acted as an instrument of socialization and transfer of explicit knowledge. Second, a core firm consulting division that was given the "responsibility to acquire, store and diffuse valuable production knowledge" residing within Toyota's cluster. Third, voluntary (small group) learning teams. Fourth, interfirm employee transfers. Dyer and Nobeoka (2000) have argued that the creation of a strong cluster identity reduces the cost–benefit calculus of its members when they weigh whether or not to provide access to their know how to other participants. This is again an interesting observation as it implies that the extreme calculativeness of the core company, expressed in attempts to institutionalize its own ideology with other economic actors, resulted in those other actors actually being socialized into lowering their own calculativeness.

In addition to the creation of identity-based ties, the "meat" of the governance structure consists of setting cluster wide "rules for knowledge protection and value appropriation". In practice, this implies completely opening up mainstream production operations throughout the network to all participants and reciprocal knowledge sharing. The resulting value to individual suppliers (e.g., productivity improvements) may then be appropriated by them in the short run, "but over time (they) will be expected to share a proportion of those savings with the network (*e.g., through price cuts to Toyota*)" (emphasis added). This appears very different from e.g., the General Motors (GM) driven value appropriation rules whereby supplier savings resulting from cluster-based interactions are likely to be followed by immediate value appropriation attempts by GM. Finally, the broad based cluster rules are complemented with multiple knowledge sharing processes, often in "nested" sub-clusters, involving small groups.

Toyota has attempted to replicate its successful vertical clustering approach in the United States. It has been instrumental in pushing suppliers from purely dyadic ties with Toyota towards multilateral ties with other suppliers. Mechanisms similar to those prevailing in Japan have been introduced to create a cluster identity and socially embedded ties. Interestingly, Dyer and Nobeoka (2000) view Toyota's US supplier cluster as "still less mature" than the Japanese one, because of the comparatively lower dependency of US suppliers on Toyota in terms of percentage of total sales going to this one buyer.

The Toyota approach is heralded as a great success. The only long run dangers recognized are that identity-based ties could reduce "variety generation" in the cluster and an excessive inward focus could reduce adaptation to changing external circumstances. Indeed, more "distance" among cluster participants may be more conducive to fundamental innovation, whereas the presence of more strongly embedded social ties in identity-based clusters may be more conducive to the efficient transfer of existing knowledge and incremental innovation. Current research fails to recognize the problem of the full reliance on the institutionalization of Toyota "recipes" as the dominant logic, indeed, the sole logic guiding the cluster functioning. In fact, this approach illustrates a lack of national responsiveness on Toyota's part. Yet, efforts to engage in mutual adaptation with suppliers may well be required when functioning in foreign clusters that are much broader than the core set of suppliers whose bread and butter largely depend on the actions of the lead firm.

It should be recognized that Toyota's calculativeness never did equate short run profit maximization with supplier squeezing, although this does occur in the US automobile industry. In addition, the calculativeness was to some extent driven by constraints exogenous to the core firm's management. First, the employees' own perceptions that their functioning in a large organization such as Toyota and their loyalty to it were dependent on long term employment guarantees not found in smaller supplying firms, effectively precluded vertical integration. Second, it was Japanese government policy to protect weak suppliers. The calculativeness did consist, however, of the knowledge that explicit and formal supplier cluster management, through institutionalizing Toyota-determined rules of the game, would in the longer run greatly benefit Toyota's productivity and profitability.

In contrast to the Toyota-case, Rugman, Verbeke, and D'Cruz (1995) description of multinational, flagship based clusters, still largely driven by the institutionalization logic of the core firm(s) offers some interesting lessons about managing broader, inter-industry clusters with many participants. Specifically, such a cluster includes: a leading 'flagship firm' which is a multinational enterprise; key suppliers; key customers; selected competitors, and the non- business infrastructure (NBI). The NBI comprises government, the non-traded service sectors, educational institutions, social services, trade unions, trade associations, and non-profit cultural organizations. The cluster's governance structure depends upon asymmetric control of the cluster's strategic purpose by the flagship firm. The flagship firm's resources and global perspective enable it to develop global strategies which can capitalize on the capabilities and knowledge of all partners. Because partners may compete in business systems not related to that of the cluster, it should be emphasized that the flagship firm's asymmetric strategic control extends only to those aspects of its partners' business systems committed to the cluster. The co-evolution of cluster participants is therefore always partial.

Cluster relationships decrease the need to establish elaborate internal MNE structures and systems with high bureaucratic costs. As noted above, such costs are high if the various (potential) sub-units face very different sets of required cognitive specialization, assets, skills, and coordination and control routines. Organizations that choose to participate in such a cluster, realize that the demands of global markets may preclude any given firm from having the capability to be competitive in every aspect of its current business. The rapid pace of technological change, product obsolescence, and market growth places heavy burdens on companies if they wish to remain competitive. Many corporations now understand that they are competing against global business systems as opposed to within broadly defined industry groupings (Rugman 2000). Restructuring and outsourcing those activities in which the partner has no core competence (Prahalad/Hamel 1990) lessens investments in 'non-core' assets and particularly, those in which the partner has less knowledge. Consequently, the likelihood of investment in assets which quickly become 'non-performing' is decreased. When partners focus on investment in core assets and the exploitation of their core capabilities they are better able to follow, predict, and adapt to market changes which affect their operations. If all cluster partners assume similar approaches, then the boundaries of the cluster can shift more easily to accommodate changes in the global market. The cluster, therefore, benefits from the permeability of its boundaries and its shared strategic purpose.

The flagship firm's experience in international markets is vital for the cluster's determination of which markets to serve and what products/services to produce. Essentially, the flagship firm's visible hand guides its partners toward a strategy of global competitiveness for the cluster as a whole.

The flagship firm's assumes its strategic leadership position by (1) stimulating the development of a common resource and knowledge base, as well as shared relationships and routines: (2) re-engineering the division of labour among cluster participants, especially regarding innovation activities; and (3) benchmarking all key value added activities performed by cluster participants against international best practices.

In practice, it is the cluster partners who determine that strategic leadership by a flagship firm offers rewards that could not otherwise be obtained. Because cluster partners understand that internalization may fail to structurally position the firm for competitiveness, they are willing to engage in more open-ended relationships based on knowledge sharing, not knowledge protection. Such firms organize their structures to change with the market. The form of relationship, on the surface, appears to be traditional: joint ventures, supplier development, market-sharing arrangements, technology transfers, etc. However, the method of implementation, through managerial interaction and joint working teams, rather than static contractual arrangements, is devised to encourage co-operation and knowledge development.

Organizational Characteristics of Clusters

In the two cases described above, the dominant logic of core firms, and the institutionalization of routines they consider appropriate, determine the cluster's functioning. Paradoxically, much of the modern international business literature revolves around the concept of national responsiveness and adaptation to host country cluster requirements, thereby reducing the potential of institutionalization. Many clusters now exist in which foreign MNEs perform the role of core firm, but subject to their willingness and ability to be nationally responsive or, in more general terms, to participate in mutual adaptation processes with other cluster participants.

This implies that host country clusters in which MNE subsidiaries participate may lead these subsidiaries to view these clusters as an alternative for the internalization of specific activities, which before might have been performed within the hierarchy, thereby generating positive spill-over effects. Second, and perhaps more importantly, they may also have negative spill-over effects on the internal MNE functioning and the interactions with the home country cluster. This occurs when adaptation by subsidiaries to foreign cluster requirements seriously impedes the corporate headquarters' ability to institutionalize firm-level routines in the subsidiaries themselves. In transaction cost terms: the administrative costs of managing the remaining internal activities may increase. This "cost" must then be weighed against the learning benefits in the form of "subsidiary specific advantages" at the level of the affiliates (Rugman/Verbeke 2001a).

The above analysis is illustrated in Figure 2 which describes four types of asymmetrical, core firm based clusters.

Figure 2. Organizational Characteristics of Clusters

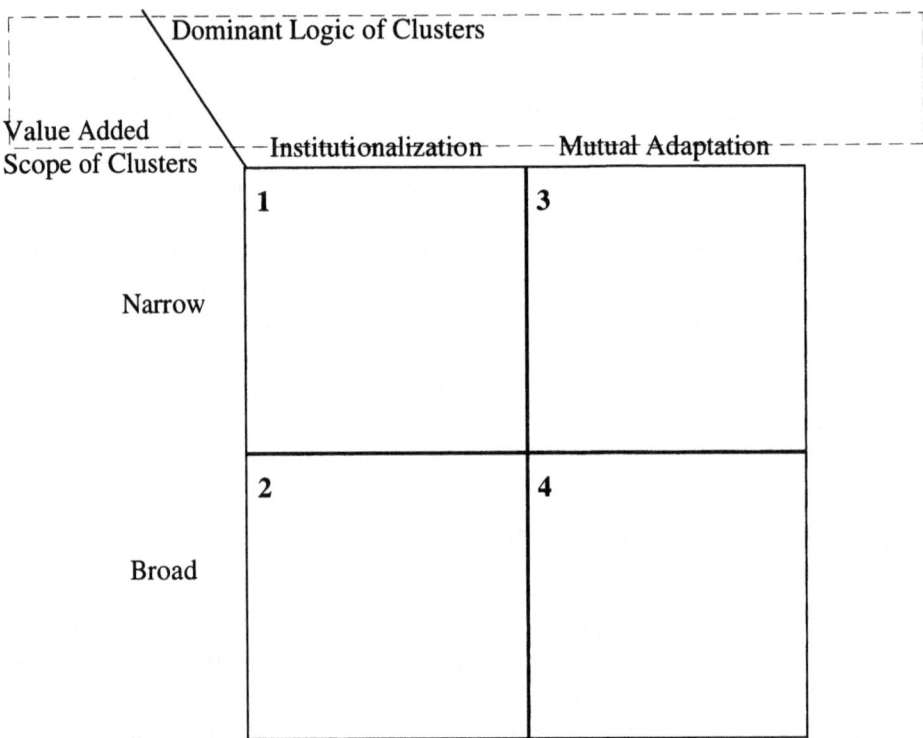

On the horizontal axis of Figure 2, a distinction is made between two types of "dominant logic" that may characterize a cluster. Here, we find the institutionalization logic versus the mutual adaptation logic, with national responsiveness as a typical (but not exclusive) expression of the MNE's willingness to participate in mutual adaptation processes.[2]

The vertical axis investigates the value activities' scope of the cluster, which may range from a rather narrow scope (e.g. a supplier-based cluster) to a very broad scope (with a high variety of participants' roles, potentially even including non-profit organizations and government agencies).

Quadrant 1 represents the positioning of the Toyota supplier cluster. The broader scope of the Rugman and D'Cruz (2000) flagship-based cluster allows a positioning in quadrant 2. The typical R&D clusters in strongly geographically concentrated districts and in which large, foreign MNEs actively participate without an institutionalization attitude but rather with an approach of isomorphic flexibility, are now representative for clusters in quadrant 3. Finally, the clusters in quadrant 4 may pose specific problems for MNEs, as described by Rugman and Verbeke (2001a). Here, adherence to broad, localized clusters in host countries may lead to SSAs embedded in host country operations of the MNE and these SSAs may be non-transferable to other parts of the MNE (and to the home country cluster).

Conclusions

This paper has focused on the contribution that foreign-owned firms can make to the development of clusters. Building upon the seminal insights of Porter (1990a, 1998) we have extended his "diamond" framework to include the role of MNEs in fostering knowledge development in localized and transborder clusters. More specifically, we have developed a two-stage framework that allows us to synthesize the relevant literature and to clarify the set of potential cluster opportunities open to firms.

First, we focused on the cluster's geography, which can have domestic, single diamond, Porter-type characteristics, or transborder, multiple diamond features. We also made a distinction between symmetrical and asymmetrical clusters and provided examples of these cases. Second, we examined the organizational characteristics of asymmetrical, transborder clusters. We related the narrow or broad value added scope of clusters to the dominant logic of the clusters, i.e., either institutionalization or mutual adaptation.

The overarching conclusion is that the introduction of the core firm concept on the one hand and the recognition of the importance of international linkages on the other hand, provides a richer set of conceptual and practical insights into the role of MNEs in cluster development, than the domestic clustering approach of Porter. For example, the flagship framework is built around the institutionalizing role of the MNE as a core firm, and it allows us to describe the purposive behavior of an international, rather than just a domestic firm. In contrast, when focusing on the functioning of the MNE in host countries, the SSA-concept recognizes that, once established in a localized foreign cluster, and operating according to principles of mutual adjustment, MNE subsidiaries may face difficulties in diffusing their knowledge base to other affiliates or even to be responsive to the needs of other parts of the MNE and its home country cluster. The current literature on clusters now needs to move ahead by taking on board flagship and SSA-related concepts.

Endnotes

1 From the MNE perspective, participation in a foreign cluster may lead to several benefits: access to knowledge, which otherwise would have remained out of reach; the potential leveraging of this knowledge throughout the firm's internal network; the transfer of global best practices; the monitoring of rivals active in the foreign clusters, etc. Yet, actually obtaining these benefits in practice is not easy. Different sub-units within the MNE may have a specialized knowledge base and a specific technological trajectory, which may be inconsistent with the knowledge absorbed in a foreign cluster. In addition, the MNE unit involved in the knowledge absorption process may be faced with difficult choices between maximizing convergence of its own operations with the other parts of the MNE-network, and maximizing convergence with the functioning of the localized knowledge cluster in which it is physically embedded.
From the perspective of the domestic participants in the localized knowledge cluster itself and the governments/public agencies that may want to foster the growth and international competitiveness of this cluster, the entry of foreign MNEs is equally challenging. First, how can MNEs be attracted that may contribute to the cluster's development? Second, could MNEs perform the role of 'bumble bees' through cross-fertilization (knowledge exchange) among the various clusters in which they participate? Third, will foreign MNE-activity mainly contribute to cluster upgrading, or could it be a threat leading to e.g., the reduction of both the cluster's stability and its insulation against imitation of innovation processes elsewhere. Fourth, will reliance on foreign firms reduce domestic entrepreneurship and innovation in the long run?

2 Mutual adaptation need not be restricted to solely responding to the needs and requirements of domestic actors in a host country, but may include adaptation to other international and even global actors in the localized cluster.

References

Birkinshaw, J./Hood, N., Characteristics of Foreign Subsidiaries in Industry Clusters, *Journal of International Business Studies*, 31, 1, 2000, pp. 141–154.
Birkinshaw, J./Solvell, O., Leading-edge Multinationals and Leading-edge Clusters, *International Studies of Management and Organization*, 33, 2, 2000, pp. 3–9.
Blois K., Vertical Quasi-Integration, *Journal of Industrial Economics*, 20, 3, 1972, pp. 253–272.
Cartwright W. R. Multiple Linked "Diamonds" and the International Competitiveness of Export-dependent Industries: The New Zealand Experience, *Management International Review*, 1993, 33, pp. 55–70.
Davies H./Ellis P., Porter's Competitive Advantage of Nations: Time for the Final Judgement, *Journal of Management Studies*, 37, 8, 2000, pp. 1189–1213.
Dunning, J. H., *The Globalization of Business*, London: Routledge 1993.
Dunning, J. H., *Alliance Capitalism and Global Business*, London: Routledge 1997.
Dunning, J. H./Rugman, A. M., The influence of Hymer's Dissertation on the Theory of Foreign Direct Investment, *American Economic Review Papers and Proceedings*, 75, 2, 1985, pp. 228–232.
Dyer, J. H., Specialized Supplier Networks as a Source of Competitive Advantage: Evidence from the Auto Industry, *Strategic Management Journal*, 17, 4, 1996, pp. 271–293.
Dyer, J. H./Singh H., The Relational View: Cooperative Strategy and Sources of Inter-organizational Competitive Advantage, *Academy of Management Review*, 23, 4, 1998, pp. 660–679.
Dyer, J. H./Nobeoka, K., Creating and Managing a High-performance Knowledge-sharing Network: The Toyota Case, *Strategic Management Journal* 21, 3, 2000, pp. 347–376.

Enright, M. J., The Globalization of Competition and the Localization of Competitive Advantage: Policies Towards Regional Clustering, in Hood, N./Young S., *The Globalization of Multinational Enterprise Activity and Economic Development*, London: Macmillan 1999, pp. 303–331.
Hirschman, A. O., *Exit, Voice and Loyalt*, Cambridge, MA: Harvard University Press 1970.
Hite, J. M./Hesterly, B. S., *The Influence of the Firm-life Cycle on the Evolution of Entrepreneurial Dyadic Networks*, Mimeo 1999.
Hood, N./Young, S. (eds.), *The Globalization of Multinational Enterprise Activity and Economic Development*, London: Macmillan 1999.
Koza, M./Lewin A. Y., The Co-evolution of Strategic Alliances, *Organization Science*, 9, 1998 pp. 255–264.
Markusen, A., Sticky Places in Slippery Space: A Typology of Industrial Districts, *Economic Geography*, 72, (3), 1996, pp. 293–313.
Porter, M., *The Competitive Advantage of Nations*, New York: Free Press 1990a.
Porter, M., The Competitive Advantage of Nations, *Harvard Business Review*, March/April, 1990b.
Porter, M., *On Competition*, New York: Free Press 1998.
Powell, W. W./Koput, K. W./Smith-Doerr, L., Inter-organizational collaboration and the locus of innovation: Networks of learning in biotechnology, *Adminstrative Science Quarterly*, 41, 1996, pp. 116–145.
Prahalad, C. K./Hamel G., The Core Competence of the Corporation, *Harvard Business Review*, 90, 3, 1990, pp. 79–91.
Rugman, A. M., *The End of Globalization*, London: Random House 2000.
Rugman, A. M./D'Cruz J., *Multinationals as Flagships Firms: Regional Business Networks*, Oxford: Oxford University Press 2000.
Rugman, A. M./van den Broeck J./Verbeke A. (eds.), *Research in Global Strategic Management: Volume 5: Beyond the Diamond*, Greenwich, CT: JAI Press 1995.
Rugman, A. M./Verbeke, A., Foreign Subsidiaries and Multinational Strategic Management: An Extension and Correction of Porter's Single Diamond Framework, *Management International Review*, 33, 2, 1993a, pp. 71–84.
Rugman, A. M./Verbeke, A., How to Operationalize Porter's Diamond of Competitive Advantage, *International Executive*, 35, 4 1993b, pp. 283–299.
Rugman, A. M./Verbeke, A., Subsidiary Specific Advantages in Multinational Enterprises, *Strategic Management Journal*, 22, 3, 2001a, pp. 237–250.
Rugman, A. M./Verbeke A., Location, Competitiveness and the Multinational Enterprise in Rugman A. M./Brewer, T. (eds.), *Oxford Handbook of International Business*, Oxford: Oxford University Press 2001b, pp. 150–177.
Rugman, A. M./Verbeke A., Internalization Theory and the Functioning of the Multinational Enterprise, *Journal of International Business Studies*, 34, 2, 2003, pp. 125–137.
Rugman, A. M./Verbeke A./D'Cruz J., Internalization and De-internalization: Will Business Networks Replace Multinationals? Boyd, G. (ed.), *Competitive and Cooperative Management: The Challenge of Structural Interdependence*, Aldershot: Elgar 1995, pp. 107–128.
Saxenian, A., *Regional Advantage*, Boston: Harvard University Press 1994.
Storper, M., *The Regional World: Territorial Development in the Global Economy*, New York: Guilford Press 1997.
Tallmann, S. B./Jenkins M., *Structure, Knowledge and Performance in Open Regional Clusters*, Mimeo 2002.
Van Den Bulcke, D./Verbeke, A., *Globalization and the Small Open Economy*, Aldershot: Elgar 2001.
Young, S./Hood, N./Peters, E., Multinational Enterprises and Regional Economic Development, *Regional Studies*, 28, 7, 1994, pp. 657–677.
von Hippel, E., *The Sources of Innovation*, New York: Oxford University Press 1988.
Westney, D. E., Cross-Pacific Internationalization of R&D by U. S. and Japanese Firms, *R&D Management*, 23, 2, 1993, pp. 171–181.

mir *Edition*

Doris Lindner

Einflussfaktoren des erfolgreichen Auslandseinsatzes

Konzeptionelle Grundlagen – Bestimmungsgrößen –
Ansatzpunkte zur Verbesserung

2002, XX, 341 Seiten, Br., € 59,00
ISBN 3-409-11952-3

Die fortschreitende Internationalisierung bringt eine zunehmende Zahl an Auslandsentsandten mit sich. Die Einflussfaktoren erfolgreicher Auslandsentsendungen geraten damit verstärkt in den Fokus internationaler Unternehmen. Anhand einer empirischen Untersuchung werden die Ursachen für den Abbruch von Auslandsentsendungen eingehend analysiert und differenziert. Daraus lassen sich Ansätze zur besseren Gestaltung von Auslandseinsätzen entwickeln.

Betriebswirtschaftlicher Verlag Dr. Th. Gabler GmbH, Abraham-Lincoln-Str. 46, 65189 Wiesbaden

Management International Review

Neuerscheinungen

Joachim Scholz
Wert und Bewertung internationaler Akquisitionen
2001
XXII, 365 S. mit 40 Abb.,
(mir-Edition),
Br. € 79,–
ISBN 3-409-11602-8

Joachim Wolf
Strategie und Struktur 1955–1995: Ein Kapitel der Geschichte deutscher nationaler und internationaler Unternehmen
2000
XXXII, 673 S. mit 156 Abb.,
7 farb. Abb. (mir-Edition),
Br. € 94,50
ISBN 3-409-11637-0

Dodo zu Knyphausen-Aufseß (Hrsg.)
Globalisierung als Herausforderung der Betriebswirtschaftslehre
2000
XVIII, 285 S. (mir-Edition),
Br. € 64,–
ISBN 3-409-11719-9

Laila Maija Hofmann
Führungskräfte in Europa. Empirische Analyse zukünftiger Anforderungen
2000
XXVIII, 414 S. mit 89 Abb.,
129 Tab., Diss. Augsburg 2000
(mir-Edition),
Br. € 64,–
ISBN 3-409-11704-0

Frank Niederländer
Dynamik in der internationalen Produktpolitik von Automobilherstellern
2000
XXVIII, 296 S. mit 111 Abb.,
36 Tab., Dissertation Eichstätt 2000
(mir-Edition),
Br. € 59,–
ISBN 3-409-11722-9

Jan Hendrik Fisch
Structure Follows Knowledge. Internationale Verteilung der Forschung und Entwicklung in multinationalen Unternehmen
2001
XXII, 247 S. mit 84 Abb., 10 Tab.
(mir-Edition),
Br. € 49,–
ISBN 3-409-11802-0

Betriebswirtschaftlicher Verlag Dr. Th. Gabler GmbH, Abraham-Lincoln-Str. 46, 65189 Wiesbaden

mir *Edition*

GABLER

Jan Hendrik Fisch

Structure Follows Knowledge
International Distribution of Research and Development in Multinational Corporations

2001, XXII, 247 pages, Br., € 49,00 (approx. US $ 45.–)
ISBN 3-409-11802-0

While the general factors influencing the internationalization of research and development are well-known, there exists neither an embracing approach to explain the international distribution of R&D activities nor one to design it efficiently.

The author develops a new model of the R&D subsystem of multinational corporations. Using modern quantitative methods the model determines both the optimal distribution of R&D activities among countries and the optimal assignment of tasks. The empirical test of the model suggests that at present not all multinational corporations show an efficient internationalization of their R&D activities.

The book addresses lecturers and students of international management, innovation management and organization theory as well as scientists and axecutives in R&D management and organizational planing.

Betriebswirtschaftlicher Verlag Dr. Th. Gabler GmbH, Abraham-Lincoln-Str. 46, 65189 Wiesbaden

Management
International Review
© Gabler Verlag 2003

EDITORIAL OBJECTIVES

MANAGEMENT INTERNATIONAL REVIEW presents insights and analyses which reflect basic and topical advances in the key areas of International Management. Its target audience includes scholars and executives in business and administration.

EDITORIAL POLICY

MANAGEMENT INTERNATIONAL REVIEW is a refereed journal which aims at the advancement and dissemination of international applied research in the fields of Management and Business. The scope of the journal comprises International Business, Transnational Corporations, Intercultural Management, Strategic Management, and Business Policy.

MANAGEMENT INTERNATIONAL REVIEW stresses the interaction between theory and practice of management by way of publishing articles, research notes, reports and comments which concentrate on the application of existing and potential research for business and other organizations. Papers are invited and given priority which are based on rigorous methodology, suggest models capable to solve practical problems. Also papers are welcome which advise as to whether and to what extent models can be translated and applied by the practising manager. Work which has passed the practical test of successful application is of special interest to MIR. It is hoped that besides its academic objectives the journal will serve some useful purpose for the practical world, and also help bridging the gap between academic and business management.

PUBLISHING · SUBSCRIPTION · ADVERTISEMENTS

Published quarterly, fixed annual subscription rate for foreign countries: Individual subscription 108 Euro (approx. US $ 112.–), institutional subscription 212 Euro (approx. US $ 219.–), single copy 59 Euro – (approx. US $ 55.–). Fixed annual subscription rate for Germany: Individual subscription 99 Euro –, institutional subscription 206 Euro. Payment on receipt of invoice. Subscriptions are entered on a calendar basis only (Jan.–Dec.). Cancellations must be filed by referring to the subscription number six weeks before closing date (subscription invoice); there will be no confirmation. There may be 1 to 4 supplementary issues per year. Each supplementary issue will be sent to subscribers with a separate invoice allowing 25% deduction on the regular price. Subscribers have the right to return the issue within one month to the distribution company. – Subscription office: VVA, post-box 7777, D-33310 Gütersloh, Germany, Tel. 00 49/(0) 52 41-80 19 68/80 28 91, Fax 80 96 20. Distribution: Kristiane Alesch, Tel. 00 49/(0) 6 11/78 78-3 59. Reader-Service: Britta Christmann, Tel. 00 49/(0) 6 11/78 78-1 29, Fax 78 78-4 23. Advertising office: Thomas Werner, Tel. 00 49/(0) 6 11/78 78-1 38.
Editorial Department: Ralf Wettlaufer, Tel. 00 49/(0) 6 11/78 78-2 34, e-mail: ralf.wettlaufer@bertelsmann.de. Annelie Meisenheimer, Tel. 00 49/(0) 6 11/78 78-2 32. Production: Gabriele McLemore, Betriebswirtschaftlicher Verlag Dr. Th. Gabler GmbH, Abraham-Lincoln-Straße 46, D-65189 Wiesbaden, Tel. 00 49/(0) 6 11/78 78-0, Fax 78 78-4 00. Internet: Publisher http://www.gabler.de; Editor http://www.uni-hohenheim.de./~mir; Managing Director Dr. Hans-Dieter Haenel; Publishing Director Dr. Heinz Weinheimer; Senior Publishing Editor Claudia Splittgerber; Sales Manager Gabriel Göttlinger; Production Manager Reinhard van den Hövel. Produced by Druckhaus „Thomas Müntzer" GmbH, Bad Langensalza – Contributions published in this journal are protected by copyright.

© Betriebswirtschaftlicher Verlag Dr. Th. Gabler/GWV Fachverlage GmbH, Wiesbaden 2003.

No part of this publication may be reproduced, stored in a retrieval system or transmitted in any form or by any means: electronic, magnetic tape, mechanical, photocopying, recording or otherwise, without permission in writing from the publisher. There is no liability for manuscripts and review literature which were submitted without invitation.

ISSN 0938-8249

GPSR Compliance
The European Union's (EU) General Product Safety Regulation (GPSR) is a set of rules that requires consumer products to be safe and our obligations to ensure this.

If you have any concerns about our products, you can contact us on

ProductSafety@springernature.com

In case Publisher is established outside the EU, the EU authorized representative is:

Springer Nature Customer Service Center GmbH
Europaplatz 3
69115 Heidelberg, Germany

www.ingramcontent.com/pod-product-compliance
Lightning Source LLC
LaVergne TN
LVHW080313260326
834688LV00038B/1100